The
Average Man
Fights
Back

The Average Man Fights Back

David Hapgood

IN COLLABORATION WITH RICHARD HALL

Doubleday & Company, Inc., Garden City, New York
1977

Portions of this book first appeared in
The Washington Monthly.

Library of Congress Cataloging in Publication Data

Hapgood, David.
  The average man fights back.

  Bibiography: p. 265
  Includes index.
  1. Consumer protection—United States. I. Hall,
Richard H., 1934–   joint author. II. Title.
HC110. C63H358   381'.3
          ISBN: 0-385-11285-8
Library of Congress Catalog Card Number 76–18350

Contents

10 PROGRESSIVES IN THE
        STATES   218

11 ACTION LINE   237

12 GOOD NEWS IN HARD TIMES   249

    Bibliography   265
    Index   268

Acknowledgments

RICHARD HALL HAS been a versatile and talented collaborator. Most of the research was done by him, but his role has far exceeded that of researcher. The final shape of the manuscript owes a great deal to his ideas and insights.

Richard Hall is also the author of Chapter 10: "Progressives in the States."

People too numerous to list have helped us along the way. We would particularly like to thank the following for reading drafts and offering their advice in the areas of their specialties:

LAW: Murray Teigh Bloom, William D. Dalsimer, Jethro K. Lieberman, Stephen Meyers, Robert S. Nathan, Pierre A. Tonachel. HEALTH: Gordon Chase, Dr. Sidney M. Wolfe. GUILDS: Paul Gillette, Karen Green, Bonnie Naradzay. INSURANCE: Joseph M. Belth. AGING: David Affeldt, Frederick R. Eisele, Mary Adelaide Mendelson. PROPERTY TAXES: Steven Cord, Cathy Covell, William Newcomb, Perry Prentice, Jonathan Rowe. ACORN AND OTHER SEEDS: Madeleine Adamson, Pablo Eisenberg. PROGRESSIVES IN THE STATES: Neal R. Peirce. Others who have read and commented on parts of the manuscript are Richard Hamilton, Craig Jacobson, Andrew Levison, and, closest to home, Janice Hapgood.

We would also like to thank Joseph M. Belth, editor and publisher of *The Insurance Forum*, for permission to quote from his interview with a student at Indiana University; Jeffrey L. Steingarten, a Fellow of the Institute of Current World Affairs, for permission to quote from his Institute newsletter JLS-21; *The Washington Monthly*, for permission to use material from articles by Richard Hall and Arthur Levine, the latter of which we draw upon in chapter 11, and *Trial* magazine, for permission to quote from an article by Danny Jones.

1

Fighting Back

THE AVERAGE MAN is getting smarter. Through the gloom that has settled over us in the mid-seventies, it is possible to see fragments of a different landscape. In this dimly glimpsed place, the average person is increasingly aware of the ways he is being screwed and is beginning, here and there, to find out that it doesn't have to be that way.

Progress is uneven. Sometimes it is as wide in scope as a Supreme Court decision that outlaws the sacred right of professional associations to force their members to impose minimum prices on the public. Sometimes, notably in law, it is members of a profession breaking ranks with their colleagues and finding ways to deliver better service at less cost to the public. Sometimes it is just one person who points the way for others—Christine Winter of Chicago, for example, who took a course in auto mechanics so she could avoid the flat-rate labor swindle, or Ralph Charell, author of *How I Turn Ordinary Complaints into Thousands of Dollars*, who is listed by the *Guinness Book of Records* as the world's most successful complainer. Sometimes it happens in the belly of the dinosaur: state regulators beginning to control the insurance industry for the public benefit; federal bureaucrats showing a renewed interest in battling monopolies.

Often it is local groups, unknown outside their territory, who are successfully battling some screwing in their town or county or state. Often, too, it is public-interest groups or individuals who by lobbying and just putting out information are building a constituency that one day may put a set of swindlers out of business. It doesn't add up to Utopia, but it is undeniably there: something is happening that in its own way is as important as the much more obvious cluster of reasons for selling our shares in tomorrow while we can still find a buyer.

Credit for the average person's growing awareness might, in a more innocent time, have been claimed by the education industry, pointing with pride to school attendance figures as evidence that the public was getting smart because it was consuming more of the industry's product. Today, with the educators in disgrace, that claim would draw little more than a snicker. Our skepticism about the educators symbolizes the many types of expert whose claims on our credulity and our cash have worn thin as we reach the end of the years of prosperity. We don't believe as easily as we did.

The average person first met many of the experts during those prosperous years—the great quarter of a century of steady growth in the standard of living from World War II to the mid-sixties. (As we use the term "average" here, we mean those who earn their income by work and take home less than $25,000 a year. They are the net losers in our system.) Before that, when he was in working-class poverty, the average man had little occasion to patronize the experts. Now, however, he sought them out to guide him through the novel complexities of middle-class living. "They" were lawyers and real estate men, doctors and insurance men, and a whole host of other organized professionals: today's counterparts of the medi-eval guilds. In those first transactions in his new world, the average man was not likely to question what the ex-pert was selling him. Indeed, the very fact that he was dealing with the experts conferred on him a status his fa-ther never had, and that was reason enough not to look too closely at the price tag nor ask just what he was buy-ing or why. The average person bought gladly, and the experts thrived and they multiplied.

By the seventies, most of those innocent first encoun-ters with the experts were in our past. The average person was likely to be more blasé, to ask more questions, the second time around. When in the great government-sub-sidized suburban boom of the fifties, the average man bought the first home anyone in his family had ever owned, he did not linger during those rites of passage marking his entry into the middle class to ask the experts at the closing why he had to buy anything so silly as title insurance. But twenty years later the typical buyer has owned before or is from a homeowning family. This time he may stop to ask why the paperwork costs so much more than the woodwork—and the day that he asks that question, a whole coterie of experts is in mortal danger.

In the forties he went to college on the GI bill, the first in his family, and a white collar job was waiting for him off-campus. His son served his time for the same diploma, but no job was waiting for him and so he asked what he had bought with his four years. The stock market did its part to educate the average man. When, in the fifties and sixties, he for the first time had some savings to place, the market offered him both investment and, through learn-ing its vocabulary, the delightful feeling of being an in-sider: he could turn knowledgeably to the stock tables, just like Mr. Merrill and Mr. Lynch. Millions who had never bought stocks before accepted Wall Street's invitation. Then came the colossal crashes of the late sixties and early seventies, costing investors $300 billion, ten times the public's loss in the 1929 crash, and there was no point looking at the stock figures because the garbage he had bought from Merrill and Lynch was worthless. Knowing the words was cold comfort, now that the market wasn't playing his tune anymore. Even when the market turned upward in 1975–76, small investors were noticeably reluctant to get back into a game in which they had lost so heavily only a few years before.

The experts were disgracing themselves in other ways. Even the doctors, experts of all experts, found it hard to keep their haloes in place when the cost in blood and money of unnecessary surgery became widely known, and the recurring Medicaid scandals revealed them to be clawing for the public dollar with all the zeal we normally ascribe to a used-car dealer. Similarly with the lawyers, who in the seventies were showing up increasingly on the far side of the bar of justice. The high-level transgressions that drew the most publicity had nothing to do with the humdrum daily legal screwing of the public, but their exposure made the point that protection of the law was too important to be left to the lawyers: the step from Watergate to challenging the bar's minimum fee system is not a long one.

The experts had overreached in their eagerness to catch up with the Rockefellers, but it wouldn't have mattered had the average man still been making money too. During the golden years most people turned a deaf ear to those who announced that they were being screwed by the experts. It might be true that Rockefeller was banking ten dollars each time the average man pocketed a dime, but that average man was getting more than he ever had before. He wasn't as well off as the rich kept telling him he was, but most years he inched ahead a bit, and certainly he was doing much better than his parents. Besides, lots of middle-class people had hustles of their own going, and who am I to cast the first mudpie? But then in the seventies the average man's real income started falling, and suddenly his world took on a browner hue. Millions were pushed back down into the poverty that their parents had endured and from which they thought they had escaped for good. The arithmetic of net screwing now turned up a negative balance. Net screwing —the difference between the individual's gains at the expense of society and others' gains at his expense—had not captured most people's attention when times were good. Now, as his income slid, the average man began recalculating where he figured in the over-all accounts—and found himself to be a loser. This, inevitably, turned more people's attention to the possibility of reducing the nips that others were taking out of their hides.

The average man's prospects were fading. Two of the essential badges of middle-class status—stigmata of the winners in the net screwing exchange—were being priced out of his reach. Fewer than one in five could afford a new single-family home, that basic module of the suburbs, in 1976; a generation earlier two thirds of us could afford the equivalent house. The future too had dimmed: not only did the college diploma, academic equivalent of the single-family home, buy less in the job market than it used to—its value as an investment dropped by one third in only five years—but now fewer of the average man's children could afford to buy even that depreciated paper. In 1974, for the first time, the percentage of children of the middle class attending college dropped.

Inflation whipped up the public's anxiety. Where a stagnant economy just means we have to put down our heads and postpone our dreams in the hope of better times ahead, inflation threatens to take away what we already have. Inflation is an undeclared tax on our earnings, but it also reaches out to take whatever we've managed to put aside. Ten years ago, when inflation and savings account interest both were running around 4 per cent, the average saver was merely being robbed of any return on his capital. By the mid-seventies, inflation cost twice as much as savings paid—the saver's capital was being eaten away while he looked on helplessly. Inflation hit the powerless average man harder than those above him on the ladder. In the first half of the seventies, while the wage-earner's real income was falling, business executives were increasing their take at better than 10 per cent a year. The government stepped in to help its friends: during the Nixon administration's brief venture into wage and price controls, wage increases were held to 4.2 per cent a year, less than the pace of inflation, while managers' pay was allowed to rise by 9.3 per cent, more than twice as much. The wealthy in any event were comfortably padded against inflation. For a family taking home $10,000 a year, a fall in real income meant less real food on the table, while the millionaire could contemplate his paper losses without changing his brand of caviar. If, that is, he suffered any loss even on paper. Inflation erodes the value of money, which is how the average man gets his pay, while the rich can invest in forms of wealth whose value goes up with rising prices: the land hoarder, for example, can increase his real wealth during inflation.

Of all the experts, none drew more of the average man's resentment than those government officials who were supposed to guide him to an ever-more prosperous economy. While mismanaging a distant war received from most people attention as peripheral as the war's location, the average man's faith in the system was rudely disrupted when government at home began behaving like a pitiful, helpless giant. Nothing seemed to work out right any more. Government trotted out its stable of experts to explain that the public would have to suffer recession, or inflation, or both plus acid stomach, because somehow full employment and stable prices were incompatible. It was always someone else's fault: the Arabs and the price of oil; the weather and the price of grain; or maybe it was the sunspots after all. This was less than convincing to those who remembered the good years of only yesterday, when the nation enjoyed low unemployment, little inflation and a steadily rising standard of living. Those days seem distant, when even the artificial recovery staged in honor of the nation's forty-eighth presidential election offered little hope of recouping the average person's losses, much less setting him back on the long march upward.

Worse still, the suspicion grew that recovery was not just around the corner—that there might never be light at the end of this tunnel. We had reached, or so we were told, the limits of growth. The pie was not getting any bigger—the average man would be lucky if his share didn't shrink. The only way he could get more was at the expense of someone else's slice—if, that is, the theory as told to us was correct. Wild talk was heard of triage in the lifeboat: shoving someone, always someone *else*, overboard to keep the rest of us afloat. Since those nominated for sacrifice never included the officers, the main effect of talk about triage was to keep the passengers fighting among themselves.

But if the pie is no longer to grow—if the bad news of recent years is all the news we're ever to get—that fact knocks a major prop from under the structure of fakery that disguises the screwing of the average man. The prop is youtooism: the system tells the average person that, though others may be getting the hog's share, he too is getting a bit more on his plate. Government uses youtooism to mask its favors to the rich. But youtoo costs money—you have to keep giving the public something— and that requires continued growth. Youtooism has been essential to papering over any complaint about the respective shares we get—the answer to each and every question was more growth. (This was known as Keynesian liberalism, and was in fact a perversion of the thought of the late John Maynard Keynes.) But now the politics of growth—of which Hubert Humphrey has been the longest-winded proponent since anyone can remember—has lost its economic base, and so the average person is forced to see the hollowness of youtooism. When, for example, he first got to itemize his tax deductions, he felt like a winner, sharing a loophole with the likes of Rockefeller. But when his income stopped rising and began to slip back, he became receptive to the message that Rocky was hogging so much of the loophole that the average man was pushed over into the losers' column. And, when he could no longer afford to own a home, he lost a set of tax privileges that identified him—in his own mind, if not in reality—as one of the winners. An increasing number of taxpayers began to see the accuracy of Catch-85, which holds that when a privilege like a tax loophole is offered to the public, the average person will end up paying extra so that the 15 per cent at the top can come out ahead. Once youtooism had stopped paying off for him it was easy—if painful—for the average man to figure out that he was among the 85 per cent of losers.

If the average man is more receptive now, he is also being offered a lot more information to mull. In recent years a host of new people and new organizations—ranging from Ralph Nader to your local Action Line—have begun pumping out a steady stream of explanations of the specific ways in which the public is screwed. We are nowhere near the state of grace—which we might describe as a situation when 90 per cent of us understand 90 per cent of the screwings practiced on us—and yet we are far ahead of where we were only five years ago. Take, for example, the government's third-party screwings in the favored fail-to-collect form. This consists of collecting from the average man while not collecting from the system's friends—tax loopholes and the interest-free deposits governments make in selected banks being the most notorious examples. The assumption is that we are less likely to notice the transaction because no money changes hands, and in fact for many years no one seemed to pay attention. It was not till 1968 that Stanley Surrey, then an assistant secretary of the Treasury, published the first list of what the loopholes cost those who pay taxes, and only in 1972 did the Joint Economic Committee compile a price list of all the subsidies that government was giving to its favorites. Public awareness that the tax system punishes those who work in favor of those who don't has been growing steadily. Two Washington-based organizations— Tax Analysts And Advocates, and Nader's Tax Reform Research Group—pump out a steady flow of information about the tax system. Some of the people that information reaches have gotten aroused enough to fight back. Bob Loitz is one example. Loitz is the owner of an upholstery shop in Akron, Ohio, whose frustration over the inequity of the tax system overflowed in early 1972. He got on the phone and eventually he circulated a nationwide petition demanding that the federal tax system give the average man a better break. Loitz is the founder of the Ohio Tax Equity for America Party that has begun to lobby for local tax reform. A dozen or more similar groups have sprung up around the country; many of them have short life spans, but when one expires, another is born. Their numbers are small, compared to the population as a whole, but they didn't exist at all a few years earlier. The effects of the tax reform movement are already visible. No longer is it so easy for Washington to create new tax privileges under the cover of darkness, and, while the tax system still favors the wealthy, the tax acts of 1975 and 1976 treated the average man better than any of their predecessors in recent years. Taxes of course are not collected only in Washington, and in chapter 7 we shall see how local groups have forced improvements here and there in the way the property tax is imposed.

A surprising number of other groups are out there trying to blow away the fog that conceals the working of one or another screwing. Hardly any of these groups existed in the 1960s. During that headlong decade, the economic system was denounced in millennial language that, like the thunder of a Fundamentalist preacher, made no connection with the day-to-day concerns of the average person. By the 1970s a wide variety of reformers were aiming at targets like life insurance, the privileges of professional associations, the high cost of health care, utility rates, and the like. These issues have identifiable solutions —ways of descrewing the public—and often that solution is found close to home. Thus, instead of a demonstration in Washington, that setpiece event of the sixties, we find myriad citizen groups fighting for their interests in city hall, or the state legislature, or at the utilities commission. They have been winning a series of victories, no one of them spectacular, that add up to a steady stream of good news for the average person.

Reform movements tied to specific issues are beginning to provide a political alternative to the failed two-party system. That system, as indifferent to its clientele as any other shared monopoly, has for a generation excluded the screwing of the average man from political debate. Competition at election time between the parties turns about as much on issues concerning the average person as

competition between General Motors and Ford turns on
quality and price. In both cases preserving the shared monopoly by excluding dangerous competitors is more important to the monopolists than the exact share of the
market held by each party or firm. Almost never has it
been possible for us to vote against any one screwing or
set of screwings: elections are not contested on the Social
Security payroll tax or how life insurance is marketed or
the privileges of professsional associations. The system
worked during the good years, when the average man
was getting his, or at least more than he had yesterday,
whatever the politicians did not do or say. But when youtooism lost its magic, the public became uneasy and resentful. One symptom was the declining trust in government and business expressed in all the polls. Another was
withdrawal, a refusal to play a two-party game increasingly perceived as meaningless to the public interest. The
number of Americans identifying themselves with either
political party declined steadily—by 1975 half the people
under forty claimed no party allegiance—and so did the
percentage that bothered to go to the polls on election
day. From 63 per cent in 1960, voter turnout for presidential elections dropped to 55 per cent in 1972; the 36
per cent that voted in the 1974 congressional election was
the lowest since 1942 and outside the South, where newly
registered blacks raised the total, was the lowest turnout
in more than a century.

In the short run this was to the benefit of the two-party
monopoly for, although they must never get caught saying it, an apathetic public is the surest guarantee that
officeholders can continue to profit in peace from their al-
liances with those who screw the public. But loss of faith
in the two-party system also provides a potential consti-
uency for a new kind of competition in politics, threat-
ening the existing order just as surely as the automobile

monopoly would be threatened if people found ways to get from here to there without buying a car. The reform groups playing politics outside the two-party system are drawing with considerable success on that constituency. Examples include the organizations that represent the elderly, which we describe in chapter 6, and local political groups, ACORN in Arkansas and a number of others, which are the topic of chapter 9. The political potential in discontent has even been glimpsed within the monopoly, as we shall see in later chapters, where some politicians are building careers on issues that only yesterday were excluded from political debate.

Now—lest the foregoing sound like the ravings of some Pollyanna parachuted into the wrong end of the century —it must be said that the grounds for pessimism are at least as solid. Wealth continues to trickle up to the rich, and the average person in many ways is more victimized than he was a decade ago. The times are ugly, and ugly times are dangerous. Apathy need not produce more competition in politics; it can simply breed more apathy, a self-proving guarantee that politics is futile for anyone but the special interests. The specter of unemployment can make us fear to take risks. Loss of faith can lead, not to more skeptical and self-reliant political beliefs, but to falling for the next persuasive pitchman. Inflation, by terrorizing us in the present as well as menacing our future, can make people easy prey to the most grotesque of political faiths; the German experience is too recent to forget. As the recurrent swings of inflation get worse, so do the political dangers they present.

Paranoia flourishes, that sure sign of disappointed hope, and conspiracy theorists attribute all our troubles to the conscious design of evil men. Paranoia is the clay from which our great novelist, Thomas Pynchon, fashions his art. Walter Karp, in *Indispensable Enemies*, views the two-party system as a knowing conspiracy against the public. Each day's news fuels this interpretation of the current scene, for, as Shana Alexander observed on "60 Minutes," "yesterday's paranoid nut is today's prize-winning journalist." Persuasive though it is, the paranoid interpretation is ultimately innocent, for it assumes that the evildoers must meet—at the Bilderberg Hotel, the Council on Foreign Relations, or perhaps the Chase Manhattan Bank's office at 1 Karl Marx Plaza, Moscow—in order to serve each other's interests. History suggests otherwise. The baron on this side of the river has always justified the tribute he levied on his people as needed to defend them against the enemy across the river, and yet—though each enemy was necessary to the other's prosperity—no evidence exists that the two barons had to meet in midstream to orchestrate their cover stories. Similarly, the two political parties in present day America can collaborate smoothly against the public interest without exchanging so much as a wink.

Indeed, the critical weakness of antitrust laws (drafted by people who evidently took a paranoid view of their targets) is that they require proof of conspiracy in restraint of free trade, while the big shared monopolies have demonstrated repeatedly that they need not talk to each other to accomplish their uniform pricing and fixed market shares. Adam Smith's Invisible Hand, which in the ideal free market shoves all participants toward performing for the maximum public good, has as its counterpart in the monopolized market a sort of Invisible Handshake by which the participants reach unspoken agreement on how to screw the public without leaving behind even a memo to be shredded. On those rare occasions when monopolizers are caught in a demonstrable conspiracy, it simply proves that they are unusually clumsy or, more likely, that they are operating in a market that retains vestiges of free enterprise.

If we believe that the system is not a monolith, but rather a set of organisms typically as indifferent to each other's welfare as they are to the public interest, then we can see a lot of possibilities for a better life. This is true even if the limits-of-growth theorists are right, even if that pie is not going to get any bigger from now on. For one thing, we are being forced to look more closely at how the pie is cut: should the rich continue to have and to hold so much at the expense of the rest? Should they and their wealth be exempted from taxation at the expense of income earned by work?

We are also beginning to look at just what goes into that pie—is it the best of fillings? A lot of filling provided by the monopolists is just plain waste, a kind of economic cornstarch, and if people stopped manufacturing waste in favor of other products we'd all be a lot better off even without a "bigger" economy. No one knows just how much waste is produced, but everyone except those in the waste business agrees it's a lot (and those in one waste business are often happy to point the finger at another's useless product). Beverly Moore* says waste totals twenty-five cents on every dollar—that's $2,500 on an annual income of $10,000—and he considers his estimate modest. Many would agree in general with Moore, though others have not spelled it out as carefully as he. Imagine, then, the improvement in the average person's lot that would result if all that waste—more realistically, *much* of it—were eliminated in favor of some useful activity.

Words are used here to conceal reality. "Goods" is one

---

* In *A Modest Proposal for Reform of the Capitalist System*, 1974. Available from the Center for the Study of Capitalist Institutions, 4914 Belt Road, Washington, D.C. 20016.

of those words, and "GNP" is a set of them made into initials. Take, for example, the plant that produces three dollars' worth of product, and at the same time causes us, through air pollution, two dollars in medical bills and two dollars at the dry cleaners (both bills of course inflated by their respective guilds). Common sense might tell us that we're coming out behind—three dollars of goods minus four dollars of bads seems to put us one dollar in the hole. But no: the bads aren't counted as bads. Worse: they're counted as *goods*.† So, in the insane accounting of economic statistics, the plant that produces that four dollars of bads and three dollars of goods is worth seven dollars to the economy—while another plant that produced the same goods and no bads would be worth only three dollars.

Bads are beginning to be recognized, even by economists, as something we should subtract from our goods in calculating where we stand. "Nones" are less well known. A none is something of no value that we are forced to buy. Professionals specialize in nones. The purest example is perhaps the requirement in some states that all corpses, even those to be cremated, must be embalmed: it does no good, it does no harm, it simply transfers some money from survivors to undertakers. Title insurance is a none familiar to almost all homeowners. If you have to hire a lawyer for a simple transaction that a non-lawyer, or you yourself, could have handled were it not for lawyer-imposed restrictions, much of the bill you will get is a none; if, as is often the case, the transaction itself was unnecessary, it is a pure none. Often nones are found in combination with bads, as when a doctor puts you in a hospital for an operation you didn't need. (In a sense, any none is a bad, even if it does no direct harm, simply because it

---

† Technically, they're called "services," but that doesn't affect the point being made here.

wastes resources that could have been used to produce a good.) Government is a major producer of nones. Some government agencies pass their time administering themselves without doing any good, or even harm, to the public; debate about these agencies frequently centers on how well they do their jobs rather than on whether the job is worth doing. The military industries of course provide the most colossal examples of the type: a nuclear aircraft carrier, in the unlikely event it is used, is a good or a bad depending on your point of view; most likely, however, it will rust peacefully away as a billion-dollar none.

A falling standard of living and a rising tide of skepticism provide promising conditions for efforts to reverse the screwing of the average man. Much more information is available about how screwings can be avoided, and many more people are absorbing that information and acting on it. The results appear in three distinct ways. People are finding that even as lone individuals they can stand up to an expert and ward off a swindle. People in groups are achieving similar results on a somewhat larger scale; their achievements hold lessons for the rest of us. Finally, signs of progress are visible in combating those screwings that can only be reversed by society as a whole.

In the immediate, these struggles are about whether we shall continue to be swindled by the complexity of a life insurance policy or robbed by the utilities or overtaxed so others can enjoy a free ride. In a deeper sense, however, the struggle is to decide who—ourselves or others—shall design the shape of our lives. The evidence of the last few years is that a growing number of us have come to realize that our present rulers can no longer be trusted to determine the circumstances under which we live. We are beginning to do it ourselves.

2

Lawyers: The Crumbling
Monopoly

THE LEGAL SERVICES industry is in the throes of a transformation that ultimately will affect most of our encoun-
ters with the law. The storm came up suddenly. Only yesterday the fortress seemed secure enough to last a
thousand years. By patient effort over the years, the lawyers had established a monopoly that guaranteed that
whenever a legal transaction took place a lawyer would
get paid for it. Under cover of the principle of "unau-
thorized practice of law," they had driven out all competitors and had entered into non-aggression pacts with other
professionals, such as collection agencies, that delineated
their respective territories. The number of lawyers was
held down and, within the guild, free enterprise was
effectively throttled by imposing minimum fees on the
members and forbidding them to advertise. Administration of the rules of the game was safely in the hands of
the bar association itself. As he reached out to punch the
clock that would meter his bill at twenty-five dollars to
one hundred dollars or more an hour, the lawyer could
reflect that his profession was doing as well as any this
side of organized medicine.

Now these certainties have all come unstuck. The
events of the past decade have fueled a growing skepti-

cism about experts of all kinds, and none has suffered
more from this healthy trend than the lawyer. It is increasingly obvious that justice is for those who can afford
it, and that most of us are priced out of the market. In the
old days that didn't matter too much, because only the
rich hired lawyers, but as the average man moved into
middle-class life he became entangled in legal transactions, and eventually he began to question the cost of the
services he was buying. Within the professional guild, a
minority, mostly young lawyers, was publicly challenging
the equity of the established order. Occupational birth
control broke down: law firms had only one job for every
three graduates. The oversupply of lawyers pumped out
by the law schools raised this question: if there are too
many lawyers for the caseload, and millions of people out
there who aren't buying our services, might there not be a
way to bring the two together? Jeffrey O'Connell, one of
the fathers of no-fault insurance, first asked whether the
automobile really had to guzzle as many lawsuits as it did
gallons of gas, and then asked a similar question about
the fast-growing field of product liability. Others asked
whether the routine transactions of the law really required the expensive skills of the lawyer; could we not
hire someone cheaper or even, the ultimate heresy, do it
ourselves? As the answers to these questions began to
take shape, the average man could look forward to a time
when, as Jethro K. Lieberman, legal affairs editor of *Business Week*, put it, we would have both less and more lawyering: more when we need it, less when we don't.

Much of what is happening can be seen in the case of
prepaid law, currently the hottest growth stock in the industry. Prepaid is legal insurance: instead of paying a fee
for each legal service, you pay an annual premium that
entitles you to certain kinds of legal services, either free
or at reduced rates. The idea is recent: first discussed in
the fifties, the earliest existing prepaid plans date from

the late sixties (a couple of earlier ones died in infancy). They grew slowly at first, not just because the idea was new, but because the organized bar went into court to try to argue prepaid law out of existence. The bar didn't like the prospect of salaried lawyers handling what should be fee-for-service work, especially if it meant lower costs. In Illinois, for example, the bar succeeded for a time in stopping the United Mine Workers from hiring a salaried lawyer to handle its members' workmen's compensation cases at a fraction of the fee-for-service cost, and in Virginia the bar convinced the state court that the NAACP was "soliciting" when it offered to take its members' cases without charge. In both cases, however, the bar lost the last round in the Supreme Court.

Resistance softened enough so that, in 1971, the American Bar Association agreed to join the Ford Foundation in sponsoring an experimental prepaid plan. It was in Shreveport, Louisiana, and the participants were members of the Laborers International Union Local 229. For a family premium of $40 a year, a member was entitled to $100 worth of consultation, $250 of office work and $325 in court costs. The plan was financially possible because only one family in five used it in any given year. But that was twice as often as the members previously had sought out a lawyer's services.

That last statistic gave the bar pause. Twice as much legal work out there? Today Shreveport, tomorrow the world? As legal opinion wheeled toward prepaid, the ABA began noising around numbers that it had not previously considered worthy of notice: only one American in ten could afford a lawyer, we were suddenly informed, and only the poorest one fifth were entitled to free representation through Legal Services or Legal Aid (though the supply is only a fraction of the demand); that left 70 per cent of us unlawyered. Most Americans, in fact, have been getting through a lifetime without seeing a lawyer more than once or twice. With lawyers now in surplus, that huge market, the average person in his many millions, just had to be brought within the orbit of the law.

The medical analogy intruded itself ever more insistently. Lawyers began asking whether prepaid might not be the M&M of their profession. M&M: that's not the candy, it's Medicare and Medicaid, and the sweet rewards those programs have brought to the health industry. M&M, and before them Blue Cross, had successfully severed the link between patronizing the professional and paying his bill. What law clearly needed was some similar mechanism to deafen the customer to the sound of the lawyer's meter ticking away at fifty dollars an hour, without of course stopping the clock. Prepaid was the obvious candidate.

Institutions began adjusting their principles to these new perceptions. In 1973 Congress amended the Taft-Hartley Act to permit employers to pay into union-managed employee prepaid law plans. This gave the union bureaucracies more money to administer, on top of health and pension plans; Teamster officials were among the first to spot the gravy on the plate. The unions were able to tell their members the legal services they would be getting were "free" because they were paid for by the boss, although in fact the workers paid the premiums in foregone wages; all that happened was that they became forced buyers of prepaid law whether or not they consumed any lawyering. Insurance companies saw a new product they could sell. As usual there was a tax angle. The IRS has always taken the view that benefits supposedly paid by the employer are in fact employee income and therefore taxable. In 1976 the advocates of prepaid were lobbying to get prepaid law declared tax-exempt, a loophole already enjoyed by health and pension plans, so why not us too? This is the third-party loophole system: the industry, in this case the lawyers, would get a subsidy, not directly, but via a tax exemption on income used to buy its services.

Finally, in 1975, the ABA abandoned most of the restrictions with which it had tried to keep its members out of prepaid law. The boom was on. By 1976, according to the organization that promotes prepaid law, the Washington-based National Consumer Center for Legal Services, some two million people were members of four to five thousand prepaid plans of one variety or another. Union-negotiated plans, of which there were about two hundred, are of course available only through the place of employment, but there are a growing number of other ways to get prepaid law. Some universities provide it for students; in Utah you can get it through credit unions, and, in a triumph for one-stop shopping, Blue Cross of New Mexico is marketing prepaid law along with its own product. One of the early non-union plans was Consumers Group Legal Services of the Berkeley, California, Coop, an 80,000-member food co-operative. Subscribers, who must be members of the food co-op, paid thirty-nine dollars the first year, thirty dollars thereafter. For that they got two free half-hour consultations a year, plus access to a wide range of legal services at prices well below the prevailing rates, and such tidbits as a set of instructions—"Keep this in your car in case of accident"—for recording the essential facts about your next collision. In its fourth year, the Berkeley legal group had just over 2,000 members, with a 37 per cent renewal rate; not spectacular figures, but it may be that people attracted to the food co-op are not the kind most likely to be interested in prepaid law.

The cost of prepaid law, which in most union plans runs from fifteen dollars to eighty-five dollars a year, depends mainly on how much law the plan provides. None covers every legal possibility, and many require members to pay part of the cost of some kinds of cases; some provide a fixed amount of lawyer time. In the first four years of the Shreveport plan, domestic relations (divorce and custody) and the automobile, including traffic tickets, each provided just over one quarter of the caseload. Real estate and criminal defense were the next biggest categories.

An issue of consuming interest to lawyers, less so to clients, is the distinction between "open" and "closed" plans. In an open plan, you can use any lawyers who will accept your case at whatever rate the plan will pay him, while in the closed variety you are restricted to the lawyers, often on salary, who participate in the plan. Bar associations much prefer the open plan, for the same reason organized medicine prefers the Blue Cross and Blue Shield to the prepaid health plan with salaried doctors: under the open plan, the new money can be expected to flow to the same lawyers who collected before, and no salaried lawyers threaten the sacred fee-for-service system. The bar, whose restrictions have done so much to make informed choice of a lawyer impossible, argues that it is merely trying to protect our freedom to choose any lawyer we want.

The growth so far of prepaid is, in the view of its enthusiasts, only a sample of what's to come. Here, sounding like an early Forty-niner, is Danny Jones, vice-president of Midwest Mutual Insurance Company, known as the "pied pipers of prepaid," touting its benefits to the profession in *Trial* magazine:

"What are those economic fruits which the legal profession can harvest? The most obvious market for insured legal services is the American middle income segment. The market is composed of 128 million people who earn between $5,000 and $20,000 a year. If the insurance industry can penetrate 60 per cent, then there will be 46 million new, fee-paying legal matters annually. The reported average claim of the Shreveport . . . plan is

$142.00. This translates into an annual new income of approximately *SIX BILLION DOLLARS* [his caps, not ours] to the legal profession or approximately $20,000 in new fees per year per lawyer, based on a projected lawyer population of 500,000 by the year 1985."

Six billion—twenty thousand per! These figures, while doubtless intoxicating to a third-year law student, may well cause the average man, as a member of that middle-income "segment," to wonder who is going to pay for all those helpings of legal caviar. If the third-party principle is working right, the source of the money will be so muddied that it will be clear that no one is paying—but that of course means everyone, so the average man will once again receive the bill. The figures in any event seem drawn from hope rather than reality. Writing in *Juris Doctor*, David Weinstein, a consultant studying prepaid plans, questioned how many of Jones's 128 million target population would in fact turn out to be clients. "Not even the most rambunctious or ambitious seven-year-old is likely to hire a lawyer," Weinstein observed. Weinstein added that a public opinion survey by the ABA had found that "the incidence of problems for which consulting a lawyer is generally considered was very low. The median number of problems (chosen from a long list) was 3.4 in a lifetime—and this figure included traffic tickets. So if the average person has about fifty adult years, then he is likely to have a problem about every 15 years which can in some sense be defined as 'legal.' And he is unlikely to seek a lawyer's services even when he has such a problem." (He may, of course, avoid the lawyer not because he doesn't want him but because he can't afford him, or because he senses the lawyer would just make things worse.)

Michael Kinsley, a newly minted Harvard lawyer, also questioned whether the average person needs all that new litigation. While acknowledging that many people are screwed for lack of a lawyer, he did not see a wheel-barrowful of prepaid law as the best or only solution. Writing in *The Washington Monthly,* Kinsley asked if the person who got through the year without legal help missed it any more than he did the services of, say, a glass cutter or a flower arranger. While it may be a good idea to see the dentist once a year (some would say twice), does our law decay at the same rate as our teeth? Kinsley concluded with a dismal picture of a world engulfed by universal litigation "where the portion of the population that went through a typical year happily oblivious of the legal profession slipped from two-thirds, to one-half, to one-quarter, to none at all."

Although prepaid may never reach the size of Danny Jones's dream and Michael Kinsley's nightmare, it seems certain to become one of the ways in which legal services will be delivered at a price the average man can afford. Not the only or primary way, however, for prepaid, like its medical counterpart, the Health Maintenance Organization, will not reach the part of the market made up of those many people who do not believe their law requires enough attention to justify paying an annual premium. To such people, prepaid's notions of "preventive law" and "regular legal checkups" can only be reminiscent of the old French movie *Doctor Knock* in which Louis Jouvet solved the problem of excessive health in a peasant village by putting everyone in bed for preventive treatment. For those who want to hire a lawyer only when they need him, and yet do not belong to the one in ten who can afford today's meter rates, the emerging answer is the legal clinic.

The first, most successful and the best-known of these is the Legal Clinic of Jacoby and Meyers, which has three offices in the Los Angeles area. Since its opening in 1972, it has become a major producer of low-cost legal services. In contrast to the practice of most lawyers, who avoid talking fees until the client is hooked, the clinic posts its prices in the office. The comparison shopper will like what he sees. For the kinds of transactions they handle, Jacoby and Meyers charge from one-quarter to two-thirds less than the prevailing rate. A flat fee of $15 gets you an initial interview, after which you can leave if you don't like what you hear. The clinic's growing volume of business suggests that quality has not suffered because of low prices, and testimonials from satisfied clients are numerous. An actress was delighted to find that, despite the progress of inflation, she could get a divorce with property settlement from the clinic for $250—her previous divorce had cost her twice as much for no greater service. For Judith and David Hamilton of Pacific Palisades, there was no alternative to the clinic. A roofer had bungled the job, and the Hamiltons wanted their $800 back. A standard law firm wanted $900 to take the case, putting the Hamiltons $100 in the hole even if they won. They couldn't go into small claims court—the maximum there was $500. But Jacoby and Meyers took the case for $300, and won, netting the Hamiltons $500 and a redress denied them by the rest of the legal system.

The clinics—Jacoby and Meyers, and the others that have sprung up after them—are able to work at those prices because they've improved the delivery system. They accept only the categories of cases in which they've specialized, though these include most of the routine transactions the average person needs. They employ paralegal assistants, at greatly reduced cost, for much of the work that doesn't require a lawyer. Perhaps most important, Jacoby and Meyers shortened preparation time by breaking down the standard procedures in different kinds of cases and organizing them in work kits that summarize the pertinent law and list the information that must be gotten from the client. The savings are great. When, in a 1975 radio interview, Stephen Meyers said the clinic could show a profit on a $135 uncontested divorce, the interviewer said that the lawyers who charge $400 (the bar association's "suggested" fee) for the same job must be taking it home in a truck. Meyers disagreed: the difference, he said, lay more in waste than in profit. The typical general practice lawyer will take on any kind of case, then scramble on the client's time to learn the law; he uses none of the clinics' time-saving techniques. As a result, it takes him a lot longer to reach the same goal. Now the clinics are bringing the cold wind of competition to a business that had been a comfortably featherbedded monopoly. Because the clinics don't play monopoly by the guild rules, they are, in Meyers' words, an "economic threat to local attorneys."

The California bar agreed, and in 1973 it brought charges against Jacoby and Meyers. Skirting the touchy issue of prices, the bar accused them of advertising. No one said they had taken ads—"go broke with us, and save $75 on your bankruptcy"—in the local press, but they had answered reporters' questions about the clinic, and in their early days that publicity was crucial to getting the volume of business the clinic needed to survive. Like other professional guilds, the bar considers advertising "unethical"; such rules banish the specter of free enterprise and protect established firms against upstarts. It is all right, of course, to get your name in the paper, for example, by running for office—if you're not cutting prices. (Anyone who believes that overregulation is a government monopoly might contemplate the insanely detailed rules lawyers impose on themselves: your local zoning code's rule on the size of the sign a lawyer may hang out pales by comparison with the New York Bar Association's ruling that its members may not use blue paper for their business cards.) The chilling effect of the California bar's action was felt by the half-dozen clinics that had opened after Jacoby and Meyers. Unable to advertise, fearful of retribution if they even got their names in the papers, three clinics had to close; their volume of cases, ample for an old-style high-cost firm, was not enough to sustain their low-price operations. By 1975, there were fewer clinics than a year earlier. With even the founding fathers staring down the barrel of the California bar's canon of ethics, it seemed that organized law had successfully squelched the industrial revolution and that the legal clinic was to be relegated to the history books, like the steam engine invented in Ptolemy's Alexandria, as an innovation whose time had not yet come.

This time history went the other way. In that same year of 1975, a Supreme Court decision shattered one of the pillars of the legal monopoly, the minimum fee system, undermined another, the ban on advertising, and sent shock waves through the structures of the other organized professional guilds. Minimum fees have been an integral part of the legal featherbed. It is, as Mark J. Green reminded us in the New York *Times Magazine*, a long time since the Cincian Law of 200 B.C. forbade Roman lawyers from taking any fees at all. Starting in the late nineteenth century, those days when professional guilds were spreading faster than railroads, minimum fee schedules were adopted by one bar association after another; by the time of the Supreme Court decision, 750 local bar associations had rules setting forth the minimum amounts their members must charge for their services. Their purpose was most baldly stated in 1960 by the Illinois Bar Association: "The respect for the legal profession and its influence in the individual community will be raised when the lawyer occupies his proper place at the top of the economic structure." The case that brought this happy state of legal affairs to a conclusion was started by Ruth and Lewis Goldfarb against the bar association of Fairfax County, Virginia. Appropriately, the object of their suit was a title search, the most egregious of the make-work services the would-be homeowner is forced to buy. When they set out to buy a house in Reston, Virginia, the Gold-farbs asked local lawyers their price for a title search (a service worth, at generous estimate, perhaps $50): all nineteen who replied quoted a price of $522.50, the bar association minimum. The Goldfarbs rebelled, and Alan B. Morrison of the Nader Public Citizen Litigation Group took the case all the way to the top. When the Goldfarbs' case reached the Supreme Court four years later, the bar association argued that as a "learned profession" it was exempt from the antitrust laws, but the court found, by 8–0, that minimum fees were just plain old price-fixing. (The "learned profession" argument, as we note in chapter 4, has fallen on hard times recently, a casualty, no doubt, of the general decline of the expert.) Alan Morrison happily proclaimed the decision to be "a big shot in the arm to the little guy who has to deal with lawyers."

Lawyers' fees did not come tumbling down immediately in the wake of the Goldfarb decision, though Alan Morrison reported that the cost of a title search in northern Virginia dropped by one third. But the feeling was widespread that, with minimum fees outlawed, the ban on advertising would be the next monopolistic practice to go. Lawyers generally agreed with Chesterfield Smith, former president of the ABA, that "now that the court has clearly put lawyers under the antitrust laws, all of the ethical principles of the existing professional code that restrict competition will have to be reexamined. . . . The present prohibition on advertising cannot now survive a court challenge."

The challenge was not long in coming. Within a week of the Goldfarb decision, Carl E. Person, a New York law-yer who also trains paralegals, brought a federal case against the advertising ban; so three months later did two lawyers in Virginia; others followed, including a Con-sumers Union suit against the California bar. The FTC, which, as we report in chapter 4, has been attacking the prohibition of advertising by other guilds, said right after Goldfarb that it was launching a year-long study of the effect on fees of the advertising ban in southern California, locus of the bar's attempt to put Jacoby and Meyers out of business. And the head of the antitrust division of the Justice Department, Bruce B. Wilson, invited the lawyers to do voluntarily what the courts seem certain to do for them. In February 1976, the ABA gave in and abandoned its opposition to advertising. Its action did not overturn the bans on advertising maintained by state and local bar associations, but it did not seem that the locals could hold out long against the combined pressure of the law and the national bar.

The Goldfarb case, and the imminent freedom to advertise, saved the legal clinic from probable extinction. In Phoenix, the Bates & O'Steen clinic took an ad in the *Arizona Republic* that started out with "DO YOU NEED A LAWYER? Legal Services at Very Reasonable Fees" and went on to list the prices of five common services. The clinic also filed a suit seeking to establish its right to advertise. Already the bar had begun issuing sounds of qualified approval, the qualification having to do with the incomes of those who would have access to the clinics' cheaper services. Earlier the bar had approved government-paid legal services for the poor; since the poor weren't about to hire lawyers in any event, the only result of legal services for them was more work for lawyers, the bill being third-partied to the taxpayers without affecting the rates lawyers could charge their existing clientele. Perhaps the clinics could similarly be boxed in to the lower brackets. Thus, when the organized bar decided to support an "experimental" clinic of its own, an ABA committee came out strongly for a clinic limiting itself to people making less than $10,000 over one with a $20,000 top. The latter, the committee explained to the president of the ABA, "is going to generate intense hostility from the practicing lawyers in the vicinity where the clinic will operate, who will feel that the clinic is taking away their clientele who really can afford their fees and really do know how to find lawyers." The idea for the "experimental" clinic followed a conference to which the bar invited the operators of all the existing clinics—except Jacoby and Meyers. It was no more than a rearguard action: of the clinics existing in 1975, only one limited its clients by income, and with the legal barriers demolished there seemed no reason why future clinics should turn away a client just because he could afford another lawyer's exorbitant fees. (In addition to saving the low-cost clinic, the repeal of the advertising ban will help the average person who, when he sets out to choose a lawyer, would like to know the lawyer's specialty and how much he charges. The bar has valiantly resisted efforts to make that kind of information available to the public. When Consumers Union tried to make a survey of lawyers in Arlington County, Virginia, preparatory to putting out a directory that would include lawyers' prices and specialties, the local bar hopped right down to the courthouse and got the judge to put a stop to it.)

The legal clinic, more than prepaid law, is the prototype of a system that will deliver legal services to the average person at greatly reduced prices. Because they are paid not by the hour but by a fixed fee for a given service, both clinic and prepaid practices will be forced into a continuing search for greater efficiency. As competition grows, fueled by the oversupply of lawyers, existing law firms will be forced in the same direction. Ultimately the pressure of competition may convert lawyers into crusaders for efficiency in parts of the legal system that lie outside their own offices. They may find that the calculated boondoggle of the title search—title insurance combination is no longer in their interest, and, in a broader sense, once the lawyer is not paid by the meter, he will no longer stand to gain from the vast waste of the court system. Thus the effects of introducing competition into legal services will reach far beyond the issues in the Goldfarb case.

Paradoxically, the future of the law includes fewer and larger law offices along with more competition, because many of the cost-cutting innovations in legal work—computer research and the machines that write standard texts are examples—cannot be easily adopted by the very small firm. One innovation, however, is helping the smaller firm against the giants, and cutting costs at the same time. This is the legal research firm. Winning the usual case turns less on Perry Mason dramatics than on careful research of the law, and the small firm of two or three lawyers has neither the time nor the specialized skill—nor, frequently, does the client have the money—to be an even match for a big opponent. The research firms help equalize the match by selling research work at a price low enough—most charge less than twenty dollars an hour—so that the client can get up to twice as much work as he would had his lawyer researched the case. "Expert legal research puts us into the big firm category," a small firm lawyer, quoted by Edward Tivnan in *Juris Doctor*, said after he won the first case he tried with outside research. The business is booming. Tivnan's 1975 article listed five research firms, some with several offices. The first and largest, The Research Group, Inc., dates from 1969 and is now a two-million-dollar a year business with fifty-five full-time lawyers. The research firms, unlike the legal clinics, are able to advertise because they sell their services to lawyers, not to the public, and because they do not "practice law" in the sense that they do not appear in court. The savings that result from outside research do not go directly to the client, but in the developing competitive market, the lawyer will ultimately have to pass on most of his lower costs to the public.

Another area in which law is evolving in favor of the average man is product liability. Today the person injured by a manufacturer's product has a better chance than ever before of collecting some kind of compensation. The field is distressingly large: each year some twenty million among us are injured in the home in the use of a consumer product, and of these 30,000 are killed and 110,000 disabled. (Those figures do not include on-the-job or highway injuries.) The electric fan alone lops off 13,000 fingers a year. "It's the age of consumer body count," product-liability lawyer John Hayward said. "They're keeping track to find an acceptable death level. Insurance companies ask all the time, 'How much is a person going for these days?'" The answer is that our price is going up.

Product liability has come a long way. In the early days of the industrial revolution, the injured customer had virtually no recourse: the law protected the manufacturer with the doctrine that, since he had signed no contract with the buyer, no grounds existed for suing him if his product was defective. The first decade of this century, a time, much like the present, of shoddy products and a rapidly rising cost of living, brought widespread demands for making industry responsible for what it put on the market. The law began to change in 1916 when Benjamin Cardozo, then on the New York Court of Appeals, found against Buick, despite the absence of a contract, in favor of a customer whose car's wooden wheels were defective. But the doctrine of negligence—that the injured person had to prove the manufacturer had been negligent in making the defective product—still made it extremely hard to collect. Then, in 1944, came the case of the Coke bottle that exploded in a waitress's hand. Ruling against the company, California Supreme Court Justice Roger

Traynor put aside the need to prove negligence and laid down what is now called the doctrine of strict liability: "The purpose of such liability is to insure that the costs of injuries resulting from defective products are borne by the manufacturer that put such products in the market rather than by the injured persons who are powerless to protect themselves."

Other judges accepted Traynor's precedent, the number of product liability cases multiplied, and the victims' batting average improved. In less than a decade the number of cases rose from 50,000 a year to ten times that number. The injured person won more often: 54 per cent of the verdicts in 1974, compared to less than half ten years earlier. And he was winning more: the average verdict, $11,644 in 1965, was $79,940 in 1973. California, the state with the greatest number of product liability cases, was bringing in an average of ten $100,000 verdicts a *week*. The lawyers were also winning more. Products law had once been "the guffaw of the bar," Jonathan Evan Maslow wrote in *Juris Doctor*, but now "personal injury lawyers are migrating to products law in a great stampede" and finding there "a land of milk and honey, a deliverance from tormented wanderings in the desert of no-fault," the latter of course being the way of settling injury cases without litigation.

But if the person maimed or mutilated by the industrial machine's output has a better chance than ever of collecting, that chance is still pretty poor. "Most injuries to consumers go uncompensated," the National Commission on Product Safety concluded; one estimate is that compensation covers less than 15 per cent of the total loss. Product liability cases are extremely technical and hard to prove, and lawyers are reluctant to take a claim for less than five or ten thousand dollars. The injured person's lawyer must, as one of them put it, "overcome, in a very short time in a courtroom, years of people's training to believe in products through advertising." His opponent, the manufacturer's lawyer, comes to court flanked by platoons of engineer witnesses whose testimony no one understands but who are clean-cut and therefore obviously sincere. Rather than make their products safer, the manufacturers are trying to improve their record for safety in the courtroom, with the aid of something called the Defense Research Institute, a think tank which does for product-liability defendants what, from its name, you might have thought it was doing for the weapons industry. In his book *Ending Insult to Injury*, Jeffrey O'Connell commented that "the recipients of money which could help to compensate injured consumers are for the most part a few highly skilled lawyers on both sides, a few highly skilled engineers and technical experts, and a few casualty insurance companies, constantly complaining about how much money they are losing on the whole operation."

O'Connell has an idea for increasing the amount that trickles down to the victims. It's the same idea he had before, and the lawyers aren't going to like it this time either. It's the no-fault principle that O'Connell and Robert E. Keeton introduced to auto-injury cases (and which is the principle of workmen's compensation for on-the-job injuries). O'Connell argues that manufacturers could carry no-fault insurance on their products that would, by eliminating litigation, cost them less and still better compensate the injured. The idea is far more complex and problematic than auto no-fault, but, on his record, O'Connell may one day be creating another no-fault desert in the lawyers' latest land of milk and honey.

No-fault is part of the second way of improving legal services for the average person: less lawyering when we don't need it. Auto-injury no-fault, which now exists in what O'Connell considers "genuine" form in fifteen states, has in fact begun to reduce the flow of traffic through the courtroom. No-fault divorce is also progressing. Since California started it in 1970, thirteen states have eliminated the need for finding fault in the process of putting asunder those who were unhappily joined in matrimony; eleven other states have limited forms of no-fault divorce. In all those states, divorce is cheaper and less painful than it would otherwise be.

Those who would like to do their own lawyering, because the amount is small or the lawyer's fee large, or for whatever other reason, will find the path less difficult than it was only yesterday. Lawyers have always frowned on the amateur in the courtroom: he doesn't know a tort from a tortilla, nor, for that matter, law from justice, and besides he's costing some brother a fee. Judges have typically done their best—sometimes more than their legal best—to prevent people from representing themselves; a judge, after all, is only a lawyer who knows a governor. Sometimes the legal defense is remarkably ingenious, as Paul Gillette found out. Gillette is a writer, maverick psychologist, and eloquent critic of professional monopolies who also likes to represent himself in court. Having won a couple of cases elsewhere, he tried again in Lackawanna County, Pennsylvania. Gillette started by asking the judge for the local rules of procedure. The judge referred him to the county bar association, and the answer Gillette received there made everything perfectly clear: "Please be advised that the Lackawanna Bar Association published the local rules of court and distributed same only to members of the Association. There are no extra copies available for distribution." The system's delaying tactics worked: Gillette ran out of time and had to abandon his case.

But the experts are in eclipse, and the trend is toward letting people have their day in court without a lawyer. In June 1975, the Supreme Court, by a 6–3 vote, guaranteed that right for criminal cases. (Chief Justice Burger dissented on the grounds that the defendant must be protected from his folly by the expert and, in another dissent, Associate Justice Blackmun quoted the old line: "One who is his own lawyer has a fool for a client." These two opinions, by the Court's supposed conservatives, remind us that in America conservatism and the defense of individual liberties do not go hand-in-hand.) Six months after that decision, the Associated Press reported a great increase in self-defense: in Los Angeles County, for example, the number representing themselves had tripled. One reason many gave was that public defenders and Legal Aid lawyers were too quick to plea-bargain away their claim to innocence.

The right to do it ourselves is not enough, except for the Paul Gillettes of this world, without some idea of how to go about it. Many of us, contemplating the notion of going it alone on some routine civil procedure, are likely to be discouraged by the fine print of the paperwork couched in a dialect calculated to drive us back onto the lawyer's meter. At such moments of indecision, the do-it-yourself kit may determine whether the customer saves some money or a law school graduate gets a job. In the last decade there has been a proliferation of manuals designed to help people do without a lawyer in various legal transactions. One of the oldest and best known is Norman Dacey's *How to Avoid Probate*. Up in Greece, New York, James Winder's bumper sticker proclaims, "Stop Government by Lawyers"; in keeping with that point of view, he sells a divorce-yourself kit ($90), and has added wills ($6.00), separation ($35) and bankruptcy ($55). Divorce-yourself kits are also available in Texas and Washington. John Slavicek of San Francisco sells a bankruptcy kit for $50, and the customers like it better than does Judge Robert L. Hughes. Hughes, whose court handles two to three hundred bankruptcy cases a month, had this to say: "Before Mr. Slavicek started operations, there would be five to ten that filed without a lawyer. Now we get about fifty who filed without a lawyer. This is primarily because Mr. Slavicek advertises so heavily." The organized bar has tried repeatedly to put this kind of bathtub law out of business, and most of the time the bar has lost. Winder hired a lawyer when the bar went after him, and the bar won the first round. On the appeal, Winder took his own prescription and represented himself; this time he won.

Of course, not everyone who buys a kit actually uses it. One publisher of manuals, Nolo Press of Berkeley, has tried to estimate its products' effect in the marketplace. Nolo, run by a group of lawyers, puts out titles on subjects as diverse as *How to Legally Beat the Bill Collector* to *Sex, Living Together and the Law*. Their first title, *How to Do Your Own Divorce*, was little noticed till it was denounced by the president of the local bar association; since that promotion, it has sold more than 100,000 copies. It's an attractively designed, clearly written volume, with occasional offbeat asides: "If there are times during your dissolution when you feel tense or down, it should be no surprise. . . . Take a break sometimes and get into the artwork in this book. In many drawings, the shapes are not of anything in particular, but are pure energy and motion. Get lost in the forms, perceive the motion and the feeling. Relax and stare at the art a while—you'll like it." Fine . . . and where were we? Yes: the book does not assume you're necessarily going to do it yourself, but provides helpful advice if you intend to retain a lawyer for part or all of the process. The author, Charles E. Sherman, who used to be a Legal Aid lawyer, estimated in 1975 that using *How to Do Your Own Divorce* had saved its readers about $40 million in legal costs.

Still, a book cannot answer all our ignorant questions, and that fact alone will scare off a lot of would-be selfdivorcers. For them, California offers the Wave Project. Wave has twenty-eight offices around the state where you can get help on a lawyer-free uncontested divorce for $75 (far below the usual lawyers' fee of $300–$500 and up and only half of Jacoby and Meyers' $150). The help is provided by laymen trained in a few days by Phyllis Eliasberg, Wave's director, whose headquarters is in Van Nuys. Eliasberg, who is a lawyer, says that the Wave laymen are "at least as competent to help in the dissolution proceeding as any lawyer. Perhaps they are more competent since they are not trained in the adversary process and do not have such a large financial stake in the outcome of the proceeding that dissolution becomes inevitable." (The name Wave, in case you were wondering, is not an acronym. Eliasberg explains: "A wave is an energy force. It meets obstacles but can go around them and come together again.") Wave has grown rapidly, and by 1976 was handling divorces at the rate of three thousand a year. It was part of what, by comparison to other states, was a tidal wave of do-it-yourself divorce: one in every five California divorces was being done without a lawyer, for a saving of around $8 million a year and a lot of lawyer-induced conflict. Phyllis Eliasberg hopes eventually to branch out into other kinds of legal services, beginning with probate, that can be efficiently and inexpensively handled by a group of laymen supervised by a lawyer. If Wave survives. Like Jacoby and Meyers, Wave came under the cold eye of the California Bar Association, and, like them, Phyllis Eliasberg was charged with price-cutting, or, as the bar calls it, advertising. But, whatever the outcome of Eliasberg's case, the bar was obviously playing King Canute to the Wave of the future. The ban on advertising cannot long endure, and, when it goes, the pattern set by Wave is sure to be replicated all over the nation.

Another way of doing it yourself is the small-claims

courts that exist in varying forms in all the states. In theory, this is where the average man could pursue a small-scale dispute without hiring a lawyer or getting enmeshed in the cumbersome and expensive machinery of the judicial system. In practice many small-claims courts discouraged his participation and some were mainly used by collecting agencies. In recent years, however, there has been renewed interest in small claims and a number of states have been impelled to make those courts more useful to the average person. Perhaps the most important improvement, and the one most resisted by the legal establishment, is raising the limit on the amount you can sue for in small claims; in most states the limit is still under $1,000. When the limit in New York City was raised from $500 to $1,000, the Council of Judicial Associations, representing judges, protested on the grounds—you may not believe this—that the increase would mean the loss of millions of dollars in filing fees in the higher courts. Consumer groups here and there have put out guides to small claims and have pushed for making them function better by, for example, holding evening and weekend sessions and by making it easier to collect if you do win your case.

The barrier to doing it yourself has been eliminated, in two states, in the field of the most lucrative legal makework—probate. Probate is the process of distributing what we leave when we die; because it happens only once per person, and because to the heirs it is unearned income, the lawyers have been able to carve a large slice for performing what are mainly routine duties that many laymen could do if the system permitted them to. Appropriately enough, the breakthrough occurred in Wisconsin, where in a notorious case less than ten years ago the state supreme court blocked a citizen's attempt to probate his mother's will without a lawyer. (As noted in chapter 5, Wisconsin is also the only state that sells cheap life insurance.) Wisconsin adopted do-it-yourself probate in 1973, followed by Minnesota in 1975. When he signed the law, Governor Patrick J. Lucey said, and for once political rhetoric matched reality: "Wisconsin's probate-reform act represents a great victory for the individual citizen. No longer does the law assume that the average man or woman cannot handle his or her own personal affairs. No longer is the citizen required, in effect, to pay a legal tax amounting to hundreds or thousands of dollars for a service he wants to perform for himself."

Murray Teigh Bloom, who had described probate hustles in his book *The Trouble with Lawyers*, now explained how the new law works (in the *Reader's Digest* for July 1975). Under its system of "informal administration," a non-lawyer, typically a member of the family, can probate the will if all the heirs agree. (If there is a dispute, it can be taken to court.) The probate court, which previously had done all in its considerable power to discourage do-it-yourselfers, now encouraged them. In, Dane County, for example, the local probate register, a lawyer, offers free advice, and two booklets—the *Layman's Guide to Probate* ($1) and *Probating an Estate in Wisconsin Without an Attorney* ($.65)—are also available. The new law also ended some time-honored probate boondoggles. Title to jointly owned property could only be changed by paying a lawyer 5 *per cent* of the total value; now it takes $10 and a simple affidavit. Survivors are no longer required to pay an appraiser a substantial fee for looking up in *The Wall Street Journal* the value of the deceased person's stocks, nor are they required to pay a court-appointed lawyer to act as special guardian of any minor children mentioned in the will.

At the time Bloom wrote, more than 400 Wisconsin residents had chosen to do their own probate. The estates ranged from $10,000 to $100,000 and were relatively uncomplicated; if an estate is large and complex, a lawyer who knows how to thread a tax loophole can save many times his fee. (Especially if he is hired before death. In his *Estate Planning Desk Book*, William J. Casey compares ten methods of transferring a $300,000 estate and finds that the cost of transfer can range from a low of 4.13 per cent to a high of 40.62 per cent.) Some do-it-yourselfers also used a lawyer when it seemed necessary, at much less cost, usually under $400, than under the old system, because the lawyer didn't do the routine paperwork. Bloom offered the example of Joanne Casey of Greendale, who probated her father's fifty-thousand-dollar estate, saving $1,000 or more in legal fees. Mrs. Casey later commented: "I have only a high school education. If I can do it, anyone can." Bloom also described the case of the widow who probated her husband's estate, worth about $50,000 plus life insurance of $20,000, on behalf of their two children and herself. The estate was settled in four and a half months, far less than the average time. The job cost the widow about thirty hours of her time and just $45 in cash. And, in implied response to the lawyer's claim that amateurs are bound to screw up the paperwork, Bloom reported that no laymen's probate had resulted in litigation.

The benefits of the new law are not limited to those who take advantage of it. The very existence of the do-it-yourself option breaks the lawyers' monopoly on probate and thereby puts pressure on them to hold down their prices to those who choose to use their services—still the large majority in Wisconsin. The savings from this threat of competition may add up to more than the benefits gained by those few who practice do-it-yourself probate.

No change of such magnitude happens by accident. In Wisconsin it was the fruit of a campaign led by state legislator David Berger of Milwaukee and backed by a statewide petition bearing no less than 350,000 signatures; the bill passed the legislature over the intense opposition of probate lawyers and judges. Such a triumph for the average man is unlikely to be duplicated elsewhere without a similar political effort. Some states—eleven at last count—have adopted the Uniform Probate Code, a less ambitious reform. Even in those states, the simplified procedures of the uniform code have greatly decreased the cost of probate. Bloom compared probate costs in Idaho, the first state to adopt the uniform code, with Michigan under the old system: a widow inheriting $100,000 would have lawyer bills of $900 in Idaho, compared with $4,800 in Michigan, and another $2,000 if the lawyer was also executor; court costs would be $32 in Idaho, $947.50 in Michigan.

The American court system remains as an imposing barrier between the average person and the ideal of justice that is both cheap and speedy. Our courts are run along the lines advocated by the Chinese Emperor K'anghsi: ". . . lawsuits would tend to increase to a frightening extent if people were not afraid of the tribunals and if they felt confident of always finding in them ready and perfect justice. . . . I desire therefore that those who have recourse to the tribunals should be treated without pity and in such a manner that they shall be disgusted with law and tremble to appear before a magistrate."

The American who goes to court on, say, a personal injury case may well come away "disgusted with law." He can afford it if his lawyer takes it on a contingency fee. But the inefficiency of the courts, and the lack of any supervision of the cut his lawyer takes, mean that the lawyer won't take a small case because of the court costs, and that more than half what he is awarded is likely to vanish between costs and the lawyer's fee. For most people who get entangled in the judicial process, its agonizing slowness is probably more damaging than its inflated cost; lawyers representing the elderly say their main problem is not winning the case but getting the settlement paid

while the client is still around to spend it. Run by people
who are responsible to nobody—the ideal of every bureaucracy—our courts are models of waste and indolence that
can stand comparison with anything the weapons industry can offer. Far fewer dollars are involved, of course, the
cost of courts being a trivial item in the total bill for government; for that reason, perhaps, taxpayers seldom get
aroused over judicial boondoggling. The person who has
just gone through an endless legal proceeding—waiting
four years to get compensated for an injury, for example—
doesn't expect to be doing it again soon, never if he has
any luck, and so he is not disposed to spend his spare time
lobbying for court reform. His opponent in that case, the
insurance company, actually benefited from the delay.
The natural lobbyists for more efficient courts, the lawyers who practice there, do not today have much reason
to demand speedier justice. As long as the client doesn't
mind paying—and for corporate clients legal fees are a
minor cost—the lawyer doesn't mind sitting around waiting for the judge to come back from his three-hour lunch;
his meter is ticking all the while. As noted earlier, this
may begin to change with the spread of prepaid and
clinic law: these lawyers, paid by the case, not the hour,
will find that the present dragging out of the court
process is a cost to them, not a benefit.

That time has yet to come, but already some courts
have made noticeable progress toward better performance. In Massachusetts, for example, which had six of the
twelve counties in the nation with the worst judicial
backlog, a five-year effort has resulted in considerable
simplifying and standardizing of a hodgepodge of local
court rules; cases move faster and sometimes—because of
innovations like substituting a taped for a typed transcript—more cheaply. California has been more active
than other states in getting rid of judges who don't belong
in court, and evidently with good reason. In recent years

these events have been recorded in California courts: a judge loudly informed a rape victim that she was "nothing but a horse's ass"; a judge jabbed a lawyer in the rear with a "battery-operated object sometimes referred to as a 'dildo'"; a judge locked up a bunch of lawyers for contempt, evidently having prejudged them by ordering preparations to take them to jail even before they had appeared in court. Within the past four years, seven judges have resigned while under investigation—a record number—and the California Supreme Court for the first time in its history removed a judge who had not been convicted of a crime: that was the judge with the dildo. But neither California nor any other state has begun removing judges for simple sloth, which is the judiciary's most common sin.

The surest way to reduce the cost and time involved in the usual court proceeding is, obviously, to avoid it completely. As we have seen, in civil law no-fault and the expansion of small claims are important steps in that direction. Businessmen have been turning in growing numbers to arbitration as a way to settle contract disputes faster and cheaper than in court, and, in criminal law, a few small steps have been taken, here and there, toward keeping victimless crimes, those which are defined by state morality rather than harm to others, out of the courts.

The most interesting recent event in the courts may well be what happened in Columbus, Ohio. The Night Prosecutor program was started in 1971, with the purpose of keeping personal conflicts and minor crimes out of the cumbersome and damaging grasp of the criminal procedure. It is a kind of criminal small claims operation. The Night Prosecutor is an after-hours court that tries to handle the cases it gets with the aim of resolving the underlying conflict that brought those people there, rather than determining guilt and innocence. As an official of the Law Enforcement Assistance Administration, which funded the project, wrote: "The emphasis is on a lasting solution to an interpersonal problem rather than a judgment of right and wrong." It is aimed at the kind of conflict which, in the standard criminal process, leaves the disputants no alternative but to either accuse the other person of a crime or abandon any hope of redress—those many cases where, when all you want is for the other fellow to stop what he's doing, or give back what he took, the cop says: "Do you want to bring charges?" But getting him indicted may not get you what you want, and may be a more punitive outcome than you would prefer, while if your answer to the cop's question is "no," society will offer you no help in solving the problem.

The Night Prosecutor holds hearings, not trials, and the person running the hearing is a local law student, trained and supervised by a professor from the Capital University Law School, one of whom is on duty every night. No rules of evidence are observed, and everyone is encouraged to speak out. If the conflict cannot be resolved that night, another hearing is held. If the antagonists do reach an agreement, the Night Prosecutor's office will check back periodically with both parties to see if the treaty is still holding.

The cases the Night Prosecutor handles are mostly small: conflicts, violent or not, among neighbors, public nuisances, unleashed dogs, all the run of occasions for one of us to be aggrieved about another. Some of these can escalate into a lot of potential court business: one feud between families, resolved by the Night Prosecutor, had produced seven felony and fourteen misdemeanor charges. The Night Prosecutor has gone beyond resolving personal conflicts: it also handles bad-check and landlord-tenant cases. The cases come to the Night Prosecutor from a lot of sources: policemen on patrol, detectives, the criminal prosecutor and Legal Aid lawyers, all seeking a better way to handle the problems that land in their laps;

and, of course, angry citizens racing to tell their story first.

The record in Columbus is remarkable. In its first year, the Night Prosecutor handled 3,684 cases, of which only 84 had to be sent on to the criminal courts. By mid-1975, it had handled 30,000 cases. In bad-check cases, the Night Prosecutor brings together the merchant, who just wants to be paid, and the person who wrote the rubber check: in the first two months, of 461 cases 290 had resulted in full restitution, 156 were being held in abeyance on a promise to pay, and just 15 had been sent on to the criminal courts. The police and criminal court systems of Columbus were feeling the effects: in 1974 arrests dropped by 20 per cent, while they were escalating practically everywhere else, and cases in criminal court decreased by 10,000. This freed both court and police time for serious cases.

The Night Prosecutor program is being emulated by a number of other cities, perhaps because it's cheap: a case there costs about twenty dollars, a fraction of what it would cost in criminal court. That's not the most important statement to make about it. One of the law school participants said: "Community tensions have eased . . . the police can spend more time on patrol, less in court testifying." And Milton G. Rector, president of the National Council on Crime and Delinquency, drew broader implications:

> An arrest record is one of the most disabling things that can happen to an individual. Any process that avoids it, while enhancing justice and protecting the public, is worth its weight in gold. Americans have a great tendency to settle things by taking someone to court. For most minor offenses, this is a costly and time-wasting process. The Columbus way is faster, friendlier and cheaper, yet satisfies justice and the law.

A good idea, but not particularly new. In traditional African law that persists today, and in the legal systems of many vanished societies, the goal was to solve the problem and compensate the injured, not to afford the state the satisfaction of punishing those it had found guilty. Now, in no-fault and "innovations" like the Night Prosecutor we are groping our way back toward understanding what we all knew a few centuries ago.

That last thought—that we are just beginning to catch up with our ancestors in our conception of the meaning of law—will serve to temper the optimism of what we have reported earlier in this chapter. For the average person, little has changed as yet. If he has a three-hundred-dollar legal problem, a lawyer still costs too much and so the problem will be unresolved; if he buys a house, he will still get swindled on the title search and insurance, unless he lives in northern Virginia, where he'll be swindled a little less since the Goldfarb decision; the search for the right lawyer is still a game of blind man's buff played in the yellow pages. Yet, far upstream, the professional monopoly of law is coming apart and, just as the effects of a breaking dam can be foreseen long before the water reaches downstream, we can discern the shape of things to come in the delivery of legal services. The legal clinics show us that law can be cheaper and faster. The Wave Project in California shows us that new kinds of non-lawyers can become specialists, cheaper and less deliberately mysterious than lawyers, who will guide us through the fine print of modern life. And if what now ends up as lengthy and ulcerous litigation is converted into mediation intended to resolve the issue, not to enlarge it, then we shall surely experience a great improvement in the ways in which we deal with our fellow members of society.

3

Health: Getting a Hand
on the Wheel

It's that impatient condescension. The doctor will listen to us briefly, even though we speak barbarous English instead of his medical Esperanto, but his entire manner makes it abundantly clear that he can barely wait for the dialogue to be over. He'll work his miracles of modern science, if only we'll hurry up, and shut up, and pay the bill. And, above all, don't waste my time with questions. He is the expert in full bloom.

This lordly image of the physician, so different from the kindly family doctor of the half-forgotten myth, is at the center of the growing struggle for more public control over the vast, expensive and admittedly inefficient health industry. Much of the time it seems that nothing is happening; a new national health insurance plan is announced, and it vanishes down the drain like its predecessors; prices keep going up. Yet, down below the headlines, a surprising amount of change can be seen. The public is getting at least a fingertip on the levers of power, and the industry itself is responding in various ways to the demands on it. Indispensable to this process of change is a more informed, more skeptical, more healthy view of this most mysterious of the services we get from the experts.

We are beginning to abandon the exaggerated expectation, foisted on us, mainly by ourselves, during the years of optimism, that the health industry can solve all our problems. The miracles of modern medicine are of limited application. In *Who Shall Live?* health economist Victor R. Fuchs quotes a physician writing in *Medical Economics:*

> Fully 80% of illness is functional, and can be effectively treated by any talented healer who displays warmth, interest and compassion regardless of whether he has finished grammar school. Another 10% of illness is wholly incurable. That leaves only 10% in which scientific medicine—at considerable cost—has any value at all.

That statement is less than complete—it does not take into account the role of preventive medicine—but it serves to remind us that our health depends less on scientific medicine than we usually tend to think.

In the years to come improvement in our health will come not from medical research but from public or personal decisions about the way we live: an increase in the gasoline tax, reducing auto travel and with it pollution and accidents, would do more for our life expectancy than the next few grants out of the National Institutes of Health; so would greater safety in the workplace. The much-publicized gap between our health statistics and those of other Western nations, used as a club to beat the health industry, often has less to do with the doctors than with the rest of us. Swedish males, for example, die a lot less in the middle years than do their American counterparts, but the difference is mainly due to homicide and accident, and there is nothing the health industry can do about our national fondness for death by gun and car and industrial accident.

Even within his own sphere, the doctor's infallibility is being increasingly questioned. The evidence comes in many shapes, including that of your television screen. After years in which the network reading of popular opinion dictated that doctors must be cast in the heroic mold of Kildare and Welby, NBC in the fall of 1975 launched "Medical Story" and "Doctors Hospital," programs which portrayed doctors as being as afflicted with error and greed as the rest of us. Producer Abby Mann was aided in preparing "Medical Story" by Dr. Sidney M. Wolfe of Nader's Health Research Group, a leading critic of unnecessary surgery; the producers of Marcus Welby, who would never dream of committing any medical sin, get their cues from the American Medical Association. Johnny Carson and the authors of "Mary Hartman, Mary Hartman" took repeated jabs at the medical profession. "Medical Story" only lasted a season, and doctors still rated high in the polls on which-profession-do-you-most-respect, yet, if television either mirrors or molds public taste, what was appearing on the tube in 1976 seemed to herald a shift in public attitudes toward doctors.

Critics like Ivan Illich, author of *Medical Nemesis*, and Andrew T. Weil, tell us about the harm we do to ourselves in our overdependence on doctors, and, on a more pragmatic level, traitors to their class like Arthur Levin, M.D., have begun telling the secrets of the trade to the public. Dr. Levin is the author of *Talk Back to Your Doctor*, a particularly good example of a recent spate of books on that general theme. (Another is Dr. Marvin S. Belsky's *How to Choose and Use Your Doctor*.) On one level, Dr. Levin is providing intelligent advice on how to pick a doctor or a hospital for all our major health needs, from general care to surgery to childbirth and child care. But Levin also spells out in plain English what constitutes good medical practice in such a way that a member of the laity, which is what they call us, can tell for himself whether the doctor is doing his job properly. Anyone who has absorbed Levin's explanation of how a physical examination should be made or a medical history taken can get a pretty good idea of an important part of his next doctor's competence, even if he doesn't know a tibia from an aorta. Obviously, as Levin writes, we'll never be able to tell if the surgeon dropped a stitch during the gall-bladder operation, but so much of a doctor's work is accessible to layman's evaluation that we can see for ourselves whether we're dealing with the type of person who is likely to drop that stitch at the wrong time. Here Levin is denying the basic credo of the guild: that the layman must be convinced he can't understand anything. If he does begin to understand, or even believe that he can understand, then he'll begin to talk back. Levin writes that when people come to him with questions about a recent medical encounter, he says: "Why didn't you ask your doctor that?" The answer usually has to do with that impatient condescension; the doctor is seen as "too busy to talk to me." Levin comments: "I only wish—if I could do one thing—that I could convince people that they need not stick with a physician who is too busy to talk with them." Here Levin is reiterating a point of view expressed many years ago by Plato. Plato said a doctor should be authoritarian in treating slaves, but in treating a free citizen, he must "enter into discourse with the patient" and not start a treatment until the patient is convinced. In the modern setting, it is up to the patient to make the doctor see him as a free citizen—or, as Dr. Belsky advises, "Get off your knees."

The authors of *The Well Body Book*, Mike Samuels, a doctor, and Hal Bennett, a writer, want us to do considerably more than get off our knees and talk back. Their purpose is to teach people how to understand the body, which they call "the three million year old healer," well enough so they help rather than hinder the natural processes of healing. Samuels, in a note on "How I came to write this book," said that in his first clinical work he realized "how little most people knew about their bodies." Samuels and another doctor "decided to set up a clinic which would help people treat themselves, and that we would enjoy. We had massage people, faith healers, Indian medicine men, color healers and three M.D.'s on the staff. It was like a clubhouse where people learned how to take care of their own health problems, with us as their helpers. The clinic tried to write the book, but was too busy being a clinic." (As you may have guessed by now, all this took place in California.) So Samuels had to write the book. In a chapter titled "Create Your Imaginary Doctor," the authors describe a technique for creating within one's self an objective understanding of the state of one's health. They believe that people who understand their bodies well enough to aid the natural process of healing will need a doctor or drugs less often, and, on the occasions when he does need outside help, the patient will be an equal partner with the doctor in aiding the body to heal itself. Many readers may find themselves unable or unwilling to follow all the suggestions in *The Well Body Book*, and others may be put off by the authors' somewhat mystical style, but those who persevere are likely to find themselves more in control of their health and their lives.

Before you can take Levin's advice to talk back to your doctor, you have to choose one, and few people have access to the information necessary to make an informed choice. To provide people with something more substantial than groping around in the yellow pages, a process which will doubtless bring you under the care of Dr. Aaron Aardvark, the Health Research Group has been helping local consumer groups to compile physician directories that include such information as their training and specialties, the hospitals they use, the fees they charge, and how long it takes to get an appointment. The first directory was for Prince Georges County, Maryland, and when the local medical society heard what questions were being asked, it reacted much as God would if asked to quote a rate on miracles. But miracles do happen: the Naderites prevailed and in co-operation with Consumers Union made up a manual for putting together a doctors' directory that was subsequently used by local groups in Massachusetts and New York. The Health Research Group also put out a directory to dentists in Washington, D.C., along with general instructions, titled, perhaps inevitably, *Taking the Pain Out of Finding a Good Dentist,* and a consumer guide to psychotherapy called *Through the Mental Health Maze.* By 1976 various groups around the country had put out a total of thirty health guides: good news for everybody except Dr. Aardvark. The purpose of the directories will be greatly advanced when the Supreme Court's Goldfarb decision, described in chapter 2, is interpreted to mean that organized medicine can no longer prevent doctors from advertising.

Another and more ambitious kind of directory is the guide to health services in the Washington, D.C., area put out in 1976 by the Washington Center for the Study of Services. *Checkbook Health* does not evaluate individual doctors, but it does evaluate hospital emergency rooms, health maintenance organizations, insurance plans, abortion clinics, pharmacies, and nursing homes. The center planned to move on from health to auto services and then to other services ranging from banks to plumbers. The center's president, Robert Krughoff, said consumer groups elsewhere could use the Center's format to produce similar guides.

Getting what we need from the health industry begins by not accepting what we don't need. First on that list is unnecessary surgery. The fact that a lot of operations are unneeded has only recently begun to sink into the public mind. Within the profession, it has been discussed for decades, but only in the last few years has the message been broadcast to the laity by dissident insiders. Prominent among these is Dr. Wolfe of the Health Research Group. Using comparisons between the United States and Britain, and among Americans in different kinds of health plans, Dr. Wolfe estimated that 17 per cent of all operations are unnecessary, which works out to 3.2 million operations a year. The price tag is 16,000 deaths a year and a waste of $4.8 billion. Other estimates reach roughly the same conclusions. The reasons are clear enough: the nation has too many surgeons, surgery pays better than other medical work, and, under the fee-for-service system, the doctor who decides the operation is needed is also the one who gets paid for doing it—the legal equivalent would be for the judge to have a financial stake in the cases that come before him. The chief victims, not surprisingly, are women, children, and the poor. Hysterectomy is what surgeons like to do to women; almost 700,000 of these operations were performed in 1975, resulting in about 1,200 deaths—from 15 to 40 per cent, depending on who's making the estimate, were avoidable. As a Baltimore specialist said: "Some of us aren't making a living, so out comes a uterus or two each month to pay the rent." For children, the leading unnecessary operation is tonsillectomy; the classic example is the doctor who, when one kid shows up with a sore throat, schedules all the children in the family to have their tonsils out on the same day. As for the poor, a 1975 study found that Medicaid patients are operated on at two and a half times the rate of the rest of the population. Here greed is not the only factor: the poor provide most of the patients for teaching hospitals, and there just aren't enough sick organs around to supply the practice needed by interns and residents in surgery.

Avoiding an operation you don't need is ultimately a personal decision, but it can be powerfully influenced by the ground rules that surround the decision. Salaried physicians cut less often without valid reason than their fee-for-service counterparts: that's why surgery rates are much lower in Britain and Sweden. Thus the growth of prepaid health plans with salaried doctors, a topic we'll be discussing later in this chapter, is one way that unnecessary surgery is being reduced.

Another way is a second opinion by another surgeon who has no financial stake in the decision. This has been pioneered mainly in New York City, and the results to date are dramatic. In 1972, the small Storeworkers Union, with 8,000 members employed at Gimbels and Bloomingdale's, added a required second opinion, by a panel of salaried medical school doctors, for elective (non-emergency) surgery under its health insurance plan. They were soon joined by District Council 37 of the Municipal Employees Union, with 108,000 members, and an assortment of smaller unions with another 65,000; in these cases the second opinion was made voluntary. In 1975 Dr. Eugene G. McCarthy and Ann Susan Kamons of Cornell Medical School, which had set up the panels of surgeons to provide the second opinions, reported on what had been accomplished. In three years the second opinion had avoided 594 operations, which were no fewer than 28 per cent of the cases that had been considered. Hysterectomies and orthopedic operations were rejected at a considerably higher rate than other kinds of surgery, and specialists in those areas were found to be reaching for the knife more often than general surgeons. The program had cost $200,000 to run, and it had saved hospital costs of $1.5 million, plus a necessarily unknown number of lives.

The great leap forward came in 1976, when Blue Cross of New York began offering a free second opinion to some groups among its nine million members in the metropolitan area. "That takes a lot of courage," Barney Tresnowsky, a vice president of the National Blue Cross Association, had said of the idea when it was under consideration in New York. It was certainly a surprising act for the organization traditionally known as the hospitals' friend. But Blue Cross was being tormented with bad publicity over still another rate increase, and less surgery is one way it can hold its premiums down. In any event, the step taken by Blue Cross in New York put the second opinion in the big leagues for the first time, and what is now on its way to being standard practice in New York is likely to spread rapidly to the rest of the country. (And what of the poor surgeon, already in surplus? Economist Gelvin Stevenson suggested that he might make his living as a consultant, giving opinions about surgery instead of wielding the knife, especially if he can convince health insurers of the need for a *third* opinion, to be known as the "tie-breaker.")

Unnecessary hospital stays are, if less dramatic than the operation you didn't need, another great waste of people's time and money. It comes in two forms: going to the hospital when you don't have to, and staying too long when you do have to go. It happens because the nation has too much hospital capacity—the surplus of beds is variously estimated at from 67,000 to 250,000—and empty beds act as magnets attracting occupants. At its extreme, most notoriously in the Los Angeles area, hospitals buy patients from doctors at $50 to $100 a head; the price is right because, as one administrator said, "whenever we purchased a patient, he never got out the door until he ran the bill up to $1,000. The payoff was $100, our overhead was $400, so that left us with a net profit of $500." Health insurance often pays for hospital treatment but won't pay for the same or an alternate treatment outside, and the health financing system generally has offered few incentives for keeping people out of the hospital. Insurance that pays virtually all the costs of a hospital stay is also responsible for our choosing too often to go to the most expensive institution in reach: the operation may only be on the toenail, but, if the insurance is paying anyhow, why not choose the teaching hospital with the heart-lung machine instead of the lower-cost community hospital? The extra cost of each such decision is of course third-partied back onto the general public. The result of unnecessary hospitalization was illustrated during a doctors' strike in San Francisco in early 1975 when hospitals were closed except for emergency cases: the hospitals found there was no noticeable public demand for their missing services, and they concluded the public had been "spoiled."

The beginnings of change are visible. Walk-in surgery is increasingly available. Some 2,000 hospitals are geared to do simple operations without an overnight stay; the first to offer same-day service was Butterworth Hospital, in Grand Rapids, Michigan, in 1961. A couple of dozen surgical clinics do only walk-in surgery for a range of about 40 simple operations; some 100 more such clinics are planned. Their record for safety is evidently good: one of the oldest, Phoenix Surgicenter, has performed 26,500 operations in five years without a death and without an emergency transfer to a hospital. The savings are equally impressive; some of the Surgicenter operations cost less than half the hospital price. A dilation and curettage, for example, in 1975 cost $121 compared to $265 in a Phoenix hospital (the prices do not include doctor's fees.) The reduced-time surgery program of Southwest Ohio Blue Cross—known, we regret to say, as "Verticare" —saved $250,000 in its first two years, and its members avoided more than 4,000 hospital days. In Washington, D.C., Blue Cross was taking ads to tout same-day surgery under the headline: "In by nine. Out by five." The ad concluded: "If programs like these succeed, they'll lead to improvement of health care for everyone. They may even save money."

Abortion is an operation that, after an initial period of uncertainty, is now done primarily outside hospitals. The fact that abortion is now legal by Supreme Court decision, and in practice ever more widely available, is of course a great success story in the politics of health. When New York State legalized abortion in 1970, and it was clear that it was first going to happen on a large scale in New York City, hospitals lobbied to restrict the action to their premises. But Gordon Chase, then the city's Health Services Administrator, pushed successfully for allowing non-hospital clinics to do early abortions, again at less than half the hospital price. After five years the clinics' safety record was as good as the hospitals', and certainly far better than the bad old days: in 1974 just one woman died during abortion, while in 1969, the last year before the law was changed, illegal abortions took the lives of twenty-four women. The success of the abortion clinics undoubtedly has been a factor in persuading people that many much simpler operations can be done without an overnight hospital stay.

Blue Cross, perhaps the single most important force in the field, has moved in various ways, often under pressure, to reduce unnecessary hospital use. In 1971, Herbert Denenberg, the famous Pennsylvania Insurance Commissioner, blocked a Philadelphia Blue Cross rate increase of 50 per cent and demanded that Blue Cross renegotiate its hospital contracts to reduce costs. The new contracts provided that Blue Cross would not pay for patients kept too long and would reduce its payments for costly underused equipment, of which the most notorious example is idle open-heart surgery units. As a result of the tougher contracts, 9 per cent fewer Blue Cross members were hospitalized in 1972, and those that were spent 7 per cent less time there; Blue Cross spending rose only 2.5 per cent in that year, less than the rise in the cost of living, compared to 67 per cent in 1969–71. An increasing number of Blue

Cross plans provide for pre-admission testing: this means you have pre-surgery tests done as an outpatient, and come to the hospital only when the operation is scheduled. According to Blue Cross, this can cut two days off the average hospital stay. Blue Cross also increased its benefits for home care. Currently about two thirds of Blue Cross plans offer some form of home care, and the savings can be dramatic: Rochester, New York, Blue Cross reported, for example, that 220 of its members were being treated at home at an average cost of $18 per day, compared to $116 in the hospital. Both these moves by Blue Cross took courage, as the man said about second opinions, because they can only reduce business at hospitals already suffering from empty beds.

The effect of the various efforts to keep us out of the hospital when we don't need to be there began to be felt in 1975 when, for the first time in many years, the number of hospital admissions fell slightly, while the use of outpatient clinics rose.

Another way of minimizing our need for the health industry's services is to reduce the hazards of the workplace, where each year one hundred thousand are killed and many times that number disabled. This is a major goal of the Health Research Group, but it is not easy to make headway when safety in the workplace appears to be of as little interest to most unions and government inspectors as it is to employers. When the group took on the case of Cleam Caldwell, a District of Columbia Metro tunnel worker who had contracted silicosis and then been fired for "unreasonable questioning of safety on the job," all Caldwell had gotten as compensation was $750—plus an offer of reinstatement in the same hazardous place; his eventual settlement was for $45,000.

Progress has been made on some fronts. Pressmen at Washington newspaper plants brought hearing specialists to measure the din at work and to determine that more than half the pressmen had suffered hearing loss; with the help of the HRG, the pressmen made enough noise of their own to force the newspapers to install sound-reducing devices. Later the HRG set up a clearinghouse of hearing specialists to help other unions interested in muting the workplace. In Superior, Wisconsin, workers in grain elevators found that more than half their number were coming down with respiratory disease. With outside help from the University of Wisconsin, they uncovered the usual lax enforcement of inadequate standards and were able to force the employer to install new safety equipment; the improved standards resulting from the case will apply to 100,000 grain-elevator workers around the country. Governmental efforts to regulate safety at work, never more than a tiny fraction of what was needed to make any dent in the annual carnage, seem to be both rising and falling: the federal government's somewhat greater effort in recent years has been used by the states as a pretext to do even less than they were doing before.

The current boom in malpractice suits measures, as on a barometer, the public's rising desire to fight back and the willingness of some doctors to tattle on their colleagues. Malpractice claims are running close to twenty thousand a year. In *The Great American Medicine Show*, Spencer Klaw cites a government survey that found about half the claims to be "legally meritorious." But far fewer than half who sue actually collect anything, and, as Klaw points out, the true rate of malpractice is far higher than the number of claims, since many victims are reluctant to sue or unable to find a lawyer willing to take the case. Doctors have been howling in pain as the cost of their malpractice insurance has gone up in proportion to the judgments against them; indeed, the cost has gone up faster than the verdicts, since malpractice insurers only pay out one dollar in claims for every three dollars they collect in premiums, the rest of the money disappearing in overhead.

The doctors' anger about malpractice has mainly been directed at the lawyers—another case of two guilds at each other's throat—because the lawyers take malpractice cases on a contingency fee gamble, so that they collect 30–50 per cent of the verdict if they win, nothing if they lose. This, say the doctors, gives the lawyer a stake not in justice but in a huge award from the jury. (In case you were wondering, one statistician provides the lunatic calculation that a fatality is worth $3,786 times the number of years of life expectancy foregone by the victim.) The lawyers counterclaim that the contingency fee is the only way the average man can get a lawyer to take his case. That's true if the lawyer can smell a killing, but the average small medical butchery will never see the light of justice. Jeffrey O'Connell, one of the originators of no-fault car insurance, has proposed that doctors carry no-fault insurance for the riskier operations, on the sensible assumption that if the operation fails it doesn't really matter to the victim whether it was the doctor's fault. But only California has even discussed this solution, while other states have limited contingency fees, with the certain effect of reducing the number of victims who will be able to sue. Doctors have also made much of the idea that malpractice cases force them into what they call "defensive medicine": too many tests and a reluctance to do anything, no matter how desirable for the patient, that carries any risk of an eventual lawsuit. Spencer Klaw reports a study that showed defensive medicine to be much less prevalent than the doctors claim, and overtesting, which as noted earlier is a real problem, is more likely not to be defensive but rather the doctors' aggressive response to all that free money flowing in from Medicaid and Medicare.

One healthy effect of the malpractice boom may be to motivate doctors to do that which they've always refused: discipline their fellow physicians, including themselves. The old tacit understanding which let the other fellow bury his mistakes in silence begins to break down when his malpractice suit comes home to roost on your insurance premium. A few cases like that of Dr. John Nork of Sacramento can shake the faith of even the most sincere advocate of professional solidarity. As described by Roger Rapoport, the West Coast chronicler of medical horrors, Dr. Nork is a surgeon whose performance drew a record number of suits from patients left crippled after he had operated on them. By the time Rapoport reported on the Nork case in *New Times* in 1975, twenty-four patients had won a total of $10 million in damages from Nork and the hospitals that allowed him to use their operating rooms—and twenty-five more cases against Nork were pending in the courts. Nork was, Rapoport observed, well on his way to setting the all-time record for malpractice, though not necessarily for butchery; his lawyer said he had looked at the records of another Sacramento doctor who made Nork look good. Nork was brought down, not by his fellow physicians, but because the lawyer for one maimed patient tracked down other victims and persuaded them to sue. Many were reluctant. One of these, a medical secretary, even testified for Nork in one trial; the evidence convinced her and she then sued him for the permanent damage his surgery had done to her. Without that one lawyer's persistence Nork would doubtless be still at the operating stand. But now the huge series of verdicts against Nork's insurance company helped raise the premiums of every doctor and hospital in California, doubtless stimulating in them a more active interest in maintaining professional standards (though the doctors' immediate reaction was a protest slowdown that failed to get the premiums lowered).

A less drastic treatment is the growing use of the patient bill of rights. It provides that the patient has a right to be told, in English not Esperanto, what's wrong with him, who's in charge, and what they propose to do to him. He has the right to refuse treatment except in rare cases, and the right to refuse to be the object of experimentation. The hospital has to explain its costs to him. The bill of rights was pushed through the American Hospital Association in 1973 by a committee headed by Joseph V. Terenzio, the former Hospital Commissioner of New York City and currently head of the city's Hospital Fund. Two years later Terenzio found that a "disappointing" number of hospitals were actually using the bill; their pretext for not doing so being either that it would encourage malpractice suits or constitute an admission that the hospital wasn't doing all those good things, which of course it was. However, in New York State, the hospital code now provides that all hospital patients must be given a copy of the document. The bill of rights, which after all is just a piece of paper, works best in the small but growing number of hospitals that employ patient advocates—people whose only function is to represent the patients' interests.

Avoiding the medical care we don't need does not, of course, guarantee us the care we do need, and talking back, as Arthur Levin recommends, is of limited value if there's no one here to listen. The chronic shortage of primary-care doctors makes most people grateful to get a scrap of the physician's time; if they talk back, they fear they will soon be out on the street. If we are to be more demanding of our doctors, there must be an adequate supply of them. More primary-care doctors are needed, too, so that whatever form of national health insurance eventually takes shape does not kite the bill beyond the nation's ability to pay. Otherwise we shall repeat the experience of Medicare and Medicaid, which pumped a lot of new money into the system, increasing demand without any offsetting increase in supply, and resulting in higher prices that wiped out much of the benefit of all that taxpayers' money.

The scarcity of doctors will soon be easing, it seems, almost three quarters of a century since the AMA instituted occupational birth control with its 1910 Flexner Report that pulled the plug on half the nation's medical schools. By the 1960s, the AMA's resistance had weakened, twenty-seven new medical schools were started, and in 1975 enrollment was up by 70 per cent from ten years earlier. Physicians in practice were up by fifty thousand, with considerably larger increases expected in the next two decades. The AMA, which had recognized the shortage it created for only about forty-five minutes, now joyfully proclaimed that the problem no longer existed. If it seemed that doctors were scarce, we were told, it wasn't a shortage, just maldistribution: too few doctors in the slums and the boondocks, too many in the fat suburbs. The logic was feeble even by AMA standards, for, if the suburban practices are overcrowded, some doctors out there should be starving. But medical malnutrition hasn't been observed anywhere recently, certainly not in the suburbs, though surplus surgeons are forced, if they cannot find anyone to operate on, to the occasional indignity of treating organs instead of removing them. The increase in medical school enrollment has been fueled by federal subsidies that supply almost half the cost of the future doctor's education. When it was suggested in Congress that once he had joined the nation's highest-paid profession, that doctor might repay the taxpayers' money that got him to that exalted position, the AMA roared in indignation. How, organized medicine asked, could you make the student repay money that he had never seen, it having gone directly to the medical school instead of passing through his pocket? The idea went no-where. The consolation to the taxpayer, as he examines the bill handed him by a doctor he helped put through medical school, is that the bill would have been even higher if the federal subsidy had not increased the supply of doctors.

The new doctors will not in the short run correct the imbalance between primary care and specialization. Pri-mary-care physicians (mainly general and family practice and internal medicine) are still so much in demand that in 1975 Virginia was complaining that its newly minted family practitioners were being lured away by other states. They were "flown to Illinois where they were wined and dined," the president of the state academy of family practice reported, and some states "even intro-duced them to the girls who would work in their office"; North Carolina was the worst offender. The supply of types of doctors is controlled not by the medical schools but by the number of residencies available in each spe-ciality, and that is determined by the teaching hospitals. With the AMA's help, they have beaten off efforts to use federal subsidies to manipulate the supply of residencies. Thus the growing interest among medical students in pri-mary care will not necessarily translate itself into reality at the end of the production line. Accordingly, the nation will continue in years to come to get too few primary-care doctors and too many surgeons who will try to perform too many operations. Residencies in family practice, the most popular form of primary care, are growing rapidly—from 290 in 1970 to 3,720 in 1975—but this is offset in part by the decline in general practice, which is roughly the old-fashioned version of the same thing. Once in practice, the primary-care doctor tends to drift into a specialty more often than the specialist switches to primary care. The result is that, though the number of primary-care physicians is increasing, the number of less needed specialists is growing faster and will make up an increasing percentage of all doctors. The day is still distant when the supply of primary-care doctors is such that we can talk back to ours secure in the knowledge that the fellow across the street has room for us in his schedule.

Even the projection of an increased supply of doctors depends on the United States continuing to rob other countries which for years have been supplying the nation the doctors denied it by the AMA. As recently as 1973, almost half of all newly licensed doctors were graduates of foreign medical schools; some were Americans who couldn't find a place in school at home, but the great majority were from countries short of doctors who were lured here by better pay and amenities. The AMA didn't mind during the halcyon days of the doctor shortage: its members would get the suburban practices, while the Pakistanis worked the night shift in the city hospitals. But by 1976 there were mutterings about restricting the entry of foreign doctors. If that were to happen, if the United States were to stop looting other countries' health manpower—a good thing for both, since a doctor usually performs better in his own culture—the effect on the domestic medical market would be to cancel out the entire increase in American medical school production and guarantee a shortage of doctors for many years to come.

Tomorrow's primary care will come not just from more doctors but from a new kind of health provider who is taking over part of the physician's job. It is a reversal of the centuries-old trend toward more specialization and longer training for the same work. First the witch doctor divided into priest and physician, and later the barber-surgeon separated into his component parts (though we don't hear much these days about unnecessary haircuts).

Now a new occupation is moving onto the doctor's turf. It is called, for want of a better term, the physician extender, and, for reasons of historical accident, it comes in two versions distinguished by sex rather than function: the nurse-practitioner, female, and the physicians' assistant, male (though there are exceptions to both rules). From a cloud no bigger than a man's hand a decade ago, these two occupations have multiplied so fast that they seem certain to be an essential part of tomorrow's health care package. Today they number about 10,000, and they are being turned out at a rapidly increasing rate. Most of us will, in not too many years, be getting at least part of our health care from a nurse-practitioner or a physicians' assistant.

The nurse practitioner has moved onto the scene with little fanfare. Though the idea isn't new—the Frontier Nursing Service has been providing most of the primary care in a thousand square miles of Appalachia in eastern Kentucky since 1925—the modern era dates from Dr. Henry Silver's experiments in the mid-sixties at the University of Colorado in training nurses to assume some of the pediatrician's work. Silver demonstrated that the pediatric nurse associate, as she is usually called, can replace the pediatrician for about three quarters of his duties, and that the clients—mothers as well as children—quickly came to accept, and sometimes prefer, a visit with the PNA rather than the M.D. As for the pediatrician, he was able to carry a greater patient load, and that, a federal evaluation politely stated, "proved to be an economic boon to the physician." With Silver's experience as a model, the pediatric nurse associate has spread to other states and now makes up about half the nurse-practitioner population. Some are in private practice with pediatricians, but more are in public health institutions, with the largest single concentration being the seventy PNAs in the New York City Health Department. The city began sending nurses for PNA training at Cornell Medical Center as recently as 1972. By 1976, PNAs were handling one quarter of all patients visits in the city's network of eighty child-health stations, and they were beginning to supplant doctors in giving school physicals. (The city had also trained ten nurse-epidemiologists to investigate cases of infectious disease.) According to Margaret O'Brien, the director of Public Health Nursing who selected and supervised them, the PNAs have been fully accepted by parents, and on at least one occasion a mother whose child saw a doctor because the PNA was absent called the PNA at home to ask if it was all right to follow the doctor's advice. Some problems missed by doctors have been caught by PNAs, not, in all probability, because the PNA is more skilled but because she devotes more time to each case. At the present rate, the nurse-practitioner will in not too many years outnumber the doctor in the largest public health system in the nation. The doctors, though not happy about the turn of events, have made no organized effort to block the gradual erosion of what was once their exclusive territory.

The nurse-midwife, the second most prevalent type of supernurse, is a modern throwback. She is succeeding both the old granny midwife, who still practices in some parts of the South, and the lordly obstetrician, product of the era of scientific medicine. She is trained to handle normal childbirth—that's 85–90 per cent of cases—with a physician available in case of complication. At first the nurse-midwife served mainly the poor, and with notable success: a number of big-city clinics use them, and in Holmes County, Mississippi, the introduction of nurse-midwives led in three years, from 1969 to 1972, to cutting the infant mortality rate in half. Then, as the nurse-midwife began serving a more than poor clientele, it became evident that quite a few women preferred her services to those of the obstetrician. That at least is the experience of

Roosevelt Hospital in Manhattan, where since 1974 five nurse-midwives have been attracting a growing number of middle- and upper-middle-class women. For some the calculation is economic: the nurse-midwife costs less than half the obstetrician's price. But money is not the only, or even the primary consideration. The director of the hospital's midwifery service, Dr. Thomas F. Dillon, had this to say:

> We have tapped a group of people to whom economy is important and we have tapped a group of people that are women-oriented. Beyond that, I'm sure we've tapped much more—something else. And right now I don't know what that is.

Some of the mothers who chose the nurse-midwife suggested what that something else might be. One, herself a pediatrician, saw no place for a physician—"trained to treat the abnormal"—in a healthy childbirth. Some viewed the nurse-midwife as a welcome change from a person in whose behavior they saw the classic male chauvinist pig. For others, the objection to the obstetrician was medical: he was more likely to use drugs to induce labor, and forceps in delivery, for his personal convenience. Although they were approved by the American College of Obstetricians and Gynecologists in 1971, when business was better, many obstetricians think nurse-midwives are a lousy idea—having just shoved the old granny out the back door, they find her daughter, dressed up in a diploma and, can you believe it, a goddam stethoscope, coming back through the front door. When the birth rate's falling! The obstetrician hasn't been able to slam that door, and as time goes by childbirth will be available to more women on better terms—financial, yes, but also that "something else"—than it is today.

Many nurse-practitioners are working in the care of those chronic ailments that the physician tends to find stale and unprofitable. This is particularly important to the elderly, whose cases bore the doctor, and who find it hard to get to see him now that he no longer makes house calls. The nurse-practitioners who specialize in geriatrics —some work exclusively in housing projects for the elderly—can be a decisive factor in saving the old from the nursing home, and any nurse-practitioner can help keep people out of the hospital. Judith D. Jordan, for example, is a nurse-practitioner specialized in diabetes who works in a group practice in Gainesville, Florida. Her patients are periodically examined by a doctor, but Jordan manages those chronic problems of the diabetic for which the physician will never find time. She teaches new diabetics how to give themselves insulin, and she makes house calls on diabetic amputees for whom it is difficult to get to the office. If the patient's eyesight is poor, Jordan will prepare a set of doses to last him till her next visit. This kind of care keeps many of her patients out of the hospital or the nursing home so that, although more time is spent on each patient, the total health bill is smaller: better care for less money.

The physicians' assistant is a byproduct of war. More than ten years ago, the thought occurred to a few people that the civilian health industry could find a useful place for the thousands of medical corpsmen being discharged by the military services. These corpsmen were produced by a remarkably efficient training system, for, though the military squander our money with the abandon of the Emperor Caligula, time is too precious to waste when training men who will only be in service for a limited stay. Through a series of brief, intense training stints interspersed with active service, the military produce, in what is called the independent duty corpsman, someone who is capable of supplying the health needs of a group of men with only radio contact (if, for example, he is on a small ship) with a physician. Various ideas on how to make civilian use of this person coalesced into the concept of the physicians' assistant: someone to whom a doctor would delegate some of his tasks while always retaining ultimate responsibility for what the PA did.

The way of the PA was not easy, for, unlike his female counterpart, who grew out of the familiar figure of the nurse, nothing resembling the PA existed in the rigidly guildbound health industry. Nor was he welcome; the nurse, in particular, threatened to brain him with a bedpan, or a lawsuit, if he got between her and the doctor. The first PAs, graduated from Duke University after two years of post-military training, had to work in the university hospital. Dr. Richard Smith, designer of the imaginative MEDEX program for ex-corpsmen, toured the back country of the state of Washington looking for this prototype: a doctor with military experience who was chained to his practice because he was the only physician in that small town. Wouldn't life be easier, Smith suggested, if you had a skilled assistant, like those corpsmen you knew in service, remember? So persuasive was Smith that the law legitimizing his program was pushed through the legislature by the state medical society. But progress did not always come easily. The doctors viewed the PA with mixed feelings: he spelled money in their pockets if they charged their rate for his lower-paid work—anyone could see that, and doctors know better than anyone else how overtrained they are for most of their work; but, on the other hand, could they share the mysteries of the witch doctor, dare they let an underling read those rattling bones?

The barriers began rapidly to fall when the AMA put its seal of approval on the PA, gaining thereby a hold on his throat by which one day it may be able to strangle him. By 1976 forty states had legalized PAs and they were able to practice in most of the remaining states (nurse-practitioners in most states were able to function under their nurses' status without new legislation). More than four thousand PAs were in practice by 1976, and they were being graduated at the rate of twelve hundred a year, with that output sure to increase as training programs expanded (and drew on women and men without military experience). You could tell that the PAs had arrived when, having broken into the guild-ridden industry, they promptly formed a guild of their own: the American Academy of Physicians' Assistants. And you could tell, beyond any shadow of doubt, that the new guild had arrived from the following item from an account, in their newsletter, of the 1975 PA convention in St. Louis:

> Several drug companies sent representatives to the convention, where they distributed a great deal of literature and pertinent information through their exhibits. They also made it possible, financially, for us to have several social events including a very enjoyable evening aboard the Goldenrod Boat. Our thanks go to these companies . . .

(This did not mean the drug companies were neglecting the doctors; 1975 was also the year that six big companies banded together to start something called Physicians Radio Network. The sponsors were aiming at having twenty-eight FM stations in the network by 1977; doctors, it was said, would be given free receivers for their network, which would broadcast "medical information" twenty-four hours a day. There would, the announcement said, be eight one-minute commercials per hour.)

Accounts of physician extenders' assignments tend to focus on the exotic: Mary Breckenridge, founder of the Frontier Nursing Service, galloping off to deliver another hillbilly; PA Steve Brooks on the North Slope of Alaska, scraping injured pipeline workers off the frozen tundra. Many are indeed willing to go to locations too distant from the country club to attract doctors, but they are also moving into the mainstream where they will meet the average person. Their acceptance to date has been excellent; at this writing, not a single malpractice case involving a physician extender had been reported. Because they come much cheaper than doctors—most nurse-practitioners and PAs earn from twelve to twenty thousand dollars—they will have, and we can afford, time for those ordinary problems, boring to the physician but of consuming interest to us, that are the common coin of health care. The physician extender, coupled with the rising output of the medical schools, may restore the Golden Age of American Medicine, that legendary time before World War I when there were enough doctors to go around.

In the current turmoil about how the health industry can best be organized, plans and panaceas succeed each other like the generations of fruit flies. Everyone, even the AMA, has a plan for national health insurance; none is about to be implemented. The one new idea that has carved out a place for itself is the Health Maintenance Organization, or HMO. In an HMO, you pay a flat annual fee for all or most of your health needs; the idea is that the HMO will be motivated to keep you well, which benefits them, without either shoving you unnecessarily into a hospital or neglecting you at their own eventual expense. Most HMOs seem to work that way, though some of the newer ones, notably in California, turned out to be fronts for making off with Medicaid money. HMO members do spend less time in the hospital—an HMO sponsored by Blue Cross of New York reduced the hospitalization rate by one third in the first year. Evidently HMO members do not feel they are being undertreated, since enrollments keep growing in areas where alternative medical plans are available. Still, this does not mean the HMOs, which now have about ten million members, will engulf the rest of the American people. As Donald Meyers of Blue Cross has pointed out, even Kaiser-Permanente of California, the respected granddaddy of HMOs, has never attracted a majority of the people in the areas it serves. Doubtless one reason is that the HMO presumes a constant need for health care, whereas a good many Americans go on the healthy assumption that they don't need a doctor except in an occasional emergency: for these people, the AMA's beloved fee-for-service practitioner offers the best bargain.

Holding down the bill is the chief aim of most health reforms and the bill they have in view is the hospital's. Power to control that bill lies with those who pay it: Blue Cross and government, through Medicare and Medicaid, pay most of the nation's hospital costs. Their past record entitles us to question whether Blue Cross, the hospitals' friend, and government, nobody's friend, will make any effort to lighten the bill. But in politics there are no permanent friends, and Blue Cross has been reading the tea leaves. The message in the bottom of the cup is: With national health insurance, who needs Blue Cross? If Blue Cross is to survive, some of its leaders are convinced, it must prove it can do better than government in controlling the costs loaded onto the public by its erstwhile friends. One of its tactics, started in 1970 in New York and now practiced by many Blue Cross plans, is called "prospective rate-setting." This means that Blue Cross, instead of paying bills after the fact, sets the rates it will pay hospitals in advance; any added costs have to be swallowed by the hospitals. Unable for once to simply forward the bill to Blue Cross, New York City hospitals have held their cost increase to one third that of hospitals without prospective rate-setting. Many Blue Cross officials still don't want to think critically about the prices their friends charge, but the tide is running in the other direction: in New Jersey, for example, the hospitals in 1975 were accusing Blue Cross of going over to the other, or public, side on the issue of their costs.

Government, unlike Blue Cross, sees no threat in the tea leaves. Accordingly, in 1975, the year that Blue Cross instituted the second opinion for surgery, HEW refused a congressional request to do the same for Medicaid and Medicare, which have proven to be huge slush funds for unnecessary operations. The government's reasoning was that the second opinion was unnecessary regulation because of something called PSROs, for Professional Standards Review Organizations. PSROs are groups of doctors, mandated by a 1972 law but only recently beginning to take shape, that are supposed to oversee government-paid medical care, primarily in hospitals. The idea is so diluted that the AMA, which once opposed it, now is in the process of capturing the PSROs. According to Dr. Wolfe of the Health Research Group, about half of the PSROs in existence are nothing but organized medicine in regulatory drag: they are the creatures of the state or local medical societies. PSROs are expected to use guidelines supplied by the American College of Surgeons, hardly the place where you expect to find any zeal to wipe out unnecessary surgery. Surgery in any event will be reviewed after the fact, when it's too late to put that uterus back. Finally, the records of the PSROs—about the performance of doctors and the performance of most aspects of hospital services—will be kept secret, so that the public will never know what they have done, if indeed they have done anything at all; the temptation to do nothing will be strong. The likely outcome is suggested by the experience of an early PSRO in Utah, which disallowed as unnecessary just 24 out of its first 20,000 hospital claims. Its head told Dr. Wolfe he doubted that PSRO would have any effect on unnecessary surgery for at least ten years.

In another area, that of drug costs, government has been somewhat more active. While the Federal Trade Commission and other forces were aiming to force price competition on the pharmacists, as described in later

chapters, HEW was creeping toward a policy of not buying brand-name drugs when cheaper generics are available. After having dragged its feet for a decade, HEW
decided to apply the policy to a handful of drugs in 1976.
When its rules are in full effect, which will be 1978 at the
earliest, Medicaid and Medicare will reimburse hospitals
and other health providers only for the generic drug even
if they have bought the high-priced brand-name version.
The result, if indeed it happens, will be a substantial saving of tax money. A more directly visible reduction in the
public's drug bill is being brought about by the action of
a growing number of states—totaling ten at this writing—
to permit pharmacists to fill with the generic equivalent a
prescription written for a brand-name drug, but only at
the client's request. For this to mean anything in practice
of course, the client will have to remember to ask, and
whether he does depends on how widely it is known that
many brand-name drugs have generic equivalents that
are identical in everything except price.

The AMA roared out of its lair at these affronts to the
drug manufacturers who supply a large part of its budget,
but the AMA is no longer the king of monopolistic beasts.
By 1975 its membership had dropped to less than half the
nation's doctors, its finances were in disarray, and that
year's annual meeting drew the smallest turnout in recent
history. (With fewer doctors to entertain, the drug companies presumably had no trouble finding the money to
take the physicians' assistants on that ride on the good
ship Goldenrod.) Other signs of decay were visible. The
AMA's internal security, once the envy of the Western
world, had come unglued to the point that its secrets
were leaking out almost as fast as those of the CIA. Organized medicine's 1975 campaign against generic drugs
was mightily embarrassed by a series of documents smug-
gled to the press by a source within the AMA, who soon

became known as Sore Throat, after the Deep Throat of Watergate fame. Sore Throat's documents showed the AMA, in a successful 1970 effort to defeat an earlier generic drug proposal, had been careful to cover up its connection with the drug industry. Its lobbyist, in passing drug company propaganda to his associates, had warned them:

> I would caution that when you are discussing this matter with your respective Senators on the Senate Finance Committee that you stress the points that affect physicians and their prescribing habits rather than those areas that highlight the pharmaceutical manufacturers' interests.

Though the AMA went to court against HEW's drug-buying rules, it did not seem any longer to have the clout to repeat its 1970 victory over the generic heresy.

What organized medicine hates most, a public say in the running of the health industry, was gaining ground while the old beast was losing at least some of his teeth. In recent years citizen groups here and there have sought some degree of control over health institutions that seemed impervious to public opinion. Many, perhaps most, of those efforts have bogged down in the soggy politics of health, but they served to scare the industry into a considerable amount of response. Blue Cross, which was always supposed to have public members on its governing boards, but usually chose the banker who handled the cash-flow, now began putting on representatives of those who pay the premiums. The federal government in 1976 was preparing to launch a large-scale venture in public participation in controlling what Washington spends on health. This was a network of Health Service Agencies to be made up of public as well as government and industry representatives. The agencies

will have to certify the need for all federal spending over
$100,000 for construction and research. In the case of
hospitals, where the greatest construction overrun has occurred, the agency will be able to remove the certification
of existing hospitals, thus, or so the optimists believe,
forcing the elimination of those empty beds that attract
patients who should be elsewhere—New York City's new
agency started out by recommending the closing of no
fewer than thirty hospitals. Of course any government
proposal to give the public a greater voice should be
considered with suspicion, and public members of these
agencies may well be bored or bewildered by colleagues
who can translate the simplest thought into bureaucratic
or medical jargon incomprehensible to the average Eng-
lish-speaker. But, in the present pinched mood about public spending in general, the combination of the Health
Service Agencies and the other trends we have described
may, by cutting the supply of excess beds, provide the
one sure cure for the industry's tendency to put us in the
hospital when we don't need to be there. And that is the
biggest single contribution anyone can make to holding
down our health bill.

4

The Decline of the
Experts

LAWYERS AND DOCTORS, we all know, are organized into professional associations, the American Bar Association and the American Medical Association and their local branches, that protect their interests. So too are people engaged in such varied occupations as frog dealers, egg graders, cemetery salesmen, and tattoo artists. All are among the seven million Americans who belong to professional associations—we shall call them guilds in recognition of their medieval origins and, sometimes, behavior—that have as their purpose gaining an extra edge in their dealings with the rest of us. They gain that edge by intervening with government to throttle the competitive workings of free enterprise: guilds are professional monopolies.

For many decades the guilds made steady progress at our expense, and hardly a year went by that some occupational group did not slip through a legislature what Adam Smith two centuries ago called "some contrivance to raise prices." No one but the beneficiaries was paying attention. Recently, however, the tide has begun to turn. Many among us have become aware of the cost to the public of professional monopoly, and have started fighting back.

The citizen groups we describe in later chapters often find themselves doing battle with one guild or another. If the trend continues, the public will win back a lot of power and money that it had lost to the guilds.

The field of guilds is obscure and clouded with the ambiguities of net screwing. Most of the guild battles for protection against the winds of competition take place in the backrooms of politics, and few among us follow the details of such epics as the (unsuccessful) effort of lawn cutters in California to get themselves licensed under the title of "maintenance gardeners." The subject is ambiguous because in most cases they is us. Among those seven million guild members, only a handful in the higher professions are doing spectacularly well, and even a Park Avenue doctor is in many respects closer to the average man than he is to true Immortals like the heirs of Exxon. The great majority of guild members are thrashing around down here with the rest of the herd, both victims and oppressors. It is the classic net screw: each guild member benefits from his monopoly, and suffers from all the others, so that, unless he is a doctor or lawyer, he is hard put to tell at the end of the year whether he is a winner or loser in the game of monopoly.

The typical guild member is a small operator who, though he has avoided much of the rigor of the free market, is far from eligible for the perquisites of social-ism-for-the-rich. He goes bust by the thousands every year, while Washington's heart bleeds only for Lockheed and the Franklin National Bank. Still, the average man is being screwed by the guilds, and we need not minimize the amount just because the oil companies' take is bigger; the common estimate is that doctors' income is increased by 20 per cent by their guild monopoly. It is in the nature of things that when the average man thinks about those who are screwing him he is more likely to see the features of television repairmen and auto mechanics than the faceless abstraction of the massive third-party screwings government practices on him on behalf of the great corporate monopolies. Reform of the guilds, then, can be viewed as clearing away those swindles that divide the losers so that we can all focus on the monopolies that oppress us on a much larger scale.

The road to guild reform passes through government, because it is the government that gave the guilds their immunities from free enterprise. Government enacted into law the guild principle of mandatory licensure: you cannot practice a trade unless those already in the trade pronounce you qualified to compete for their business. Government created those hundreds of state "regulatory" boards made up of guild members who set the rules in their own interest: the drawn-out training programs and phony examinations, graded by the boards, that keep prices up by restricting entry to the occupation; the minimum price rules and bans on advertising that prevent price competition; the bans on "reciprocity," which mean that a person can qualify to practice his trade in one state but cannot do business elsewhere without going through the licensing process a second time—the lawyers and some health occupations are fond of this one.

These and other restraints of trade are there because government permitted them, and the public has no escape other than the familiar do-it-yourself route. Even that route is blocked in many cases by guilds that have put through unauthorized-practice laws preventing us from helping ourselves at their expense. In chapter 2 we saw how the bar associations try to suppress do-it-yourself lawyering, and there's the case of a California woman who was charged with practicing medicine without a license, under an AMA-sponsored law, after she advised a friend that yoghurt would relieve a vaginal itch; she was successfully defended by Phyllis Eliasberg, director of the Wave divorce-yourself project. Not all the guilds have been able to erect such sturdy fences. The auto mechanics have not, and one person's venture into that field brought her added insights into how the guilds function.

Christine Winter, a writer for the Chicago *Tribune*, took one of those courses in car maintenance that are now offered here and there around the nation. Her course was given at a local high school, and it was called "auto tune-up diagnosis for beginners." Although Winter is a consumer writer, her motives were only partly to save money; she also went in feminist indignation at the common male assumption that no woman can ever understand what happens inside a car—that assumption in turn being a special case of the standard guild belief that no one on the outside can understand the guild's business.

Ms. Winter learned to do basic maintenance that doesn't require buying more than a few inexpensive tools. As a consumer, she found out that "The amount of money you can save by basic maintenance is shocking. More important, just knowing enough to ask the mechanic to check a specific thing can be a lot cheaper than saying, 'I hear a funny noise' and leaving your bank account in his greasy hands."

She learned the swindles of the trade. One has to do with spare parts. Winter could buy parts at discount houses for as little as half what the garage would charge for the parts alone, exclusive of labor, if it installed them for her. Here she was skirting another kind of monopoly: by deliberately designed parts that only fit their own cars, the manufacturers have put themselves in a position to jack up parts prices far beyond what a free market would tolerate. The garage just transmits the screwing to the public. Ms. Winter also became witting to the swindle concealed in labor charges. When, not feeling like doing the job herself, she asked a garage for the cost of some work on her points, she was quoted a figure that included an hour's worth of labor. "Hell," Winter recalled later, "I knew I could do that job in fifteen minutes, and I'm an amateur." (On her old car; the points on some newer cars are harder to reach.) Professionals know how to charge for their time. Winter had just been introduced to the flat-rate labor system under which garages charge not for how long the work actually took but by a theoretical standard laid down in a trade manual. Theoretically, you will save money if the job takes longer than the manual specifies, but that sort of theory is best left to the civics textbooks. In the real world, garages that use the manual have simply eliminated price competition, with all the predictable effects on the public, and reward themselves with higher returns on rushed work.

Most important, Ms. Winter had lifted the veil and spied the guilty secret treasured by every guild: "The most valuable lesson I learned in my auto mechanics course is that everything in a car isn't extremely compli-cated—though professional mechanics have a marvelous ability for making it sound as if it were." This knowledge, she concluded, was worth more to her than the money she was saving: "I'll always have the satisfaction of walk-ing into an auto parts shop or a filling station and saying something like, 'I need an oil sending switch for a '67 Ford.' The expressions on those once-smug male faces is worth every bit of grease and filth on my good jeans." Take the gender out of it and Christine Winter's state-ment could apply to any of us who has found a way to match wits with an expert trying to club us into submis-sion with his superior knowledge.

Not many of us are going to emulate Christine Winter,

and in any event doing-it-ourselves doesn't make sense for most of the services we get from guild members, not after we've spent six thousand-odd years developing the specialization of labor. Opportunities to grade our own eggs are rare, for example, and making generic drugs in our bathtubs to beat the brand-name hustle is not a viable undertaking. Most of the time, then, we as individuals are helpless unless we can extract some help from government. Recently that helping hand has been stretched out, usually under public pressure, from both Washington and a number of state capitals.

The fallout from the Supreme Court's 1975 Goldfarb decision banning bar association minimum fees, described in chapter 2, is beginning to land on other guilds, where price-fixing is getting harder to maintain, at least out in the open. The Justice Department's Antitrust Division has brought suits against a number of guilds, including engineers, anesthesiologists, and accountants, which forbid their members from engaging in competitive bidding. The civil engineers gave in without going to court; the National Society of Professional Engineers lost in the Federal District Court, where the case at this writing awaits final disposition after having been up to the Supreme Court and back again. The engineers trotted out the familiar guild argument that, as a "learned profession," they should be exempt from the antitrust laws; competition, they seemed to be saying, is for people who didn't learn how to spell. But Judge John Lewis Smith, Jr., in a profoundly anti-guild mood, decided that "It would be a very dangerous form of elitism, indeed, to dole out exemptions to our anti-trust laws merely on the basis of the educational level needed to practice a given profession."

Guilds are also in a certain amount of trouble with the

Federal Trade Commission and the Department of Labor. In 1975 and '76 the FTC began bestirring itself in a manner that seemed intended to prove that you can't generalize about anything, not even the torpor of regulatory agencies. Its leadership was going around knocking fellow regulators. Wesley J. Liebeler, the FTC's director of policy planning, quoted the dismal statistics on the increased prices caused by federal regulators, and he mocked the Civil Aeronautics Board's unanimous rejection in 1974 of a British airline's offer to let us fly the Atlantic for one third the going rate; he added that as a lawyer he had to admire the elegance of the argument that preventing cheap flights to London would make America a better place to live.

In 1975 the commission's then chairman, Lewis A. Engman, was telling the states that their licensure laws were contributing to inflation. He advised them to forget the guild line that licensing is there to protect the public, observing that: "The anticompetitive and anticonsumer thrust of such licensing seems apparent on the face of it since the clamor for more licensing has always come, not from consumers, but from the trades themselves." To make his point, Engman referred to an FTC study of the condition of television repairs under different forms of regulation: California, which does not license repairmen but has a state agency that investigates fraud; Louisiana, where TV repairmen are licensed, and the District of Columbia, which at the time had no controls. There was considerably less fraud in California than in the other two jurisdictions. Licensing in Louisiana did nothing to decrease fraud—but, by artificially restricting the number of repairmen, it kept the price level 20 per cent higher than in California and the District of Columbia.

The Labor Department, for its part, has been turning

out basic information about guild practices. Much of this has been done by Benjamin Shimberg of Educational Testing Service, whose 1972 book, *Occupational Licensing: Practices and Policies*, is one of the two basic texts in the field. (The other is Jethro K. Lieberman's *The Tyranny of the Experts*, published in 1970.) Despite his position at the testing monopoly (or perhaps because of it), Shimberg got interested in the validity of licensing examinations, which he found to be more effective at keeping people out of the trade than at guaranteeing the competence of those who got in. Shimberg and Labor are looking at guilds from the other end of the telescope: how irrational testing is used to discriminate against potential entrants to a trade, and how licensing valid only for a single state prevents people from moving to where the opportunity is greatest. But their goal, letting more people into the guild, can only benefit the rest of us, since more suppliers tends to mean more service at lower prices. Thus Labor's efforts mesh with the FTC's attacks from another flank.

In 1975 and 1976 the FTC initiated a series of moves against the guilds, with state prohibitions against advertising the prices of prescription drugs and eyeglasses as the first targets. The targets were shrewdly chosen. As we shall see in later chapters, those prohibitions have been under attack by consumer groups, notably the organizations representing the aging. The FTC could also count on political support from discount chains within both industries. Finally, the FTC chose to mount its first attacks on products, whose contents are standard no matter at what price they are sold, rather than services, thus avoiding the standard guild argument that higher prices mean better quality. In both cases, the FTC proposed rules that would override state laws and guild regulations that in most states prevent pharmacists and those who sell eyeglasses from advertising their prices. The rules will not come into effect, if at all, until after a year or so of hearings, which will pit the independent pharmacies and optometrists and other professionals against the chains that want to advertise. When he announced the proposed rules, Engman said price advertising of prescription drugs would save the public $288 million. The pharmacists' main defense, limp even by guild standards, was that price advertising would encourage the public to pop more pills.

As it turned out, the public got there first through the courts. In May 1976, the Supreme Court in a 7–1 decision ruled that the states could not forbid price advertising of prescription drugs. It was a natural sequel to the Goldfarb case on minimum fees described in chapter 2, and like Goldfarb was argued by Alan Morrison of the Nader Litigation Group. The decision seemed to be the beginning of the eventual end of all guild-inspired restrictions on price advertising, although the Court's opinion did specify that it was leaving the advertising issue concerning doctors and lawyers to "another day."

What's at stake in the issue of advertising can be seen most clearly through eyeglasses. How we buy our glasses is the prize in an obscure guerrilla war between the commercial discount chains and independent optometrists, ophthalmologists and opticians.* The chains use salaried optometrists to prescribe and dispense glasses; they and the independents all get their glasses from the same manufacturers, but the independents' markup is higher. In the twenty-six states where the guilds' grip is solid, price ad-

---

* Ophthalmologists are physicians who treat eye disease; less than half also prescribe glasses. Opticians dispense glasses but do not prescribe them. Optometrists prescribe and dispense glasses, but do not treat disease.

vertising is prohibited. In the others, the chain operators flourish, to the distress of the guilds, because their prices are lower—and they can tell it to the public. In the District of Columbia, where advertising is permitted, an optometrist said banning it would be the first item on the agenda if the optometrists could get control of the situation.

Lee Benham, an economist then at the University of Chicago, found that the same glasses cost from 25 to 100 per cent more in the states where advertising was prohibited. This difference had nothing to do with quality: both commercial operators and independent optometrists (and ophthamologists and opticians) get their wares from the three companies that produce 90 per cent of the country's spectacles. Glasses made by Texas State Optical sell at relatively low prices at home, where advertising is allowed, and at high prices across the borders in Oklahoma, Arkansas, and New Mexico, no-advertising states; some residents of those states drive a considerable distance to get their glasses in Texas. It's not that the chains don't make money at their lower prices. In Texas, one chain sells contact lenses for $69.50 that costs $5 to produce, but in the restrictive states of California and Ohio those same lenses go for at least $200. In California, when the Opti-Cal chain got fined $2,000 for advertising eyeglasses at $18.90, one of its executives said: "When we sell a pair of glasses for $18.90, we are making at least a 100 per cent profit. You can imagine how much more those other guys are earning."

The difference in price had everything to do with the extent to which the optometrists guild was able to impose its will on the market: the greater their power, the higher the price (and fewer people bought glasses). Power is used to prevent information from leaking out to the populace, and the most classified kind of information has to do with prices. In Michigan, Benham found, if you want to join the optometric association so you can practice in that state, you have to score 65 points on the following scale:

	Points
Not advertising	30
Location in a professional or office building as opposed to "an establishment whose primary public image is one of reduced prices and discount optical outlet"	25
Limiting office identification sign to approved size and content	15
Professional meetings and activities	14
Physical facilities (rooms and laboratory)	8
Function facilities (equipment)	8

That means you can pass the test simply by meeting the guild requirements for keeping information away from the public, the subject of the first three categories. If we make the charitable assumption that an optometrist attending a "professional meeting" will learn more than a couple of handy phone numbers, the public interest is still limited to the last three categories, giving us a final score of Guild 70, Public 30.

Even if the optometrists succeed in fending off the FTC, they are still in danger from the courts. Given the precedent of the prescription drug advertising case, the Supreme Court would presumably rule against them, and a lower federal court already has banned California's rule on advertising, though at this writing the optometrists had prevented the implementation of the decision. In addition to their defeat in California, in Florida, Eckerd Op-

tical Centers,† a chain with forty outlets, has brought a
suit asking that the state ban on price advertising be
lifted, and in Georgia a federal court ruled that the state
optometry board cannot take away an optometrist's license because he works for a chain operation. The board
had found the offender guilty of "unprofessional commer-
cialism," which can be abbreviated to "low prices," and
the court in overruling the board noted that its members
are "economically interested in the results of the cases
they hear." The guild's reaction to all this was stated by
the *Review of Optometry:* "The rising consumer voice
holds great dangers for optometrists."

An odd footnote to Benham's work is that, when he
polled his colleagues about the results they would expect,
40 per cent of the economists and all the professors of
marketing said they thought he would find prices *lower* in
the states that prohibited advertising. Doubtless they've
been watching too much television. TV is where we find
the kind of advertising that does indeed raise prices. Typically these are ads for shared monopolies (oil, automo-
biles) or artificial monopolies (brand-name drugs) that
don't advertise prices because they don't engage in price
competition; this advertising simply saddles us with the
costs of "free" television. By contrast, price advertising—
supermarket ads are a good example—does provide us
with useful information. As Engman pointed out, it's bad
enough paying the doctor's bill without also paying twice
as much for the prescription because we don't know
about the discount pharmacy around the corner.

The FTC has also proposed rules for funeral directors
that went beyond opening up the field to price advertising. It proposed banning one of the most absurd of

---

† Its head, Jack Eckerd, is a Florida Republican who in 1975 came to
Washington as director of the General Services Administration.

guild make-work hustles: the requirement that a corpse be embalmed before cremation. As noted in chapter 1, this is one of those nones—a useless but harmless service—whose elimination can reduce, if not the cost of living, at least the price of dying. The FTC also wants to make the industry stop hiding the cheap coffins and stop taking a profit on such pass-along costs as death notices and flowers. At about the same time, FTC said that Service Corporation International, the nation's largest funeral chain, had agreed to refund some $100,000 in overcharges dating back to 1971. While all this was going on, Washington was getting another sort of insight into the funeral business. In June 1975 the District of Columbia City Council passed a bill creating a local boxing commission and tacked onto it an amendment that would allow funeral directors from states that have no reciprocity agreement with the District to get a local license without taking an examination. A councilman explained that the amendment "was tailored to the needs of Diggs personally." That's Congressman Charles C. Diggs, Jr., who's an undertaker back home in Detroit. Diggs didn't want to moonlight as an undertaker in the District, so the story went; he wanted a license so he could attend a funeral directors' convention—if one were ever held; besides, it wasn't his idea, but that of the local funeral directors who wanted him to grace their ranks with his prestige. But the locals were distressed to find that the Diggs amendment brought a flood of inquiries from out-of-towners wanting to open for business in the district, while they were still unable to invade the out-of-towners' territory. The locals had a point, in that one-way reciprocity is unfair, but that wasn't the point they really wanted to make. The real trouble, they said in classic guild fashion, is that the district doesn't have strict enough licensing, and the example they gave is that Diggs's home state of Michigan requires funeral directors to have a college degree. Embarrassed about the whole business, the City Council quickly moved to repeal the Diggs amendment. Back home in Michigan, you still need a college education to become an undertaker.

The FTC has also taken on the most powerful of all the guilds. In the wake of the Goldfarb decision, it charged the lordly AMA with illegally preventing doctors from advertising, and, as we noted in chapter 2, it sought to help make Goldfarb a reality in the marketplace by investigating the effects of the advertising ban on lawyers in southern California. In 1976 the agency was looking into restrictive practices by real estate brokers, veterinarians and hearing aid dealers.

Some of the eleven regional FTC offices were beginning to fill a political vacuum by acting as public advocates against the guilds. The Chicago office prepared briefs supporting an Indiana case against that state's drug-advertising ban, and another attacking restrictions on licensing optometrists in Illinois. In Michigan, the FTC lobbied against a proposal to license auto mechanics (which if adopted presumably would prevent Christine Winter from fixing her neighbor's car).

Out in the states, where most of the action ultimately has to take place, the picture is muddled but laced with hope. The guilds of course are still making end runs around the public interest. Horseshoers got themselves licensed in Illinois, for example, and the psychiatrists and psychologists are continuing their campaign in several states to pry everyone else's hands off our heads. But the guilds aren't scoring as easily as they used to. Several states have added public members to boards once exclusively occupied by members of the occupation they regulate, though how valuable this will prove depends largely on whether the public members are informed enough to resist the professionals' claims of superior expertise.

Some thirty states have set up umbrella agencies to supervise boards that previously were responsible to no one. Since these agencies can also advise the legislature, they are potentially important in changing the politics of the guilds. Most guilds other than doctors and lawyers do not have much muscle; no one need flee in terror from the frog dealers or rainmakers. They've won in the past because no one paid any critical attention to them. If, say, the beauticians are sponsoring a bill to stifle competition in their trade, a member of the legislature will get two or three calls or letters from beauticians in his district. That's not much, but it's all he hears. No one lobbies him against the bill, no one even bothers to tell him it will raise the cost of beauticians' services to his constituents. Why lose three votes over an obscure bill that no one cares about anyway? He votes for the bill, and a moment later he has forgotten it. An agency that would at least tell him what was involved in the bill, and might even lobby publicly against it, would go a long way toward righting the political balance.

Here is a sampling of good news that has been coming out of the states:

VIRGINIA: all licensing bills now go to an office headed by Ruth Herrink, considered by some the most effective of state guild overseers. The legislature appears to heed her recommendations. Mrs. Herrink believes that "licensing is not the answer to fraud and incompetence." She has repelled attempts to gain licensure by electronic repairmen and data processors.

OHIO: the state attorney-general, William J. Brown, won an antitrust settlement against the state's architects under which they agreed to give consumers price information. An added feature of the settlement was that the architects agreed to distribute a brochure titled: *Consumer Rights Under the Antitrust Laws in Selecting and Compensating an Architect.* Brown also brought an antitrust case against price-fixing by professional engineers.

IOWA: Joan Lipsky got interested in guilds by reading Shimberg's book. Since she is a member of the legislature, the end result of her interest was a 1975 law that: put all fees collected into the general fund, rather than reserving them for each board's use; put at least two public members on each board, and removed the requirement, common in guild-ridden states, that professional members be chosen by their respective guilds. Later on, in a letter, Ms. Lipsky reflected on guild politics:

> One of the ways we got our bill passed was by firmly refusing to consider licensure of any new groups of any type until we had adopted the uniform procedures bill. That immediately gave us some groups who were supportive—hearing aid dealers, psychologists, social workers, laboratory technicians, veterinary assistants, etc., etc. The list of groups who want to be cloaked with exclusivity via the law in the name of the public interest is of fantastic length. . . . In general, the professions are so arrogant that they don't really know how to exert much political muscle. The trouble is that the public is fantastically apathetic . . . It is difficult to find an intelligent spokesman for the consumer. Usually the consumer groups come off as soreheads or equally arrogant and querulous as the professions.

NEW JERSEY: This state violated all the principles of expertism by putting its licensing boards under the control of what should be the representatives of the unwashed populace, the state Department of Consumer Affairs. It also put at least one public member on all nineteen boards. Public members are of course likely to surrender when confronted with a phalanx of professionals explaining why high prices for, say, beauticians are good for the consumer. To counteract this possibility, Walter McCale, deputy director of Consumer Affairs, said that he attends all board meetings with a state attorney: they have a voice, though not a vote.

Massachusetts has attacked the same problem from a different angle. A state consumer affairs official observed of the public members that

> many have been totally coopted by the professional members of their boards . . . the public member function of independent consumer watchdog or lone voice was not encouraged . . . They did not have easy access to alternate sources of information and certainly had few allies on the board when the interest of the public was at variance with the interest of the professional.

The state created a public member "caucus" at which the members were to be told how they could inform themselves sufficiently to play their intended roles: at the first meeting, for example, they heard from the FTC and the Massachusetts Consumers' Council about the resources available to them.

FLORIDA: The guilds brought it on themselves. Maddened perhaps with power, the Construction Industry Licensing Board in 1973 flunked every single one of the 2,149 aspirants who took its exam to become a general contractor. That act, though reversed under pressure, inspired the legislature to launch an investigation not just of the construction board but of the twenty-six other licensing boards whose practice of the economics of scarcity had been cloaked in more discretion. The investigation, headed by one John Phillip Halstead, found that the licensing exams generally did not test the applicants' competence, and that boards without public members are "accountable to no person or agency for their action or inaction." Eighteen of the twenty-seven boards reported "an undersupply of practitioners in their fields"—though presumably they were bragging rather than complaining —but only eleven had reciprocity agreements with other states and only eight of those had actually licensed anyone under reciprocity. The fees they were collecting and keeping seemed excessive to Halstead. The Real Estate Commission, for example, maintained a staff of 133 on a budget of $2 million, and a surplus of about $1 million—yet none of this activity had done anything to dent Florida's reputation as the playground of real estate hustlers.

Finally, in Alaska, passage of a law requiring disclosure of all sources of income over one hundred dollars sent the licensing boards scurrying toward the North Slope. As reported by the newsletter of the National Council on Occupational Licensing: "This has completely crippled Alaska's occupational licensing functions. Seven major licensing boards resigned in toto and most other boards had resignations to the point that it has become extremely difficult to raise a quorum . . ."

The attack on the guilds enters new dimensions when it takes on those who practice mental therapy, the most important guilds being the psychiatrists and psychologists. Here the issue is only secondarily money, but let's dispose of that first. By roping off their territory to the extent possible, the mental therapy guilds have created the familiar effect of artificial scarcity and high prices. In the case of the psychologists, who basically subsist on the psychiatrists' leavings, the effort has not been entirely successful. The American Psychological Association busily promotes legislation to regulate such competitors as marriage counselors; the bills are often passed, but, at least in California, the vanished marriage counselor was miraculously reborn as a "personal counselor" or "counselor in family problems." The psychiatrist, by contrast, has inflicted on us one of the most resounding nones to be found on the professional market. Psychiatrists go to medical school in order to learn how to advise people about their daily lives —as Paul Gillette puts it, "they are trained in the health business but they work in the happiness business." By defining their field as mental *health*, they foster the illusion that their training in the physical functions of the body makes them expert in the workings of our psyches. So the client (including the taxpayer, since many psychiatric bills are third-partied onto the public) pays for the psychiatrist's ability to take out an appendix, which he will not do, in order to get his advice about happiness, which the psychiatrist's training did not particularly qualify him to give.

The more fundamental issue—unless you happen to be looking at that bill at the moment—is one of power. Without a great deal of public notice, the psychiatric professions have amassed considerable control over our lives. Nowhere is this more evident than in mental hospitals, those institutions where we jail troublesome or unwanted people whom we cannot sentence to a prison or nursing home. (The Russians have of course been doing much the same, ever since their government abandoned Stalin's more sincere methods of dealing with those he wanted to get off the street.) The psychiatrist can sentence us to a mental hospital without our having been charged, much less convicted, of any definable offense. There will be a hearing, but the judge won't understand what the psychiatrist is saying—if indeed it has any meaning—because they speak different brands of professional pig Latin; what both of them know is that they'll get in less trouble for committing a harmless person than for releasing one who later causes trouble. Someone accused of crime is represented by a lawyer, if only a court-appointed time-server, but no lawyer or adversary psychiatrist is required to defend the person whom someone wants to put away.

Jeffrey Steingarten, a Fellow of the Institute of Current World Affairs, observed that only about one in twenty people up for "sanity" hearings in the New York City courts were represented by a psychiatrist. Once in the bin, you cannot simply serve out your time, because the sentence has no time limit. Only the psychiatrist can turn you loose, but no rules of evidence control his decision, and he is on the institution's payroll, and the institution doesn't like empty beds. You are at the mercy of the expert.

It's all right, in the expert view, because it's for our own good. Punishment must be regulated to prevent abuse, but who needs rules when the other fellow's just trying to help? And would like to help even more. The current fad for behavior modification—if you haven't heard about it, that's occidental brainwashing—provides a promising area for growth, and the most ambitious guild leaders have trained their sights on the summit. The head of the American Psychological Association, Dr. Kenneth B. Clark, proposed recently that the president and other "power-controlling leaders" be required to accept "psycho-technological, biochemical intervention"—whatever that may be; it sounds terrifying enough to make anyone who hasn't already had his lobotomy drop out of the primaries. Dr. Arnold A. Hutschnecker, who had his moment in the sun as Richard M. Nixon's reputed therapist, offered his clinical opinion that had Abraham Lincoln enjoyed a psychiatrist's attention he "could have been helped to understand the nature of the anguish produced by his inner conflicts . . . and perhaps there would not have been any need for the bloody killings of the Civil War"—a historical interpretation that makes Dr. Hutschnecker's famous patient seem comparatively sane. On a more modest level, Paul Gillette notes, the trade is trying to extend the requirement for psychological certification for a driver's license from Pennsylvania, where the sorry practice began, to North Carolina and, presumably, the other forty-eight states.

Psychiatrists and psychologists rival their medical colleagues in their claims to knowledge withheld from the rest of us. Practitioners like Robert Carr are rare indeed. Carr is a psychologist at a federal prison who, when Mike Wallace asked him why so many convicts were repeat offenders, replied: "I dunno." The usual stridency of the psychiatrists' claims may be due to an uneasy sense that the foundations of the trade are eroding. As P. B. Medawar recently wrote,

> The opinion is gaining ground that doctrinaire psychoanalytic theory is the most stupendous intellectual confidence trick of the twentieth century: and a terminal product as well—something akin to a dinosaur or a zeppelin in the history of ideas, a vast structure of radically unsound design and with no posterity.

Posterity would at least be freed of any unwanted help, if the abolitionists have their way. The abolitionists are the members, most of them therapists of one kind or another, of the American Association for the Abolition of Involuntary Mental Hospitalization. Their goal is simpler than their name: to liberate people from imposed psychiatry. Any kind at all, but most especially treatment imposed on people confined in a hospital, where, the abolitionists believe, the forced attentions of a psychiatrist will do as much for our mental state as the regulatory ministrations of the Interstate Commerce Commission do for American transportation. The abolitionists have discouraging answers for those who, however little they may value psychiatry, are afraid of the possible consequences of abolition. If someone has done something proving him "dangerous," he should go to jail through the criminal process, in the abolitionist view, while retaining his right not to undergo psychiatric treatment. But what about that crazy who hasn't done anything yet, and who, if they don't lock him up, may come around and murder me and my family? In a time when crime is booming, and especially violent crimes that make little sense to the rest of us, we would desperately want to believe that someone, anyone can identify the Richard Specks and Lee Harvey Oswalds before it's too late. The abolitionists answer that it's impossible.

Dr. Grace Robinson, a New York therapist, states the abolitionist view that there's no evidence that psychiatrists (or anyone else) can predict tomorrow's killer. When Bruce Ennis and Thomas Litvak, a lawyer and psychologist respectively, studied the record they found that psychiatrists' predictions have been so dismally poor that in many cases flipping a coin would have yielded more accurate results. All studies of subsequent behavior showed the psychiatrists' predictions were wrong at least 50 per cent of the time; sometimes the rate of error was much higher. Like any totalitarian, the psychiatrists always overpredict danger; they do not err in favor of the individual. Several years after the court-ordered release of 969 people confined by psychiatric order to a maximum-security mental institution in California, 7 had been found troublesome in other kinds of institutions, 2 committed felonies, 3 were back in maximum security. The rest—that's 957 out of 969, or 99 per cent—were free and neither dangerous nor troublesome but just plain innocent: such a rate of preventive overkill would doubtless have impressed Stalin himself. Another study of post-release behavior found the rate of violence among those the psychiatrist found "dangerous" to be the same as among those they classified "not dangerous." Viewing this record of unrelieved incompetence, Ennis and Litvak asked, how on earth did the psychiatrist ever get to be an expert witness and why should the judge listen to him? Note that the healthy precedent of testing expert forecasting against results might well be extended to other professionals—economists and stockbrokers come to mind.

Other researchers have tried to discover just what it is that causes the psychiatric professionals to declare us to be mentally "ill." Being poor increases your chances of being "sick." So does having the wrong political attitudes; the most dangerous attitudes to hold—reminiscent again of Stalin—are those critical of the professionals themselves. In a newsletter to the Institute of Current World Affairs, Jeffrey Steingarten describes the 1974 Braginsky study that reached that conclusion:

> The researchers videotaped two staged psychiatric interviews, using the same college senior to play the patient in each. The first section of both tapes was the same: the "patient" complained of sleeplessness, irritability, poor appetite, fatigue. After that the tapes diverged. When the patient was asked about his political beliefs, he expressed in the first tape a middle-of-the-road philosophy and decried radical tactics. In the second tape, he expressed a New Left philosophy. At the end of each interview, the patient was asked for his views on the mental health profession. The middle-of-the-road patient criticized the profession for destroying traditional values; the radical criticized it as the handmaiden of a repressive society.
>
> Each tape was played to a different audience of mental health professionals. After each section, the audiences were asked to rate the degree of pathology they observed in the patient. As you'd imagine, the first part of each tape (where the symptoms were the same) produced the same average rating—mild pathology. But as the interviewer delved into politics, the middle-of-the-road patient remained stable while the radical was seen as increasingly disturbed. Then as both patients began to criticize

the mental health profession, their mental health took a grave turn for the worse. To test these extraordinary findings, the [researchers] revised the last section of the radical's tape, having him praise the profession. The new tape was shown to a new audience. Up until the end, the pattern established in the first experiment was duplicated —the radical was judged as increasingly disturbed as he expressed his New Left beliefs. But then, when he praised the mental health profession, the raters astonishingly promoted him to normality.

The abolitionist goal of reducing psychiatric power has made considerable progress in recent years. In general the institutional psychiatrist's domain has shrunk with the dramatic decline in the number of people imprisoned in mental hospitals from 559,000 in 1955 to less than half that number in 1975. This has been made possible in part by the rapid growth of community mental health centers, which provide a much milder alternative to the total institution—four fifths of the people they treat are outpatients not prisoners. Federal funding of the centers was renewed in 1975 over a presidential veto. One wonders if the President knew about Drs. Clark and Hutschnecker's plans for his involuntary mental treatment; the bill he vetoed would at least make it possible for him to get his treatment as an outpatient.

State law has shifted somewhat against the psychiatrist. In 1975, for example, California put through a bill guaranteeing mental prisoners the right to refuse psychosurgery—that's lobotomy—and electric shock treatment; the psychiatric hospitals have tried to block the law's enforcement. In many states, however, it is still possible for you to have your brain cut open at the whim of a psychiatrist after being confined by another psychiatrist sporting that 99 per cent failure rate.

Incredibly, New Jersey is the only state to have begun

to provide the mentally accused with rights like those built into the criminal process. This is happening through the Mental Health Advocacy Office of the New Jersey Public Advocate, a unique institution we'll be meeting again in chapter 10. The results to date are remarkable. In half a dozen class actions, the advocates have won the right to counsel at commitment hearings and reviews (where it is decided whether the person will be freed), the right to be examined by a psychiatrist of his choice, and, once incarcerated, the right to such civil rights as voting. In individual cases, the advocates often call a private psychiatrist to testify against the institutional doctors—doubtless his forecasts will be of as little value as the other fellow's; what matters is that the victim has an expert speaking weightily, if incomprehensibly, to the judge on his behalf. For the first time, the judge hears two sides, and the outcome of these cases tells volumes about how it usually happens.

In their first year, the mental health advocates' two field offices—they were operating in only two of New Jersey's twenty-one counties—had represented a total of 825 people at commitment or review hearings. Of 609 people up for commitment, 511 won something: dismissal of the state's case, temporary freedom, or transfer to a less oppressive institution such as an ordinary hospital. Of the 216 incarcerated people up for review, 90 won either freedom or transfer. That means three out of four people involved, by the simple fact of having someone to argue their cases, won some added degree of freedom. Projecting that percentage from two counties in New Jersey to the rest of the nation gives us some idea of the number of people among us who are being locked up on the fuzzy and unchallenged authority of the psychiatrist.

The Supreme Court's widely noticed 1975 decision awarding damages to a longtime mental prisoner got mixed reviews from the abolitionists. Kenneth Donaldson spent fifteen years in Florida mental hospitals without having committed any crime or having endangered anyone, even himself. He was incarcerated because his father said he had delusions, and he was kept in partly because, as a Christian Scientist, he refused to swallow the tranquilizers that in the modern institution have replaced the strait jacket as the primary method of social control. The Supreme Court decided Donaldson could not be kept in the bin because he could make it on the outside, wasn't considered dangerous, and had not been given treatment. The abolitionists objected to that last provision for, as Dr. Thomas Szasz, one of their leading figures, wrote, the court's decision appeared to legitimize involuntary psychiatry, even though it did give freedom to Donaldson and may help others get out.

What's happened so far is a major first step toward dismantling the structures of guild monopoly, accomplished by an odd array of free-market enthusiasts, consumer groups and some responsible office holders. Awareness of what those monopolies mean to us, of the fallacy in the public interest claims of professional organizations, has increased greatly, though as usual you can always find someone barking up yesterday's tree. In mid-1975, for example, businessman W. Michael Blumenthal took to the New York *Times* Op-Ed Page to propose a new guild: "Business executives are professional people, but there is nothing in business life that corresponds to the bar associations, the American Medical Association, or the American Society of Architects. Why, then, should business people not set up an association dedicated to defining and maintaining the standards of their profession?" Though the climate of opinion is less hospitable to such ideas, only in a few instances has the difference yet been translated into hard cash for the average man. The Supreme Court's drug advertising decision and the FTC's new rules, if they survive unscathed, will bring more competition to a handful of professional markets; a few states are no longer easy marks for guild lobbyists. But no government has yet earned the Adam Smith Medal by taking the free market plunge: repeal the licensing law, abolish the regulatory agency, send the board members back home. Note that formal qualification would not disappear with the abolition of the present mandatory licensure. Under the alternative called permissive licensure, the right to use the title—realtor, say, or frog dealer—is restricted to those who meet guild qualifications, but others can practice the trade, without the title, if they can get customers. John Stuart Mill put the case in his 1859 essay *On Liberty:*

> Degrees or other public certificates of scientific or professional acquirements should be given to all who present themselves for examination and stand the test; but such certificates should confer no advantage over competitors other than the weight which may be attached to their testimony by public opinion.

The essential difference is that under permissive licensing we are free if we so choose to buy our homes or frogs from an untitled dealer, and that this competition, or even the threat of it, will serve to keep the titled professional's fees in line.

The savings to the public from breaking up professional monopolies, though far from trivial, may not be as important as the act of extricating ourselves from the web of net screwing caused by the guilds. If we and the television repairman can face each other knowing that the government is no longer rigging the market in one or the other's favor, then perhaps we can confront the really big screwings that oppress us both.

5

Insurance: Live and Die in the Right State

LAKE ERIE, WE are told, is very gradually getting a bit cleaner, though to the passerby it still looks awfully polluted. So it is with the insurance industry. The average man confronting an insurance agent across the kitchen table is still likely to be found staring glassy-eyed at yards of fine print written in a foreign language; the agent is still likely to leave with the customer's signature on a policy that he wouldn't have bought had he been able to understand it or had he known about the alternatives available, or, most simply, had he ever figured out for himself just what he needed.

But the odds, like Lake Erie, are getting a little bit better. The criticism showered on insurance practices in recent years has made much of the public less willing to buy the industry's incomprehensible product on faith. A lot more information is available—in English, not actuarialese—to those who want to base an insurance decision on something more than the advertising put out by the industry. The better state insurance commissioners (not numerous, but the category was uninhabited only a few years ago) have begun to strip away the layers of complexity and featherbedding rules by which the industry and its friends guaranteed high prices to the buyer and high profits to themselves. Under these various pressures, the industry is beginning to offer the public a better deal. Cheaper, more efficient types of insurance, like savings bank life insurance and no-fault, are spreading.

The current vogue for telling the public what insurance is about can be dated from a *Consumer Reports* series on life insurance in 1967.* During his meteoric passage as Pennsylvania Insurance Commissioner in the early 1970s, Herbert Denenberg put out a dozen consumer guides to insurance, including the celebrated best-buy, worst-buy ratings that made him the industry's public enemy number one. These guides, which include advice on dentists and lawyers and avoiding unnecessary surgery as well as buying insurance, are now available in a paperback edition as *The Shopper's Guidebook*. Close to a dozen other books have appeared in recent years on how to buy insurance or including chapters on insurance.

For the person who's willing to spend a couple of evenings getting ready to decide about life insurance, an excellent guide is Joseph M. Belth's *Life Insurance: A Consumer's Handbook*. Belth leads the reader through the questions he has to answer in order to decide how much life insurance he needs (as protection) and wants (as investment), how much of it should be term insurance, and how much, if any, in whole-life. He shows how to compare the cost and value of different policies, and how to check out a company's financial standing to make sure it will still be around to pay off the survivors. (Belth includes a warning about the difficulty of telling one company from another; there are, for example, no fewer than ten companies whose names begin with "Lincoln," though

---

* A second series in 1974 is available as a pamphlet: *A Guide to Life Insurance*.

insurance wasn't Honest Abe's game.) The reader who gets this under his belt should be able to brush aside the agent's propaganda and buy what he wants, and no more. He can reverse the industry dictum that life insurance isn't bought; it is sold.

That doesn't mean the policy will be easy to read. Complexity is the essence of the insurance hustle, and the way the policy is written guarantees that you will not easily comprehend what you're buying or how much it's going to cost you. Denenberg dramatized this with a brilliant stunt when he had policies scored on a readability scale that showed some of them more difficult to read, though clearly narrower in scope, than Einstein's Theory of Relativity.

The policy has to be readable by the average person if we're to know what we're getting, especially since the industry typically loads its policies with trivial frills that serve mainly to disguise the basic simplicity of the transaction. We also need to know how much it's costing us. That can get fairly involved, and one who tries to follow a couple of insurance experts debating alternative costing methods can easily develop a headache and the wish that the whole question would go away. But that of course is just what the industry wishes us to wish; its representatives are forever proclaiming that the problem is beyond the capacity of the human mind, and so let's continue business as usual. It's not *that* complicated, if we bear in mind the basic fact that the industry's traditional way of quoting the price, known as net-costing, is deceptive. The pitch goes like this. The agent tells you that you will pay $1,000 in premiums in twenty years, at the end of which your policy will have a surrender value, should you choose to turn it in, of $1,001—we insured you free for all these years, see, and we're giving you an extra dollar besides! A naïve listener might wonder how the company stays in business if it gives away its product. But, as Milton Friedman might say, there is no free insurance. What net-costing omits is the money the company is earning, and we are not earning, by investing part of the premiums we paid over those twenty years. And a policy that calls for larger premiums in the earlier years will cost more than one under which payments are concentrated later on, even though the cash outlay is the same, because we've lost the use of more of our money over a longer time. Thus any pricing system that makes allowance for our foregone income is a great improvement over what the agent typically will tell us.

Making the industry give the customer a fairer deal—or at least one he can understand—is mainly up to the states, which have the exclusive power to regulate insurance. The industry likes it that way, and it vigorously opposes any federal role in insurance. (That wasn't always the case. Back in the late nineteenth century, when state legislatures were infected with populism and Washington was safely in the robber barons' pocket, the industry sang the praises of federal regulation. It took the death of populism and Woodrow Wilson in Washington to convince the industry of the logic of state regulation.) State regulation means the deal you can get from the industry depends in part on where you live. Four states, as we shall see later in this chapter, allow cheaper forms of insurance that do not exist in the other forty-six. Insurance sold to groups in a single transaction, which is cheaper and more efficient but also threatens the agents' livelihood, is banned in many states for one or another kind of insurance.

Until very recently, the industry had no more cause to complain about state regulation than the oil industry does about the Texas Railroad Commission. The good old days, which still prevail in most states, can be seen in Illinois in the 1960s as described by Karen Orren in her *Corporate Power and Social Change: The Politics of the Life Insurance Industry*. The legislative committees that dealt with insurance were controlled by insurance agents or lawyers with insurance connections, and the industry typically supplied the state with its own commissioner: of nine commissioners of insurance from 1933 to 1965, seven had been lawyers for big insurance companies, the eighth was an agent, and the ninth was a director of an insurance company. The then commissioner, John F. Bolton, was happy to have the industry tell him how much of his attention it needed: ". . . they broke down the number of companies that might have to be examined in the next year, they divided it by the number of examiners, field examiners, I now have . . . and they suggested to the Legislature that we employ 'this many' people." This many, under the industry-prepared budget, was 80 examiners for 1,300 companies. At that time New York, along with Pennsylvania the only state with enough staff to make a pass at regulating the industry, had 322 examiners for 913 companies—which is one reason why so many companies choose not to seek a license to sell in New York. The industry was properly appreciative; when Bolton's "reform" program was unveiled in the legislature, 900 industry executives paid twenty dollars a head to attend a testimonial dinner in Bolton's honor. In Illinois as in other states, the industry benefits from the legislative perception that it deals with a hopelessly complex subject in which the electorate takes no visible interest. An Illinois insurance lobbyist put it this way: "Strength comes from having a group of people who tell a story that is logical and reasonable to a group of people who don't have the slightest idea what you're talking about." Lobbyists for causes as diverse as brand-name drugs and nuclear aircraft carriers could say the same.

That's still the way it is in most states most of the time, but not all of the time in all fifty. In the last few years, since Herbert Denenberg showed that you could achieve fame as an insurance commissioner, a number of commissioners have been bestirring themselves in the public interest. The results are uneven and often transitory—insurance commissioners' span of office averages three years—but it's a lot more activity than has been seen in this field for decades.

Here are some examples of what's happening. Tighter rules on cost disclosure to the public have been put into effect in Pennsylvania of course, but also in Arkansas, Wisconsin, California, and New York; in the latter state, net-costing was banned in 1974. At this writing, a cost bill was in the works in Maryland. Rules on readability of policies—a difficult subject to regulate—are in effect in Arkansas and North Carolina, as well as Pennsylvania. In 1974, Denenberg's last year, Pennsylvania passed an Unfair Insurance Practices Act which bans misleading marketing and discrimination in giving out policies, and attempts to ban unfair settlements of claims. Though it is too early to measure its impact, the law itself was formidable enough for an industry writer to call it a "sleeping giant" that the industry must be ready to treat "with the respect it deserves."

Shoppers guides modeled on the Denenberg originals have been put out by New Jersey and Ohio. Most state commissioners at the time joined the industry in disapproving of the guides on the standard grounds that it's too complicated to compare one insurance policy with another. In 1973 the insurance superintendent of the District of Columbia, Edward P. Lombard, fought an unsuccessful rear-guard action to prevent market information from leaking out to his constituents. Arthur E. Rowse, columnist and president of *Consumer News*, put the first two

Denenberg guides on sale in Washington. (Rowse later edited all the guides into the paperback volume now on sale.) Superintendent Lombard, who hadn't liked the guides in the first place, reached back into the dustbin of history and dragged out a local law making it unlawful to publish anything "defamatory of any company now or hereafter doing business in the District . . ." That, Lombard told Rowse, was just what he was doing, and he'd better desist or Lombard would take legal action. "It's fraught with peril to horse around with this stuff," said Lombard. But Rowse paid no attention to the threat, and apparently neither did Lombard, for the legal action never took place and the guides remained on sale.

Some states have also tried to crack down on the more egregious of the industry's hustles. One of these involves campus life insurance. In their restless prowl for new customers in the world's most heavily insured populace, and doubtless having heard the rumor about gold in the youth market, the companies lit on students as a potential target —ITT, the ubiquitous conglomerate, was in the field with its ITT Life Insurance College Executive Plan. Now, life insurance is not likely to be a high-priority consumer item for students, at least not while beer, grass, stereos and long-distance phone calls are still on the market. So the companies resorted to asking the student for a minimum in cash, as little as ten dollars, with the rest of the cost financed by a promissory note signed by the student, a process that can be spread over several years. The student, that is, is paying his premiums with borrowed money. Though few may know it, the student is legally responsible for paying off on any notes he has signed, plus interest, whereas someone who takes out a policy in the usual way and lets it lapse has no further obligation. At times the companies resorted to other dubious sales tactics. What has been happening on campus can be seen in the following extracts from a remarkable interview by Joseph M. Belth (B) with a student (s) at Indiana University†:

B: Who would receive the money if you died?

s: My father is the beneficiary.

B: Would your father receive the entire proceeds of the insurance?

s: Yes.

B: As far as you know, no one else would receive any proceeds from the insurance?

s: No. Oh, besides Indiana University.

B: Indiana University?

s: I gave 2 per cent of the proceeds to Indiana University.

B: You indicated that 2 per cent of the proceeds would go to the University?

s: Yes.

B: Was it actually to be paid to the University?

s: No, to the School of Business.

B: Do you know whether it was to the School of Business Development Fund or just to the School of Business?

s: Just to the School of Business.

B: So if the benefits were, say, $30,000, then if you should die 2 per cent of that would be about $600.

s: Yes.

B: How did you happen to get the idea to have 2 per cent of the proceeds payable to the School?

s: It was suggested by the agent who sold the policy to me.

B: Did he simply suggest it, or did he give you some reasons why it might be a good idea?

s: He gave some reasons.

† From an eight-page booklet entitled *The Campus Transcript*. Copyright © 1975 by Insurance Forum, Inc., P. O. Box 245, Ellettsville, Indiana 47429. Reprinted with permission.

B: What reasons did he give?

S: Besides just giving the money, he said it might be helpful in getting a job, because I might get letters—one of them might be from President Ryan. He said it might help in getting a job.

B: Helpful in getting a job?

S: Helpful on applications. He said it might possibly be used as a reference.

B: Was he thinking of placement interviews during your senior year, possibly?

S: Yes.

B: And that this would be something that would be in your file, or did he mean that it was something you might have that you would show to a recruiter?

S: Yes. That might possibly be helpful.

B: Do you recall how much you have paid so far on the policy?

S: $10.75.

B: You did indicate that the premium was $384.

S: $384.75.

B: That was the first year premium also?

S: Yes.

B: Every year?

S: Right.

B: How did you go about arranging the first premium?

S: They have a way that you pay for the first year's premium. You don't have to start paying on it until—in my case—April of next year, and then you don't really even have to pay then. You can wait until the fifth year when you get an anniversary payment which would cover the first year's premium and the interest that they tack on. It would take care of something like 95 per cent of the first year's premium.

B: How is it actually done then? How would you describe the transaction? You paid $10.75, but you didn't pay the rest, and you can wait and do that later. How do you describe that kind of a transaction? Do you understand what I'm asking?

s: No.

b: Have they simply allowed you to postpone payment of the premium?

s: Because I'm not getting enough income right now to be able to pay for it.

b: You are a junior now, is that right?

s: Right.

b: And next April there will be a $384 premium due for the second year. What do you expect to do then? Do you figure on being able to pay the $384 for the second year?

s: You wouldn't be paying it all at once, though you would be making monthly payments, which wouldn't be that difficult for me.

b: Do you know what the monthly payments would be?

s: Something like $31. I talked to him about maybe not being able to pay the $31. He said I could reduce my benefits to make it a little easier for me to pay.

b: You could reduce your benefits?

s: Yes, after the first year, if I wanted to, and if I didn't think I could meet the payments.

b: Do you know what he meant by reducing your benefits?

s: Taking off two additional benefits besides the basic death benefit. I can't remember what those were but he said I could drop one or two.

b: Do you know what would happen in the event that you are unable to pay the premiums starting in April next year?

s: You mean if I was disabled?

b: No. Suppose you just didn't have any money. You're a senior and you're struggling to pay your bills and you haven't gotten your job yet. Let's say you can't pay the premiums. Do you know what would happen?

s: He told me and I can't quite recall what it was, but they make adjustments for it.

b: Do you plan on going to graduate school?

s: No.

b: But suppose for one reason or another you didn't have a job even after you graduated, either because you decided to go to graduate school or because you just didn't get a job, and you didn't have any money. Are you aware of what would happen then?

s: No, because mostly he just concentrated on the idea that I would have a job and we never really went into that.

b: Dennis, do you know what a promissory note is?

s: I've heard of it.

b: Do you believe that you signed a promissory note?

s: Yes.

b: Was this discussed in your conversation with [the agent]?

s: We did not discuss the promissory note.

This student got out early, but others have not been so lucky. The hustle is no longer so easy in all states. South Carolina now requires students to put up at least 10 per cent of the first-year cost in cash, which should discourage the most absent-minded buyers, and Michigan and Arkansas also require a clearer disclosure of what the student is getting into. In general, *Consumer Reports* has found campus life policies overpriced, and Belth observed with impeccable logic that the way to protect students is to insure parents' lives, not the students'.

Another hustle has to do with scaring clients out of their rights. The Maryland Insurance Commissioner in February 1975 laid fines totaling $100,000 on the Liberty Mutual Insurance and Liberty Mutual Fire Insurance Company. The fines, which were unusually large (until reduced by a court to $25,000) resulted from how the companies handled claims. Belth described the order accompanying the fines as "one of the most chilling documents I have ever read." Its centerpiece is a company memo describing a "loss control campaign." Here are some of its highlights, as reported by Belth:

> 3. . . . we are to determine the amount we wish to pay and to mail our check for that amount to the automobile owner without any discussion with him regarding the difference between that amount and the amount of the estimate coming from his garage.
>
> 9. Are we being extremely resistive to automobile rental claims from third parties? On the rare occasion when we do pay, do we pay only for the going, daily rental fee in the area for a compact and do we limit our payment to the time which it takes to repair the vehicle, refusing to pay for any time involved because the garage is too busy to get at the repair job or because parts are not available?
>
> 16. Are we holding homeowners' losses down by persuading the policyholder to do the work himself?
>
> 20. Are we standing firm in the face of complaints?
>
> 22. How extensively are we using the Persuader . . . ?"

(The Persuader was not a firearm but a notebook to be used to convince the unhappy client that he'd be better off not using a lawyer but dealing direct with the company.)

In the distinct field of auto insurance, no-fault has made considerable progress since it was first introduced in Massachusetts in 1971. No-fault attempts to reduce the overhead costs of the liability system, most of which go to lawyers, by eliminating the requirement that one participant in an accident must be found responsible before a claim can be paid. By 1976 twenty-five states had some form of no-fault. In 1976 the lawyers mounted a propaganda offensive that succeeded by four votes in the U. S. Senate in defeating a bill that would have required all the states to adopt no-fault. The gist of the lawyers' case was that premiums were going up in the no-fault states, and where the limits are low—in New York, for example, no-fault applies only to medical costs under $500—people are encouraged to pad their bills so they can sue instead of accepting a no-fault settlement. In fact, all that the lawyers were proving was that no-fault worked weakly in states with weak laws, and that inflation is shoving all costs up. As the nation's biggest insurance company, State Farm, pointed out, premiums were indeed rising in no-fault states by an average of 3.2 per cent a year—but in states operating under the fault system beloved of the lawyers the increase was an average of 13.5 per cent a year. Despite the 1976 setback, no-fault seems certain to expand rather than contract in the coming years. By contrast, group insurance for both auto and property policies remains banned in most states. Group saves overhead costs because a single contract is negotiated for the entire group, in place of individual contracts for each of its members. The politics of the two cases differs. Most of the insurance industry favors no-fault because it would get the lawyers off what the industry deems to be its own turf. But group insurance cuts into the agent's income, because he is negotiating far fewer contracts. This benefits no one except the average man, so group has no organized lobby working for it.

Title insurance is another distinctive category, and one of the purest forms of expert make-work that our society has to offer. This is the insurance the new homeowner has to buy because the real estate industry finds it more profitable to avoid installing an efficient record-keeping system that would reveal whether there were any claims on a property being sold. No state has taken the pains to eliminate title insurance, but New Jersey has at least reduced both the bite and the kickback to the lawyer in-

volved. The result can be seen in the corrections a New
Jersey lawyer made under the heading of title insurance
in the form letter he sends to clients he represents at a
real estate closing:

```
                                    3.50
      The premium for the guarantee is $5.00 for
each $1,000.00 of insurance protection.  A por-
tion of the premium paid to the insurance com-
pany is returned to us to pay for the additional
work involved in obtaining the title policies.
```

The more active insurance commissioners have even
formed a dissident group within the National Association
of Insurance Commissioners. The NAIC is pretty much
what you expected: a somnolent trade association which
meets usually in some central location—Mexico City and
Las Vegas are recent examples—to enjoy the industry's
hospitality and doze through a few committee reports.
Finding this less than fulfilling, three commissioners in
1973 started holding their own meetings. They are known
as JAM for the initials of their states: Jersey, Arkansas,
Michigan. JAM sessions have been joined at times by Illinois, North Carolina and Texas, whose chairman, Joe
Chrystie, is particularly admired by insurance reformers.
New Hampshire was a progressive state while John
Durkin was insurance commissioner. But Durkin's cost
disclosure bill was beaten by the industry.

Giving the average man a break on life insurance is not
a new idea. Earlier bursts of reform, some dating back to
the early years of the century, have left their mark in four
of the fifty states (Wisconsin, Connecticut, Massachusetts, and New York) where distinctively less expensive and better forms of insurance are available to the
public. All four of these legacies of the past operate under
severe restraints imposed by the political power of the in-

dustry; none has spread to other states; all are currently enjoying a mild renaissance.

The state of Wisconsin has been selling life insurance since 1913. In all those years, the Wisconsin State Life Fund has had little impact either at home or abroad. Although its policies are the best buy in Wisconsin, it has never held even one per cent of the market, and not till 1972 did it amass as many as 10,000 policyholders. Yet it has survived, and its history can instruct us in the politics of insurance.

The State Life Fund was born in the heady La Follette days of the Wisconsin progressive movement. The insurance industry was in disrepute, and much was made of the fact that out-of-state companies were screwing Wisconsin residents and shipping the profits back East besides. The legislature voted the fund into existence in 1911, with the stated purpose of providing low-cost insurance for the workingman, and the first policies were sold in 1913. The reformers saw it as a great precedent, the industry saw it as creeping socialism; the years have brought neither threat nor promise but only an obscure stalemate.

Efforts to kill the State Life Fund have been mounted every decade or so, though one senses in the accounts of these efforts that the industry never committed its troops to an all-out assault. It did succeed in holding down the maximum policy to $10,000, and in restricting its outlets to a single office in Madison, the state capital (the original law had required the fund to distribute application forms through local governmental offices). The industry's victory didn't mean much except to the lobbyists' box scores, since the state had stopped distributing its forms years earlier. In 1973, the industry got the legislature to restrict the sale of policies to Wisconsin residents; the war cry this time was that out-of-state college students were

getting their parents to buy the local product. Again, it
didn't really matter, since State Life wasn't selling that
much to anyone, local or foreign. While the industry
never quite killed the fund, neither were the fund's fans
able to get the legislature to increase the maximum policy
or allow the fund to use some of its income for advertising. Indeed, about the only promotion the fund ever
gets is from its enemies. Sales went up 800 per cent in
1960 after the press reported on efforts to kill the fund,
and it scored its best day ever—still only fifteen applications—after Governor-elect Warren Knowles advocated its
abolition in 1964. Surveying this history, insurance lobbyist George Hardy reached this sensible if undramatic
conclusion: "Our goal is to ignore it [the fund] and not
pay any attention to it. We would like it if others didn't
pay attention to it either. The less said the better."

Certainly the fund cannot be accused of paying too
much atttention to itself or its own excellent record. Its
overhead is low, about 3.2 per cent compared to the industry's 10 per cent. This is because the fund employs no
agents and makes no profit; it does pay taxes and receives
no state subsidy. Its seven basic policies—the fund doesn't
sell frills—cost as much as 50 to 75 per cent less than comparable private policies. Its three and a half employees
(the fraction is a part-time supervisor) have never been
suspected of scandal, nor, it would seem, of any great
desire to sell insurance.

The industry, as usual brushing aside cost as too complicated for anyone to discuss, triumphantly points to the
fund's modest sales as proof of its basic contention that
people won't buy insurance without the "professional
services" of an agent, that legendary figure you can sum-
mon at any time of day or night to figure out your "program." The experience of Congressman Les Aspin of Wisconsin suggests another explanation.

Aspin had his staff call the State Life Fund to price its

policies against a typical policy offered by a private company. This is how Aspin described what happened:

> If you are a 25-year-old male and call up the State Life Fund office and ask how much $10,000 of a . . . [particular] policy would cost for one year, the employee will politely tell you, "$135.10." Life Insurance Company A offers the same coverage for a premium of only $74.20, which is the policy's actual cost. Few potential customers would pursue the matter further. Company A is clearly cheaper—right?
>
> Wrong. What the polite employee at the State Life Fund office did not tell my staff members (at least, not before intensive questioning) was that at the end of the year, you get a dividend of $54.10 back. Company A offers no dividend. But even with the $54.10 dividend, the State Life Fund is still about $7 more expensive—right?
>
> Wrong. The State Life Fund has what is called "cash surrender value" which means that whenever you cancel your policy—whether it is after a year, six years or twenty years—you get a certain sum back. The State Life Fund's cash surrender value for the first year is $42.10.
>
> "In other words, one year of . . . [that] life insurance from the State Life Fund will really only cost you $38.90, compared with Company A's $74.20—a savings of nearly 50 per cent."

Asked about another kind of policy, the fund employees once again failed to quote the figures that showed it was comparatively a better buy. The fund has other ways of fending off any unseemly rush to buy up its product. Its brochure is one barrier. Back in 1916, the brochure shouted its policies' virtues; it was, as Aspin observed, "much more readable, forth-right and less confusing than the small-print, technical brochure used today." Opaque contracts are of course standard in the industry, but an unreadable brochure makes little sense in the marketplace when you have a legitimately superior product to sell. Even the fund's offices—tucked away on the fourth floor of a state building—are hardly placed to catch the public eye. In those offices, one senses, the three and a half employees, embarrassed perhaps by their state's lonely lurch into socialism, are content to remain an obscure footnote to insurance history.

The life insurance sold by savings banks in New York, Connecticut, and Massachusetts is a considerably larger threat to the status quo than that backroom operation in Madison, Wisconsin. Their sales volume is much higher and so is the decibel level of the industry's complaints. Savings banks do not hide their insurance virtues, and the industry does not follow its Wisconsin policy of studied inattention. Accordingly, brisk though inconclusive warfare goes on around the legislative boundaries of the banks' beachheads on the industry's territory.

Savings Bank Life Insurance, like the Wisconsin Fund, has its origins in the reform movements of the first years of the century. Its moving spirit was Louis D. Brandeis, who ironically is also remembered as an enemy of the banks. After he had participated in the 1905 Armstrong investigation that uncovered a flock of scandals in the industry, Brandeis became convinced that mutual savings banks would be a good vehicle for bringing low-cost insurance to the working public. In his native state of Massachusetts, Brandeis led a lobbying campaign that brought in 1907 the first opening for banks to sell insurance. That was that for many years. In 1938 New York succeeded on the fourth try in passing similar legislation; it was sponsored by Governor Herbert Lehman with the support of Brandeis himself, by then the elderly and sanctified Supreme Court Justice. Connecticut followed suit in 1941, under Governor Robert Hurley, and that was the last to date.

It works like this. The participating banks in each state create a central organization that designs policies, sets rates, hires actuaries and doctors, and manages a guaranty fund that stands behind all the members' policies. The banks also pool risks, so that no one bank is hurt by a lot of claims in a single year. The basic difference between bank and standard insurance is that the banks don't use agents. Although they advertise, the banks do not send anyone into your home to practice mouth-to-ear solicitation; if you want the product, you have to go down to the bank to get it. This has two happy results. The cost of bank insurance is far lower, no matter which method of comparison you use, and so is the policy lapse rate: people who buy this kind of insurance tend to keep it, in contrast to those who signed the contract mainly in order to pry the agent out of their kitchen and will drop it at the first opportunity.

Banks sell insurance under two restrictions carefully protected by that sector of the legislature owned by the insurance people. They can only sell to people who either live or work in that state: no mail-order business. Each state also imposes limits on how much insurance a bank can sell to one person; it is over those limits that bank and industry lobbyists most frequently cross swords. In New York the limit is $30,000. In Connecticut it is only $5,000, which effectively keeps the banks out of the group insurance market. In Massachusetts it is—let's see, it's either $41,000 or $5,000, depending on how you look at it. $41,000? That odd figure calls up the vision of a dawn compromise after an all-night bargaining session between the legislature's insurance agents and those members owned by the banks. But no: the rule is that one person can have $1,000 times the number of participating banks, which is currently 41. On the other hand, a bank cannot write a single policy for more than $5,000. So if you want the full amount, you have to take out nine policies at nine banks: eight for $5,000 each, and the ninth for $1,000. Is that clear? The Massachusetts rule has succeeded in the purpose suggested by that long explanation: discouraging all but the hardiest from buying savings bank life insurance.

Because of these limits, and because until recently they did little advertising, the banks have not been able to use their price advantage to sweep the marketplace. In none of the three states do the banks hold as much as 10 per cent of the market. But their growth rate is faster than the industry average. In New York, the banks increased their sales sixfold in the decade ending in 1974, much of this being due to the rapid growth of group insurance. The importance of the limit on the size of a policy, which with inflation is in fact being steadily lowered, became evident in 1975. Sales of individual policies in Connecticut and Massachusetts fell that year. But in New York, with its much higher limit, the savings banks began splashing the papers and the tube with ads inviting the consumer to compare prices: "You shop around for a car. Why not shop around for life insurance?" was the theme song. In a year when the rest of the industry was stagnating, the banks' sales to individuals rose by a record 10 per cent. They had become the state's sixth largest insurer.

All this was more than enough to make the industry view with alarm. Besides hammering down efforts to raise the policy limits in the three wayward states, the insurance people fire periodic broadsides warning of the dangers to the public of letting the banks onto their turf. The warnings take several tacks. The one with the most nostalgic appeal is a rousing defense of that potentially superfluous figure, the agent. With the bank you can only do business when they're open, while your agent never sleeps. As the Connecticut Life Underwriters explained: "The Underwriter is available twenty-four hours seven days a week to a widow or orphan." Picture yourself on Sunday morning seized with a sudden desire to talk insurance: only an agent can satisfy your need. This assumes the agent will be in the mood to trot right over. "Not my agent," says Robert J. Klein, who wrote the *Consumers Union Report on Life Insurance*. "He took my business and left me the way a frog leaves her tadpoles." Or picture Daddy dead: if, God forbid, you should pass away on Friday after banking hours, your survivors will not be able to put in the claim till 9 A.M. Monday, which is when the agent will put it in even if he was notified within the hour of the named insured's departure from this world. Some people, perhaps even a majority, will prefer the personal service of an agent—but the industry is trying to prevent us from doing without the agent if we so choose.

Marvin Kobell wouldn't want us to go away thinking that the agents oppose bankers in insurance just out of crass self-interest. Kobell represents the National Association of Life Underwriters, and when we interviewed him he explained that his constituents worry about the trend to "undue concentration of economic power in banks." He shoved across the telephone a series of reports and papers making two points: banks are getting too much of the action, and this is no good for insurance agents. While it makes sense for you and me to worry about "concentration of economic power in banks," it is faintly comic for the gigantic insurance industry to do so—somewhat like one brontosaurus advising another to join Weight Watchers. In any case, Kobell's broadsides are wide of the mark in the case of those three states: power is concentrated in commercial banks and their trust departments, not the mutual savings banks which sell that cheap insurance.

What most worries Kobell and his fellow agents is another kind of banking incursion into their terrain. By setting up a dodge called a one-bank holding company, a bank can go into non-banking businesses. It can, for example, buy or start an insurance company and locate it in the bank building, where the customer can get insurance to go with whatever banking he's doing, and where he may sense that he'll be more benevolently greeted at the loan window if he's doing business with the bank's insurance arm. That competition is unfair, the agents feel, especially in a small town where a couple of banks provide the only sources of credit.

Recently the insurance industry and the banks have been fighting on still another front: the new market in individual retirement accounts created under the pension "reform" act of 1974. So far the banks are more likely to offer a better deal, and the reason once more is the agent. If you want a retirement account from a bank, you have to go to them, but you don't have to pay a sales commission. The insurance agent will bring the deal to your kitchen table, at any hour of day or night, and he'll take 8–10 per cent off the top of everything you ever put in that account. Confronted about the difference in price, the industry offers the usual limp rationale about the great value to you of the agent's professional services, though that service presumably does not include advising that you can make a better deal across the street at the bank.

The front between those of us who can get savings bank insurance and those who can't has remained unchanged since 1941, the year Connecticut joined Massachusetts and New York. The National Association of Mutual Savings Banks, headquartered in Washington, developed an interstate plan that could be adopted anywhere as long ago as 1946, but efforts to get the necessary state legislation passed have been blocked in state after state. In those legislative battles, the life insurance agents have been joined in the opposition by the commercial banks who, though not directly involved, apparently dislike seeing the saving banks get anything that would make them more attractive to the public. Legislative change seems unlikely unless significant numbers of people in the deprived forty-seven states add their lobbying efforts to those of the savings banks.

The life insurance marketplace is beginning to reflect these various pressures. Most of the ten worst-buy policies listed in Denenberg's original guides have vanished. Some companies are putting out policies that a layman can even read. Sentry Insurance of Wisconsin in 1975 put out a car policy that was short and simple (sometimes to the point of caricature, as in: "A Car is a 4 wheel Motor Vehicle licensed for use on public roads."). Sentry's innovation caused a problem: clients often threw the policy in the wastebasket when it came by mail, evidently assuming that a document they could read must be an ad, not a policy. Also in 1975, a group of companies offered a home-owner's policy with wordage reduced from twelve thousand to seven thousand. Another company hired read-ing specialist Rudolf Flesch, who helped Denenberg on his readability scale, to put its policies into English. Ark Monroe, Insurance Commissioner of Arkansas, ob-served that the new policies introduced in his state tended to be simpler than their predecessors. Even the gi-ants in the industry made at least the pretense of letting the customer in on the secret. Prudential put out an ad leading off with: "Term and Whole Life: It's about time you knew the difference." However, the bottom line of the ad remained unchanged: "Ask Your Agent. Life Insur-ance agents are trained professionals. They know the an-swers to questions you haven't even asked. So they can certainly tell what you want to know." In case you haven't even asked, one of the differences is that your agent makes ten times as much for the same face value on whole life as he does on term.

Trends in term insurance are a good barometer of the public's sophistication. Term is death protection only, and therefore cheaper than whole life (also known as "cash value" and "permanent," though it is difficult to see how

life insurance can be permanent this side of immortality)
which essentially requires the buyer also to invest in the
insurance company. Term insures you for a limited time,
typically five years, and the premiums go up as you get
older. Whole life, by contrast, charges the same premium
from the day you sign up till you die—but its rates are far
higher, up to six times the cost of term, in those early
child-rearing and mortgage-paying years when most people need the most insurance. Whole life has cash value:
you get money back if you give up the policy. However, if
you stop to think about it, that amounts to reducing your
amount of insurance. If you're insured for $10,000, and if
you can get $2,000 any time by surrendering your policy,
it would seem the company is really only insuring you for
$8,000. You can also borrow on your whole life policy
but, since you have cash value in there already, the company is merely lending you back your own money, and
you pay the interest. Since both company and agent make
more on whole life, that's what they want you to buy.
(Agents can read the message in an industry book called
The Magic of the Whole Life Contract.) The consensus
of outside critics is that most people in most circumstances should be buying more term in preference to
whole life.

The message seems to be getting through at least to
some of us. From 1964 to 1974, according to the industry's
figures, term increased its share of new policies from 10 to
14 per cent, and in 1975, when over-all sales did not increase, term kept growing. To these figures, which admittedly are no landslide, one should perhaps add the five-
fold growth in group insurance, which is also term. Paul
Donohue, chief counsel in the Pennsylvania Insurance
Commission, saw a growing trend toward term, and so did
Denenberg himself, who was also willing to take the
credit for the trend. Even the agents' representative, Marvin Kobell, said the industry is now more "openminded

about term," though it is doubtful that the case for term is being shoved with any enthusiasm across the kitchen tables of America.

These modest advances in the deal the average man can get from the insurance industry are not the result of organized public pressure. Commissioner Monroe wrote us that Arkansas Consumer Research has supported his reforms, but that "limited resources and manpower have prevented ACR from initiating much reform in insurance." In 1974 the Naderite Connecticut Action Group investigated the handling of complaints by that state's insurance department. They found that in many cases the department did less than it might have done for the complaining citizen, and that its general posture favored the company over the unhappy client. Their report, however, was never published. That's about all.

Reform has come about through individuals, not organizations. Some, like Denenberg and the other progressive commissioners, were in public office; others, like the authors of the guides listed earlier, did their work in print. Three portraits will complete our gallery of insurance reformers.

Dean Sharp, now a lawyer in private practice in Washington, was in charge of insurance investigation for the Senate Antitrust and Monopoly Subcommittee from 1963 to 1974. He writes frequently on insurance and in 1975 was talking of starting a national consumers organization. Sharp's point is that the public pays huge extra costs for waste and inefficiency in the industry, and that this is because, first, insurance is exempt from the antitrust laws under the 1945 McCarran-Ferguson Act, and, second, because state regulators allow such anticompetitive devices as the frequent bans on group insurance. Sharp makes his case by comparing the amount the public pays in premiums with the amount that comes back in claims paid out. In the case of auto insurance, $8.5 billion in pre-

miums in 1974 produced $3.6 billion in paid claims—the
rest disappeared up the chimney. A combination of no-
fault and group auto insurance (the latter now banned in
thirty states) would reduce premiums by $3-4 billion,
Sharp says, or 35-47 per cent for the average car owner.
In a June 16, 1975, article in *Capitol Forum*, Sharp made
a remarkable comparison of the cost of delivering benefits
under alternative systems. To deliver $1 in benefits cost
$.05 under Social Security disability insurance, $.20 under
group health insurance, $.50 under workmen's compen-
sation, and a monstrous $1.36 under auto liability insur-
ance. (That Social Security provides the most efficient delivery is worth remembering the next time you hear
someone say: "Let's turn it over to private industry; they
can do the job better than government.") Sharp also
notes that the states do not have the manpower to regulate the industry even if they wanted to, and that this is
because most of them use 90 per cent or more of their licensing income for purposes other than regulating insurance. If, as we saw earlier, Illinois has too few examiners
to keep a watch over its companies, it is at least better off
than the ten states which as of 1972 had no examiners at
all. Sharp's remedies are for the states to be required to
repeal all bans on group insurance, and for the Congress
to repeal its exemption of insurance from antitrust. Any
such moves toward real free enterprise would of course
bring to Washington an even greater collection of industry executives than attended the Las Vegas meeting of
the National Association of Insurance Commissioners.

Joseph M. Belth, whom we met earlier as the author of
Life Insurance: A Consumer's Handbook, is one of a
handful of academic insurance reformers: he is professor
of insurance at Indiana University in Bloomington. Earlier he was himself an agent, and he did much of the
research for the *Consumer Reports* insurance series. Since
1974, Belth has been editing and publishing *The Insur-*

ance Forum, a four-page monthly sheet of news and opinion about industry. A typical issue will include an analysis of a new policy, a report on some regulatory action or inaction, and a selection of letters of praise or denunciation (the editor seems particularly to relish the latter). Belth is not loved by the industry he reports on; six periodicals in the tame insurance press refused to carry ads for the *Forum.* His publication is invaluable for the better elements in the industry, like the conscientious agent who wants to know the best the industry has to offer for his clients' needs, but will never get around to doing the necessary research himself.

Joe A. Mintz is a reformer within the industry. Mintz is an agent in Dallas, who has made enough noise in recent years to cause the word "maverick" to be glued in front of his name. He emerged in the late sixties complaining that neither agents nor customers could get adequate cost information about policies on the market. In 1973 Mintz testified at the Senate subcommittee hearings that if people knew and bought the best buys on the market they could get vastly greater coverage for the same premiums: a total of $300 billion for the nation, he claimed. Mintz was also primarily responsible for getting Congress to hold hearings on the Individual Retirement Accounts (IRA) that were being peddled by both insurance companies and banks after they were given a tax break in the 1974 Pension Reform Act. Mintz himself wrote a shopper's guide to IRAs, published by *Consumer News* in Washington.

Periodic noises are heard in Washington about repealing the insurance industry's exemption from the antitrust laws and introducing more competition into the marketplace. As of this writing, nothing has happened, and it is unlikely that anything more than cosmetic change will occur until the public speaks up far more loudly than it has to date.

6

The Aging: Fighting Back
After Sixty-five

THEY ARE NOT the best years of our lives. Few among us, past sixty-five or before, view the years after that watershed as the best for which the first was made; most feel that by then the best years are encapsuled in our memories. Our bleak attitudes toward the state of being old, darkened by fear of aging as well as fear of death itself, make this a subject that cannot be discussed in the bread-and-butter terms of, say, the price of eyeglasses. Most of us, in fact, would prefer not to discuss it at all: with the dissolution of the extended family, we have tried to make of ourselves as elderly a problem that government is to take care of for us, through Social Security, Medicare, and nursing homes, our role being limited to writing the checks. The result of bureaucratized aging is that growing old is no longer a gradual, lifelong process but an overnight transformation that occurs, usually, with forced retirement at age sixty-five.

That solution, if we can so call it, is coming apart under pressures that are just beginning to be felt. America is aging. The ratio is changing between those who are now working and those whom they support through government-financed retirement. Today each person drawing

Social Security is backed by more than three people at work paying the payroll tax—fewer than in the past, but more than there will be in the future. The fall in the birth rate, plus, at least in the short run, a government-encouraged state of chronic unemployment, means that the number at work will not expand in years to come, while the number beyond working age, as now defined, will continue to increase. The process is well under way; Social Security is already our fastest-growing tax. Assuming, as most do nowadays, that our economy is not going to grow at anything like yesterday's pace, it seems unlikely that working people will accept the cut in their standard of living that will be required if they are to support each retiree at anything above a dog-food diet. (Working people are also screwed by the way the payroll tax is imposed; here, however, we are concerned with the total burden rather than how it is collected.)

If we are not going to shove ourselves out on the ice with our gold watches, then we'll have to try another way —and that means demolishing the watershed of forced retirement at sixty-five, and, indeed, rewriting the entire work and retirement rulebook. Here economic and humane motives intersect, for breaking the sixty-five barrier is what some people have been advocating for a quite different set of reasons. Dr. Robert N. Butler, whose 1975 book *Why Survive?* is an angry and compelling indictment of how we treat the old, argues that when the old are incompetent, it is usually because society has told them they are; that most cases of senility are reversible; that the old could contribute a lot more to society if we would only let them. Death is inevitable, Butler is saying, but much of the emptiness and futility and misery of age is not. And, in fact, society is beginning to improve how it treats the elderly. There is, as we shall see later in this chapter, a growing effort to keep the elderly in the community: not just to bring better and more humane services to those we now neglect—the people in nursing homes, for example—but to gear those services to maintaining a person's social life as well as physical existence.

An important force in breaking the sixty-five barrier will be that growing number of people who are coming to be known as the "young old." These are people of about fifty-five to seventy-five (though they are not defined by age alone) who straddle the stereotypes of active-middle-aged-worker and idle-old-retiree. You've seen them in the ads for certain patent medicines and retirement communities: past middle life, they are in good health; fairly well off; free of family responsibilities; some are working, some not; most important, they are active in everything that younger people do. Bernice L. Neugarten of the University of Chicago, who has written extensively about the young-old, believes this age group will by its own example lead the way in creating what she calls "the age-irrelevant society" in which growing old will no longer be a cause for automatic exile from the larger world. Already the young-old are 15 per cent of the population and the main power behind the growing political clout of the aging.

That clout has been made manifest in the past decade. Although the picture on the tube of old people living in hunger, and often in terror as well, is all too shamefully accurate, it is far from a full portrait of being old in America. In some ways many of the elderly have done remarkably well. Thanks mainly to raises totaling 52 per cent in 1970–72, Social Security payments have risen faster than the pace of inflation. This makes the aging the only non-rich group in society to have gained ground during our current hard times; the real income of those on Social Security rose while that of the working class and the poor was falling. Money available for services to the elderly under successive versions of the Older Americans Act has steadily increased. The aging succeeded in getting Social Security tied to the cost-of-living index starting in 1975 and in 1974 a minimum income was provided for all the elderly, including those who did not qualify for Social Security, by SSI (Supplemental Security Income), the only kind of welfare reform to see the light of day. Twice in 1975 the aging defeated the Administration: once when it tried to cut the scheduled Social Security increase from 8 to 5 per cent and again when it tried to cut back on the food stamps that are essential to the food budgets of many older people. Both victories were lopsided. In perhaps the sincerest of political tributes, the 1976 presidential contender who advocated cutting $90 billion out of the federal budget was careful not to aim his ax anywhere near money earmarked for the aging.

The aging are winning these battles because they are the best organized of the nation's out people: better organized by far than the poor, the black, the female; better than the working class except for some unions in monopoly industries. Though it hardly fits our stereotype of the old—which seem able to withstand any amount of factual contradiction—you have to go to someone with a gun, the weapons contractors or the National Rifle Association, to find lobbying skills equal to those of the organizations that represent the elderly. Even the American Medical Association, with much more financial firepower, lost to the aging in the Medicare struggle of 1965. The successful organizing of the elderly is fairly new. Francis Townsend, a retired doctor, flashed across the 1930s preaching $200 a month for the old, but the Townsendites soon dispersed, and scholars solemnly concluded that the aging were incapable of getting it together in any continuing way. Expert opinion to the contrary, the aging have in fact learned to fight back. To determine the ends for which they are fighting we shall examine two of their organizations. The American Association of Retired Persons is the biggest, richest and strongest—it even has its own zip code, 20049—and impeccably straight in style. The much smaller Gray Panthers are calculated to lay to rest our remaining stereotypes about old people in America.

The AARP, with its sister organization, the National Retired Teachers Association, claimed in 1976 a membership of close to nine million that was growing by 100,000 a month. Membership is open to those fifty-five or over and dues are two dollars a year. It is by far the largest organization of the elderly; number two is the National Council of Senior Citizens, largely drawn from union members, which has two thousand local affiliates with three million members. The AARP has its origins in the insurance business. The retired teachers association, which dates from 1947, had gotten into selling life insurance to its members through an agent named Leonard Davis. So many non-teachers wanted the insurance that the AARP was founded in 1958, primarily to meet that demand. Leonard Davis became a multimillionaire through his Colonial Penn insurance, and AARP has been growing ever since. It is a solid financial success. AARP depends on dues for less than half its income, the rest coming from the various services it sells its members—insurance, of course, but also low-cost drugs and travel. Tying those services to membership solves the free-rider problem that plagues voluntary associations: AARP will fight for a Social Security increase that you'll get even without being a member; but if you want the services you have to join. Although its origins may show in its style—AARP occasionally comes on like an insurance man lunging across your kitchen table—it has in fact branched far from its roots both in the services it offers and the causes it espouses. Nowadays, indeed, we find the AARP doing battle, often with great efficacy, against some of the major institutions that screw the average man of all ages.

The AARP's mail order pharmacy has drawn the organization into conflict with elements of the health industry. Drugs are important to older people. They account for one quarter of all prescription sales, and, largely because drugs are not covered by Medicare, the clients pay close to 90 per cent of the bill. The burden is heavy on those who are poor as well as old: AARP found by sampling its members that they spend an average of 10 per cent of their incomes on drugs, and some spend close to half. With these needs in mind, AARP began selling drugs, both prescription and over-the-counter, by mail at prices that it claims average 40 per cent below the general market level. Money is not the only value. Invalids and those who live far from a pharmacy find it easier to buy by mail, and AARP sells to its members on credit (with, they say, only "infinitesimal" losses). Only members can use the mail-order service, but AARP runs seven cut-rate pharmacies—the first is in Washington, the most recent in Portland, Oregon—where anyone can trade. By 1975 AARP was the largest private mail-order pharmacy in the nation, filling four million prescriptions a year. It was forcing the competition to respond. Here, for example, is what a Vermont pharmacy felt compelled to say in a newspaper ad:

HERE WE GO AGAIN

AARP Prescription Prices are 20% to 40%
Below Conventional Pharmacy Prices
NOW for our own Vermont Senior Citizens
we will MEET THOSE LOW, LOW PRICES
No need to send out of State
No 7 to 10 day delay
Just present Proof of Purchase Sales Slip
from AARP, Name and Quantity of
Medication.

No one can try to sell drugs at low cost without becoming enmeshed in the politics of guilds and especially the brand-name hustle. AARP soon found itself crusading for the right to substitute generic drugs for expensive brand-name equivalents. Members were sent charts showing which cheap generic equals which high-priced brand-name drug, and when members ordered the brand-name, the shipment was accompanied by a slip identifying the generic equivalent. This led to many complaints from the doctors who write the brand-name prescriptions. It also led to drug-industry efforts in several states to ban mail-order operations; all these efforts failed, an outcome that substantiates the belief that many guilds are able to maintain their monopolies only because no one with any clout takes them on. The drug issue converted AARP into a major lobbyist in all the fifty states for freeing the drug business from guild control and price restrictions. By 1975 the industry was on the defensive, and AARP was a major force in the efforts, described in chapter 4, to allow generic substitution and price advertising of drugs.

The AARP provides a range of advocacy services through which members can get help in their struggles against one or another institution. In two cases government is the antagonist. AARP recruits and trains volunteers to give free tax advice to their elderly peers. The elderly cannot understand the deliberate complexities of the tax code any better than anyone else, and most cannot afford to pay for expert help; so about half the elderly taxpayers overpay the IRS. The AARP's 4,500 volunteers in 1975 helped 200,000 people with their returns, at a saving of at least fifteen dollars each—the minimum cost of hiring help—plus an unknown amount in overpayments that were avoided. For those who get caught in the paper gears of government programs, there is Teresa Napoli. Napoli, who used to be known on Capitol Hill as a particularly formidable caseworker for former Congressman Albert Thomas of Texas, now exercises her considerable talents as an ombudsperson for AARP. Her office gets 300–350 letters a week from people entangled in Social

Security, food stamps or Medicare. As Napoli says, neither the elderly client nor the local bureaucrat knows the intricate rules that govern those programs, and therefore many lose benefits to which they are entitled. Napoli does know the rules, and her day is spent calling agency heads to reverse injustices inflicted at lower levels: whether the agencies will behave better in other cases because of her intervention is impossible to say. For members who have been stung in the marketplace, AARP's Washington headquarters runs a consumer-assistance center which, in 1974, handled more than four thousand cases and recouped more than $57,000 for its members. Failure to deliver on mail orders, presumably not including the AARP pharmacy mail service, was by far the biggest source of complaints. When the AARP disbanded its local consumer-assistance centers, two of them were absorbed by local governments, and one, in Hyannis, Massachusetts, kept on the elderly staff recruited by AARP. These are but a sampling of what AARP does: its national office and its local chapters turn out publications, give courses, and offer services on just about any subject that might cross your mind.

Service to the members is the bedrock of AARP, but it is also a powerful lobby, in the states as well as in Washington. Any organization with close to nine million members commands respect in Washington, and AARP has a particularly responsive constituency: the aging vote more than the rest of the population, they show up to buttonhole their representatives, and forests are felled when they undertake letter-writing campaigns. The constituency is not the average elderly person. As its critics are quick to point out, AARP draws mainly on an articulate, white-collar, better-off-than-most population. The underclass of the old, those living in fear and hunger in the slums, remain isolated from this or any other organization. AARP is happy to trumpet its more than average nature when it is trying to sell something. In a 1975 letter seeking a discount from the Chrysler Corporation, for example, AARP bragged that its members have an average family income of $7,776, compared to an average of $5,868 for those over sixty-five. AARP acknowledged in passing that the two figures "are not directly comparable," which is a considerable understatement: since AARP membership starts at age fifty-five, it includes many who are still working and earning more than they will after sixty-five, when they'll drag down the average. The pitch of AARP's letter to Chrysler emerged after another five yards of statistics, all designed to show that the membership has loose cash in its pockets that it might well spend on cars: ". . . any discount available to our members could result in an even greater propensity to spend than for the older population as a whole and might contribute significantly to sales by a particular dealer where the availability of the lower rate is made known."

A family income of $7,776, the best the AARP salesman could muster, hardly makes the organization a brotherhood of the affluent. So AARP is usually found fighting for the interests of the average person who is neither poor nor rich; it tends to neglect the worst-off of the elderly. Predictably, many of its causes are the special interests of the old: it has been campaigning to ban credit discrimination against the elderly, and of course it is always around when Social Security and Medicare are on the agenda. When, as it sometimes does, AARP advocates the plugging of tax loopholes, a few lines down the page it can be found plugging for *our* loopholes: property tax exemptions for the elderly, and an even more permissive estate tax. But many issues cannot be contained within the age bracket of fifty-five-plus. AARP cannot credibly lobby for generic drugs, for price competition in pharmacies and eyeglasses, for the elderly alone, and the same is true of no-fault insurance, another major AARP cause. Controlling funeral costs, an issue on which AARP mail set records, is important to survivors of any age. When it attacks such issues, it sometimes seems that AARP is the most effective of lobbies for the average man. The logic of its membership's needs drives the organization to positions far removed from its business origins. Here is the AARP during the 1975 tax and budget debate: ". . . an even greater deficit would be preferable this year if it meant a more rapid return to a full employment economy. While acknowledging that the steps we supported would probably result in further inflation, . . . AARP asserted that excessive concentration of market power is a far more significant cause of inflation and should be dealt with." Going around asserting about "concentration of market power," a topic studiously neglected by the two-party monopoly, is a long ways from selling life insurance, and in vivid contrast to the sanctimony of those who trot out the "elderly living on fixed incomes" as a reason for preferring unemployment to inflation. If the most affluent of the organizations representing the aging talks that way, how can we retain the stereotype that the old are more conservative than their juniors?

Then there's Maggie Kuhn and the Gray Panthers. When this one-time Presbyterian Church official comes on the tube, asks permission to give the Panther rallying cry, and calls out "Off your asses!" you know that you are no longer in the land of the AARP. Their name sounds like something an archaeologist dug up from the 1960s, but the Grays have survived, while Black Panthers are seldom heard from these days, and the forgotten White Panthers were no more than a media event that expired after two press releases. The Gray Panthers' statement of their origins tells us what they are all about:

> We did not select our name; the name selected us. It
> describes who we are: 1) we are older persons in re-
> tirement; 2) we are aware of the revolutionary nature of
> our time; 3) although we differ with the strategy and tac-
> tics of some militant groups in our society we share with
> them many of the goals of human freedom, dignity and
> self-development; and 4) we have a sense of humor.

Compared to the millions of the AARP, Gray Panthers
are as scarce as their jungle counterparts. They keep no
membership, collect no dues, and claim a mailing list of
only eight thousand for their publication, *Network*
(whose logo, by the way, looks more like a kitten than a
predator). Unlike the other organizations of the aging,
the Panthers are not limited to the gray-haired. They call
themselves "Age and Youth in Action," and, in a recreation of the traditional conspiratorial alliance between
grandparents and grandchildren, their participants seem
to be over sixty and under thirty, with few in between.

The Panthers use their attention-getting style, much of
which is Maggie Kuhn herself, to deride the intangible
barriers that fence off the old. They urge their contemporaries not to accept exile from society, not to accept the
stereotypes of age. When Maggie Kuhn and five others,
all on the edge of retirement, founded the Panthers in
1970, they were seeking, not specific benefits for their age
group, but a chance to remain active in the world, and
that remains their primary goal. Maggie herself plans to
quit work "when I die." Much of their concern is with im-
ages of the old; the Panthers' Media Watch stalks the net-
works in an effort to blot out the presentation of old age
as "disease or naptime," and extracted from CBS at least a
promise to do better. Panthers often use tactics we associate with the young. Their approach to nursing-home
reform, for example, was to stage a street play at the
AMA convention in Atlantic City in which a doctor sold

patients to the Kill 'Em Quick Nursing Home; doctors' wives were reported to have glared in disapproval at what the old folks were doing. Still, the Panthers do not scorn the less cosmic issues affecting the old. In Long Beach, California, and Washington, D.C., Panthers have succeeded in getting free checking accounts for the elderly, and in Rhode Island it was free public transportation during off-hours. These victories are not world-shaking, and one senses that the Panthers' main concern is elsewhere: they want to remake the world, beginning with themselves.

The Gray Panthers are not strong on organization: they have none of the business-based bureaucratic immortality of the AARP. Just as the Townsendites scattered after the founder's death, the Panthers are not likely to long survive the eventual loss of Maggie Kuhn's charismatic presence. While they are with us, the Panthers can help undermine a few stereotypes, arouse their contemporaries to have some fun, and remind us all of an important lesson: we don't have to die till we die.

The goal of keeping the elderly in the community begins, though it does not end, with providing them a chance to do something productive, but any attempt to do so runs into the twin blocks of forced retirement and discrimination against job-seekers in their fifties and sixties (sometimes in their forties). Although something like half of us work at jobs subject to mandatory retirement, typically at age sixty-five, it makes little sense and is opposed by most of the public. There is no reason to suppose that the person capable of working full-time at age sixty-four becomes totally incompetent on his sixty-fifth birthday, and even the AMA, usually no friend to the aging, has testified that "Medicine sees in mandatory retirement a direct threat to the health and life expectancy of the persons affected" and that it is "detrimental to the best interest of society" as well. The Louis Harris opinion study on "The Myth and Reality of Aging in America" found that close to half of retired people had not wanted to quit work, and that they missed, not just the money, but the people and even the work itself. Harris found that an overwhelming majority, 86 per cent, of the public at large opposed mandatory retirement, and that even among those responsible for hiring and firing, four fifths believed those willing and able should be allowed to go on working.

Both mandatory retirement and job discrimination based on age are strongly entrenched for reasons that do not surface in answer to a pollster's questions. If you retire your fellow employees all have a shot at promotion, and the union may legitimately feel that compulsory retirement is the only alternative to forced labor past sixty-five. From the boss's point of view, the retiree goes out at the top of the salary scale, his young replacement comes in on the first rung. Private pension plans have proved to be a reason for job discrimination. The employer doesn't want to hire that older worker who'll stay just about long enough to collect a pension; he prefers the young applicant who'll either leave without qualifying or stay forty years. The personnel department finds that mandatory retirement makes their lives easier because they don't have to make an individual judgment on whether an employee is still capable of doing his job. (Similarly, at the other end of the tunnel, Personnel likes to sort young applicants by diplomas, again avoiding the need to evaluate the individual.) For all these reasons, mandatory retirement will not give way easily. Eventually, as suggested earlier, the sixty-five barrier may become too expensive to maintain as more of us live for more years past that age. Some countries have begun to break the barrier: that other aging superpower, the Soviet Union, has shifted its incentives to encourage people to keep working past retirement age, and Sweden in 1976 instituted gradual retirement between the ages of sixty and seventy. Already in this country forced retirement is under attack both in the law and by those seeking to provide more job opportunities for the elderly.

The attack on mandatory retirement has yet to score a conclusive success. Congress and a number of states have adopted laws theoretically banning discrimination by age, but many of the laws are vaguely worded, and most limit the prohibition to ages forty to sixty-five, leaving the employer free to discriminate both after and before those ages. The Supreme Court, whose members are not subject to mandatory retirement, has not seen fit in the cases brought before it to extend that right to the rest of the population. The federal government speaks with two voices: while the Labor Department brings court actions against mandatory retirement, the Internal Revenue imposes a punitive tax on the earnings of those over sixty-five who collect Social Security.

In the absence of government action, private efforts have succeeded in breaking the sixty-five barrier, but only on a small scale. Some firms specialize in hiring those over sixty-five, with excellent results. The Texas Refinery Corporation, which makes roofing materials, has more than three hundred salesmen over sixty; their average age is seventy and some are in their eighties and still selling. The company considers its elderly sales force to be good business. "This isn't a charitable thing we're trying to do," Adlai Pate, Jr., the firm's president said, and he added: "I'm grateful for what I consider the shortsighted policies of firms that enforce mandatory retirement on their employees. Every time they let one go because of age, I have another potential salesperson. Good salespeople, like good wines, get better with age." In South Norwalk, Connecticut, Fertl, Inc., which makes plant food, has a work force that averages sixty-eight years old. Hoyt Catlin, who founded the company in 1956 when he himself was sixty-five, said the firm has less absenteeism and employee turnover than comparable companies. An important factor at both Texas Refining and Fertl is that older employees are allowed to work part-time; one salesman in his seventies finds himself as productive as ever for four hours a day, but after that he runs out of gas.

Here and there agencies have specialized in placing the elderly in jobs. In Albuquerque, New Mexico, Anna Beckman, herself a great-grandmother, has been running a placement service for the AARP since 1962. By 1975 she was getting three hundred job orders a month; some were for babysitting, but she had also placed older people in full-time jobs paying over $20,000. In Chevy Chase, Maryland, the Over-60 Counseling and Employment Service has been doing the same thing for about as long as Anna Beckman. The average age of the people they place is in the late sixties: many are victims of mandatory retirement and some seek work because inflation ate up their savings. Some have trouble finding work below their level of skills. As the director of the service, Gladys Sprinkle, said: "For the most part, the public doesn't want the commodity we are marketing. It's not that these people are too old, we are told, it's that they are overqualified." Still, they place about eight hundred a year, with full-time pay averaging $10–15,000. In one case, a company's forcibly retired workers fought back in an unusual forum. The company was a utility, and when it applied for a rate increase, its opponents included a committee of resentful ex-employees: their opposition delayed the rate increase and generated unfavorable publicity for the utility and its mandatory retirement. All these examples, however, are only minor exceptions to the rule of age discrimination:

doubtless major change will not occur until enough people make the connection between mandatory retirement and the rising burden of the payroll tax.

Housing is essential to keeping older people in their community—and out of an institution. Although the Harris study found that three quarters of people past sixty-five would like to live among people of varied ages, the goal is not easy to achieve even for the relatively affluent. Those attracted to the fast-sprouting retirement communities in the sun find no young people there, not necessarily because they wanted it that way, but because the developer promised the local planning board he wasn't going to bring in any school-age children to make taxes go up. For the retired person whose health is better than his bank balance, the central problem is how to meet the payments. Some states have made this somewhat easier. As noted in the next chapter, most states provide property tax reductions for elderly homeowners, and a handful provide a similar benefit for renters; Massachusetts pioneered in allowing the elderly homeowner to postpone part of the taxes till his death, when it is paid by his estate out of his equity in the home. The same idea is the basis for what is called "split equity": making it possible for the homeowner to sell his equity in his home, to be delivered to the buyer, presumably a bank, at his death, in return for an annuity that would increase his current income. Split equity hasn't been implemented at this writing, but if it is, it has considerable potential: homeowners over sixty-five hold an estimated $80 billion in housing equity, which will buy a lot of annuities. Elderly renters, on the other hand, face a worsening squeeze as costs and rents go up. They've gotten far less help than homeowners, but in Washington, D.C., the Gray Panther housing group joined in successful campaigns for rent control (though later it was watered down) and a temporary ban on the conversions that were turning cheap rental housing into high-priced condominiums.

As the years stretch out past sixty-five, a growing number of people can no longer manage completely on their own, yet do not need the costly and constant care of an institution, usually a nursing home, where many of them are in fact found for lack of an alternative. In recent years some efforts, all modest in scale, have been made to supply that alternative. They go by such names as assisted residential housing, congregate housing, or community living, and are usually run by non-profit agencies. Here are some examples.

The Share-a-Home Association began in Winter Park, Florida, in 1969, and now includes ten homes each housing an average of fifteen people ranging in age from seventy to ninety-five. Each home has a resident manager and family, who are responsible for preparing meals and supplying all the residents' other needs. The cost, for everything except medical care, averages $325 a month per person: too much for someone who only has Social Security, though far less than the cost of a nursing home. In practice the residents tend to be middle-class people with a pension in addition to Social Security, but local church groups have subsidized some who could not pay the bill. The first home was set up by Jim Gillies, a forty-seven-year-old one-time food salesman, in a building that had been a nursing home, with Gillies and his family providing the management. The eighteen residents hold title to the home, with the mortgage financed out of their monthly payments, and in theory can hire and fire the manager. Because the homes are small, the largest having only twenty members, they can remain self-governing and free of institutional rigidity. The elected head of the Winter Park home said: "Some of the members of the family are forgetful sometimes, but here we don't think of it as senility, as they do in nursing homes. We really don't have difficulties with things like that. Everyone forgets something sometimes, but we don't mind." The family atmosphere is fostered; everyone is called "aunt" or "uncle" by the manager's kids and by each other. The Winter Park family even made their self-definition stick in court. Charged with violation of the zoning code, they said they were in fact what the code called a family—"one or more persons occupying a dwelling and living as a single housekeeping unit." After visiting the home, the judge ruled in their favor and called it "a happy, well-run family . . . a superb idea."

A similar project was undertaken in a city environment by the Philadelphia Geriatric Center. The center bought nine one-family houses in a residential neighborhood and remodeled them so that each included three small apartments, each with its own kitchenette, and a living room shared by all. The residents were supplied one main meal daily, delivered frozen, weekly housekeeping and linen service, and the recreation and social services of the nearby geriatric center. The residents, who were living before in isolation and fear, were said to be happy with what they got.

These small projects, and several others like them around the country, have shown that it is possible to keep older people who cannot make it on their own in the larger community, but they will not reach any large number of people until government reverses its present bias in favor of institutions. Medicaid is happy to pay the bill for keeping people in nursing homes; it will not pay any part of the much lower cost of keeping them out. From the point of view of the family, the government rewards the person who puts a relative in an institution, penalizes him for keeping the relative at home. In Wisconsin one program for keeping-them-out has punched a hole in Medicaid's nursing home policy.

It was the idea of Martin E. Schreiber, who has been doing for lieutenant governors what Herbert Denenberg did for insurance commissioners, and it grew out of Schreiber's experience as the state's nursing home ombudsman. Schreiber had observed that many people now in nursing homes don't need to be there—national estimates start at 20–40 per cent—and could be kept out with enough supporting services, many of which now exist in fragmented state, and enough money to pay the bills. In La Crosse County, the Wisconsin Community Organization began in early 1976 delivering those services to some fifteen hundred elderly and disabled people. Some services are strictly medical; some, like delivering hot meals and shoveling snow are not, though they are in fact health services by any rational definition. Most already existed in some form, but needed to be pulled together and paid for.

What makes the Wisconsin program different from those described earlier is that Schreiber got Medicaid to agree to pay for it. If the basic premise is proved, that it costs less this way, the Wisconsin experiment will lend muscle to the efforts to change Medicaid rules to allow payment for services that will keep people healthy enough to stay out of the institution. The sponsor of one such proposal, Congressman Edward I. Koch of New York, estimated that keeping a person on home care would cost two thousand to sixty-five hundred dollars a year instead of fifteen to twenty thousand dollars in a nursing home. (Senator James Buckley of New York proposed a benefit for families that keep an elderly relative at home, but, by making the benefit a federal income tax deduction, Buckley insured that those who benefit most would need it least.) Schreiber himself figures that home care will cost half the nursing-home bill.

Daphne Krause, executive director of the Minneapolis Age and Opportunity Center, one of the best-known and most extensive keep-them-out operations, makes the point in a more dramatic way. Krause said that if the Minneapolis center were to receive the money Medicaid saves on keeping 126 people out of the nursing home, it could pay for all these services to those 126—and provide some services to another 8,000 people besides. In the present budget-cutting mood, it is probable that home care instead of the nursing home, like measures to reduce government financing of unnecessary surgery and hospitalization, will get more favorable attention than it has heretofore. Doubtless the elderly person who is thereby saved from the institution will not quibble over the fact that those who did it were just trying to save some money.

Services of various kinds for the elderly have been created here and there around the country, most of them with stimulus of federal money from the Older Americans Act. They are usually small in scale, "tokens" in Maggie Kuhn's view, and, when fed by short-term federal grants, are likely to die off when the money runs out. Still, it's more than existed yesterday, and it indicates the directions in which a larger commitment might eventually flow. The largest undertaking is the national nutrition program which, according to HEW statistics, was in 1975 providing a quarter-million meals a day to older people at 4,200 senior day centers. Public transportation for the elderly, free or at cut-rate, can be found in, for example, Sullivan County, New York, and Hawaii; the AARP and the Gray Panthers have both observed that the rest of the population is equally handicapped by the absence of any way of getting around except by private automobile. Although most of the money for such services is either federal or charitable, Brookline, Massachusetts, where 30 per cent of the population is over sixty, decided to continue at its own expense an array of services originally started under a grant from Washington. Recognition of the particular legal needs of the elderly, who are more embroiled than the average person with the bureaucracies of government and the health and pension industries, has resulted in the creation of a variety of legal aid programs specifically for the elderly; California is training paralegal aides, some of whom are themselves elderly, to act as advocates of older people. But the total reached by any new legal service is minuscule. It should also be noted that supplying the legal needs of the elderly, as viewed by government, does not include doing anything about their status as the prime victims of crimes of violence.

Anything that helps the elderly cope with their environment is part of the effort to keep them in the community and out of the institution. The time comes when that is not enough. If, let us say, one third of those in nursing homes don't belong there, liberating them will do nothing for the other two thirds, and that's two thirds of a million people. Public attention to the nursing homes has increased considerably since the 1974 publication of Mary Adelaide Mendelson's *Tender Loving Greed,* which provided the first detailed description of how the industry was swindling the public as well as abusing the people in its custody. One of the nursing-home owners she wrote about was Bernard Bergman, whose primary base was in New York State. In 1974–75, John L. Hess of the New York *Times* carried on the Bergman story in a series of exposés that made it obvious that Bergman and other nursing-home operators were so well entrenched in the state's political structure as to be immune from any need to account for the government money they were receiving in increasing amounts, much less what they did to the patients. Nelson A. Rockefeller, when he was governor, had guaranteed this immunity by the simple expedient of preventing the state from hiring more auditors, in the face of evidence that each day an auditor worked enabled the

state to recoup twenty-five hundred dollars in overpayments to nursing homes. The industry itself was still
trying, as a headline in one of its trade publications put it,
to "Project a Positive Image!" Senator Frank Moss, chairman of the Senate Subcommittee on Long-Term Care,
complained that critics like Mrs. Mendelson were blam-
ing a whole industry for the behavior of a few bad apples,
but this defense lost whatever validity it had when the
special prosecutor in New York reported that every one of
the first seventy nursing homes he audited was overcharg-
ing the government.

The accumulating evidence eventually proved impossible to ignore, investigations started, and by 1976 twenty
figures in the industry and state politics had been indicted, including Bernard Bergman, four had pleaded
guilty, and some sixty nursing homes had been closed. It
was the most vigorous investigation the nursing-home industry had ever known, and yet there was profound pessimism about how much had been or could be accomplished. In one sense this was a recognition of the familiar
principle that regulated industries, no matter how shaken
up they may be today, will tomorrow regain their hold on
the levers of power. But those investigating the industry,
and some of the regulators themselves, were also saying
that government by its nature was incapable of playing
its assigned role as substitute for the family in the care of
people in nursing homes.

Mary Adelaide Mendelson, who had reached the same
conclusion, believed that the only lasting hope for improving nursing homes lay in the patients' relatives. Only
the relatives know the details of nursing-home abuses and
can be counted on to have a continuing interest in what
happens behind the institution's closed doors, Mrs. Mendelson argued, and only organized relatives can provide a
counterweight to the industry in the lobbies of govern-

ment. Her position was confirmed by Martin Schreiber's experience since 1972 as Wisconsin's nursing home ombudsman: of the first thousand complaints his office received, almost half (46 per cent) came from relatives, only 11 per cent from patients, who are typically fearful of retribution. (The second largest source of complaints, by the way, was nursing-home employees. All regulatory agencies together provided a grand total of 2 per cent.) Accordingly, Mrs. Mendelson set out to help form an organization of relatives. Her first goal was to organize relatives in Cuyahoga County, Ohio, which includes the city of Cleveland, and ninety-three nursing homes. In early 1976 Mrs. Mendelson put together enough financing to start a non-profit organization called the Nursing Home Advisory and Research Council, headquartered in Cleveland Heights, where she lives. She canvassed the social service workers in hospitals, who place people in nursing homes, and voluntary and religious agencies, which deal with their relatives, and drew an enthusiastic initial response. Mrs. Mendelson believed that if enough relatives joined in a continuing organization both nursing homes and regulatory agencies would have to pay attention to their demands. And, if it worked in Cuyahoga County, it could be emulated elsewhere.

The organizing of nursing-home relatives is based on the recognition that government regulation as we now know it has failed hopelessly to protect the public interest. The alternative is an organization made up exclusively of those who have a direct interest in the subject. In this case it is nursing homes. In later chapters we shall describe efforts to apply the same principle to the field of utility companies.

7

Untangling the
Property Tax

THE ONLY SURPRISE is that we put up with it for so long. If
the butcher weighed your meat as inaccurately as the
assessor weighs your property, and if he charged you one
third more so the next person wouldn't have to pay—
doubtless by now you would have switched to soybeans.
Yet that is the nature of the property tax: unfair in its
design, and incredibly sloppy in its administration. It is a
measure of the increasing sophistication of the public that
Americans are beginning to demand and get substantial
improvement in how the property tax is imposed on the
average person.

The property tax is collected in some eighty thousand
tax districts—no one seems to have an exact count—in a
bewildering variety of ways. In its complexities and con-
tradictions, the property tax mirrors the realities of local
politics; a map of the different rates paid by different
properties is also a map of their owners' respective clout.
In Boston, as described by Diane Paul in *The Politics of
the Property Tax*, single-family homes are taxed less than
apartments: homeowners tend to be long-term residents,
prosperous, and politically active; apartment dwellers are
more transient, have less money, and besides their tax is
concealed inside the rent—when it goes up, they get mad

at the landlord rather than the tax assessor. Old commercial properties are taxed high, but new businesses are offered a tax break to settle here rather than somewhere else—in Boston this is known as the "Prudential Agreement" in honor of its greatest beneficiary. In Mississippi, wealthy homes are taxed less than poor ones, poor whites are taxed less than blacks, and agribusiness, the modern plantation, is taxed least of all. Industry has been paying a declining proportion of the property tax, just as corporations are paying an ever-shrinking share of federal taxes.

All this traditionally went on without much popular attention. People noticed how much they were paying of course—the property tax usually leads the polls as the nation's most disliked tax—but few paid any attention to the boring complexities of its administration. That has begun to change. In recent years, the property tax has gotten a great deal more scrutiny, with the result that the average taxpayer in many places is getting a fairer deal than he did yesterday. As in the other aspects of our lives that we've explored in other chapters, progress is uneven, sometimes no more than cosmetic, and it has yet to attack the most basic screwings embedded in the property tax. But change is happening, and at a rate that seems to be accelerating. As we look over the scene, we see two kinds of change: improvement in the way the tax is administered, which usually means reducing the difference between your own assessment and the other person's, and, further in the distance, the beginnings of an attack on the ways the property tax, at vast cost to all of us, has distorted the way we use land in America.

The individual is not entirely helpless. The cost of a lawyer is frequently more than a property tax appeal is worth, but if you are willing to prepare your own case, and a lawyer is not required in your district, it's probable that you stand a better chance of getting your assessment (not your tax rate) reduced than of successfully appealing an IRS decision about your income tax. Many local tax boards are fairly easygoing about granting at least some reduction on an appeal, partly because the application of the property tax is so sloppy that it's easy to make your case, more because they really don't want a voting taxpayer, especially a persistent one, to go away mad. Nonetheless, the number of individual taxpayers who better their position this way is limited, first by the work involved in preparing your case, and second by the extent of benevolent indifference among local tax boards. It will be considerably easier if you live in one of the states—Hawaii, Idaho, Massachusetts, and Oregon at this writing—that in recent years have set up small-claims arrangements for tax appeals.

Groups of taxpayers are better able to put together the resources needed to beat a determined assessor. The Citizens Action Program of Chicago is an example. For years the Chicago political organization had been telling homeowners: shut up about your taxes, industry is assessed twice as high as you are. The members of CAP were able by force of numbers to do the work—not highly skilled but surely tedious—to prove the unsurprising opposite: they were taxed more, not less, than industry. They then had to fight their cases, because the Daley organization doesn't give money away, and that required individual appraisals of their homes. Appraising just one home would have cost around $200, but they were able to get a bulk rate of $25–35 per home. They won tax rebates averaging $200: as individuals, they would have just broken even; as a group they came out comfortably ahead.

Other citizen groups have been notably successful in discrediting the work of the mass appraisal firms that have sprung up in response to assessors' inability to keep their assessments up to date. The biggest of these firms is Cole-Layer-Trumble of Philadelphia, and it suffered one of its most damaging defeats in Westmoreland County, in western Pennsylvania.

Westmoreland is Mellon country. In these rolling hills are twenty thousand acres of estates belonging to the robber baron family, who hold a controlling interest in Alcoa, Gulf, and the local levers of power (and are widely known as benefactors of the arts and Pittsburgh). Our story begins, however, not with robber barons but with Mrs. Dorothy Shope. Mrs. Shope, a doctor's wife and mother of five, had just gotten a tax bill showing her assessment to be much higher than her neighbors'. Her appeal was turned down on the grounds that CLT was doing a mass reappraisal of the county's properties. Mrs. Shope and some friends formed the Association of Concerned Taxpayers (ACT) and she was elected a county commissioner.

From this vantage point, Mrs. Shope watched the results of CLT's work pour in. Some of it was grotesque, as in the case of the woman whose assessment on her home was raised from $750 to $1.4 *billion*. This was evidently the result, not of malevolence, but of sloppiness and the cutting of corners. It turned out that CLT, which had promised professional work, was hiring high school and college students at $1.50 an hour to inspect properties. Even more simply, the firm was copying many of the figures from county records—though the fact that those records were as much as forty years out of date was the reason CLT had been hired in the first place.

More than shoddy work was at issue, however, for it soon became evident that CLT's assessments fell into a deliberate pattern. Home assessments were raised by 25–75 per cent, and so were many small businesses. But two Alcoa plants were reduced by more than half, and other major industries also got their due. Nor did CLT treat the Mellon manor as it did the surrounding peasantry. The old arrangements—best symbolized by the fact

that in the file where everyone else's assessment is recorded, the family properties are represented by a card
merely saying "Special Set-up"—were continued undis-
turbed by CLT. In Ligonier Township, other homes were
raised by 40 per cent, Mellon's 15,000 acres went up by a
token 2 per cent, and one 312-acre family estate was
found to be worth just $.64 an acre—a steal at $199.68,
though doubtless it costs a lot to keep the hedges clipped.

The outside experts had managed the unlikely feat of
making the property tax still more unfair to the middle-
class homeowners who make up much of Westmoreland's
population. Soon thousands of them were protesting their
new assessments—and pointing at the Mellon estates. The
county's institutional power mobilized in defense of its
traditional way of life. The Mellon-owned newspaper
drew a veil of silence over the assessment question; the
local judge threw out a request for a grand jury investigation of CLT, and suggested instead that Mrs. Shope
should herself be investigated. A supposed opponent of
CLT, one Robert Shirey, elected on Mrs. Shope's ticket,
was in fact a tenant on a Mellon farm, and had gotten
most of his campaign money from the family. Once in
office, he voted to endorse CLT's work. Later he gave his
thoughts on barons and taxes: "There are great dangers
involved in pushing the Mellons too hard on the assessment question. There was once a time when I could pick
up a phone and get a grant for a library from the Mellon
Foundation, but now it's dried up. . . . You've got to be
careful, the family could leave the county."

If anyone was to leave Westmoreland, it was more
likely to be the homeowners, for it seemed clear that the
organization could outlast their brief revolt. Had the story
been played out only in Westmoreland, the result could
only have been another obscure defeat for the public. But
one of Mrs. Shope's followers addressed a letter to:
"Ralph Nader, Washington, D.C." The letter was actually

delivered—surely the unlikeliest event in our tale—and soon there arrived Barry Greever, a Nader organizer, and Jonathan Rowe, at the time the property tax specialist at the Tax Reform Research Group.*

The Naderites were able to move the struggle off the controlled turf of Westmoreland County. The news about the Mellon assessments, not fit to print at home, appeared in the national press. CLT went on the defensive. Mrs. Shope commented: "CLT wouldn't even reply to our charges because we were shut out of the local papers. But then the Nader people came in and arranged the news conference, and all of a sudden CLT started talking and people began to think that maybe there was something to all this after all."

Jonathan Rowe had found out that CLT had a lot to be defensive about. The firm had left a spoor of disaster in its wake, and courts had discredited its mass appraisals in places as far apart as Fort Wayne, Indiana; Atlanta; Quincy, Massachusetts, and Nashville. In Wilmington, CLT had given industrial properties $33 million in lower assessment, and had topped that with no less than one million clerical errors—a volume of mistakes that would doubtless have taken an old-fashioned assessor decades to accumulate. In Trenton, New Jersey, the local Public Interest Research Group found that land belonging to U. S. Steel was assessed at $.45 a foot, while homeowners' land across the street was at $1.70, and in Troy, New York, CLT was giving its best breaks to vacant lots owned by land speculators.

The outcome of the long struggle in Westmoreland County is unclear at this writing. The homeowners' opposition is still alive, but it has yet to win any major change

---

* *People and Taxes*, the monthly publication of the Tax Reform Research Group, is an excellent source of information on property and other taxes. See also their book *Tax Politics*, published in 1976 by Pantheon Books.

in the way property is assessed. The most significant result to date has been the widespread resistance to the methods of CLT and other mass reappraisal firms. (In 1975, California banned the use of private mass reappraisal anywhere in the state.) By demonstrating the assessors' traditional faults—favoritism and incompetence—on a colossal scale, computers and all, the mass appraisers had done a great deal to advance public awareness of the defects of the property tax, though this may not have been what the president of CLT had in mind when he said that "CLT is doing more for tax reform than Ralph Nader ever dreamed of accomplishing."

A number of states have been moving, dragging their feet and usually under court order, toward one of the most important of property tax reforms: assessing all property at full market value. Resistance has been fierce, for there is nothing this side of a grand jury summons that an assessor hates so much as full value assessment. It makes him work harder, and it makes favoritism and incompetence more difficult to conceal. Ernest H. Johnson, Maine state assessor, explained that there is an "instinctive belief of many assessors that the more mystery attached to the assessing process—and I do not believe that anyone can deny that fractional valuations contribute more than their share of mystery—the more unlikely it is that any taxpayer will successfully challenge his assessment. . . ."

Johnson observed that assessors tend to undervalue more expensive properties and overvalue cheaper ones. The example he gave was that if a $45,000 property was valued at $10,000 a $15,000 property was likely to be valued at $5,000 and a $2,500 one at $1,000.

A little arithmetic demonstrates that in Johnson's example the owner of the $2,500 property is assessed at the highest rate (40 per cent) the $15,000 next (33⅓ per cent) and the $45,000 least (22 per cent). But not many people do the arithmetic; most appear to feel that if they are underassessed they are getting away with something, even though, if others are more underassessed, the net effect is that they are being taxed at *more* than the market value of their property. One reason for this is that few property owners are aware of the local rate of underassessment—the average fraction of true value at which property is taxed. It's not something the assessor advertises, for, if at all possible, he'd like you to go on thinking that everybody else is taxed at market value. In Philadelphia, to discourage bootleg arithmetic, the tax appeal form used to state, in appropriately red ink, that property was assessed at "actual market value," until a citizen group, The Philadelphia Tax Equity for America Party, threatened to sue unless the city either dropped the statement or started living up to it. Dropping it was easier than proving it, since property was in fact being assessed at less than half market value, and that's what Philadelphia did.

None of the states has in fact achieved full value assessment, though that's what the law says in twenty-three states. A handful—Oregon, Kentucky, and Alaska—are fairly close to full value, which is enough to keep the assessor on his toes. In the last few years, court or legislative action has pushed Washington, North Carolina, and New York in the same direction. A much larger number of states, fourteen at last count, decided it was all too much trouble and discarded the full-value standard, which didn't mean much since none of them was living up to it anyway. South Carolina is in a class by itself: the law requires full value, and property is assessed at an average of 4 per cent of its value.

Where it exists, assessment at or near full value forces the assessor to keep his work up to date, not so much because the law says so—it always has—but because without the phantom of underassessment property owners are quick to challenge any appraisal that seems to exceed market value. After decades of torpor, the assessor faces real problems in meeting that challenge. Here technology comes to the rescue, for the computer can do the tedious work of accumulating and comparing sales and construction figures far faster and cheaper than people can.

Ramapo was the first town in New York State to combine the computer with full value assessment. Three years after its start in 1973, the system had succeeded in greatly reducing the inequities of local taxes. The average assessment error—the difference between the assessor's appraisal and what the property actually sold for—had been reduced to less than 10 per cent compared to a state-wide average of 35 per cent. (The national average is about 20 per cent.) More uniform assessment didn't make the people of Ramapo uniformly happy, because one man's equity is another's tax increase. About one third of the residents found their taxes going up, another third went down, and the rest stayed about the same. The losers tended to be those who had owned their properties longer, because sales cause immediate reappraisal. Also losing were the elderly and veterans who found that their exemptions had been watered down: five thousand off on your assessment means less than a third as much off on your taxes when a house is assessed at full value rather than at 30 per cent, which had been the Ramapo practice. In Ramapo, as elsewhere, the volume of complaints justified the assessors' fears about market-value assessment. Complaints rose from 483 in the last year of the old system to 3,825 two years later—even though assessment had become much fairer in that time. But by 1976 the rate of complaints flowing into the office of assessor Clara Williams had dropped back to its pre-reform volume.

Out in Pierce County, Washington, assessor Ken Johnston took the process a step further. In 1975 he started providing property owners with a preliminary assessment along with a printout of the information on which it was based: type of construction, number of rooms, and so on. This permits the owner to register a complaint about any part of the information even before the final assessment is made. In Johnston's view, his system will reduce the time both he and the taxpayers will have to spend on appeals.

Reform-minded assessors don't always find it that easy. Take, for example, Evan Doss of Claiborne County, Mississippi. Claiborne is a rural county where blacks are numerous and poor, whites fewer and better off, and each is taxed according to his ability to exercise power. Property assessment there follows the classic formula of Catch-85: 85 per cent of the people pay too much so that 15 per cent can pay too little. In the 1960s blacks began to vote, and in 1972 they elected Evan Doss, twenty-five, as county tax assessor. His platform was fair assessment. In evident tribute to the sincerity of the young man's campaign promises, the white-controlled county Board of Supervisors promptly cut the new assessor's budget from $17,000 to $13,000, and its president offered Doss his counsel: "We would expect that the assessment rolls be continued on approximately the same basis as before, with like assessments as they have been in the past." Doss rejected this advice, and for the next two years he campaigned for assessment reform with the help of outsiders who accumulated the information needed to prove the existing patterns of inequity. The supervisors were able to block any actual change, so in 1974 Doss got on the ballot a referendum that would force reappraisal of all properties. That was too much. The supervisors, perhaps with a nostalgic glance backward at Mississippi's version of the final solution, had to content themselves with having Doss jailed on a charge of refusing to sell one of them his license tags —in Mississippi that's part of the assessor's job. But Doss was soon freed, and the referendum was soon passed. Now the supervisors were mandated to reappraise everyone, though there were some fear they would turn to a mass-appraisal firm to make sure the job was done wrong. At this writing the outcome in Claiborne is uncertain; what is certain is that the property tax pattern could not even have been challenged a decade earlier. Maintaining the good old days is, at the very least, getting more difficult.

Competitive underassessment of industrial and commercial property is just beginning to come under effective attack. Everybody loves a taxpayer who brings business rather than schoolchildren into the district, so communities compete in offering tax breaks to any enterprise that is having a deliberately hard time deciding just where it wants to locate. Sometimes the business will offer a few bribes to improve, or preserve, its tax break, but often the deal is made right out in broad daylight, as in Boston's "Prudential Agreement," under which the company pays lower taxes on its new Boston office building. A recent example is New Jersey's efforts to entice the New York stock brokerage business across the Hudson; the brokers then used the Jersey promise as a threat to keep their New York taxes down. The result, under the third-party principle, is make all other taxpayers pay more. But the effect in any one district is just the opposite, and those who oppose a new industry—perhaps because it's going to pollute the place—are met with the deadly argument that if we don't get them to come here all our taxes will go up. It is, in its quiet way, one of American industry's biggest subsidies.

One major industrial area, the Twin Cities region of Minnesota, has found a precedent-setting way of at least reducing the competitive pressure to underassess. The seven counties of the region, which covers three thousand square miles and includes the cities of St. Paul and Minneapolis, reached an agreement that 40 per cent of the added tax base from any new industry would be shared by all the tax districts in the region; the other 60 per cent would stay in the district where the industry settled. Though approved by the Minnesota legislature in 1971, the deal did not come into effect until 1974 because of a court challenge, so its results are only beginning to take shape. The Twin Cities accord is far from perfect, since 60 per cent of the motive to underassess remains, and of course the region as a whole will still be competing with everyone else for industry. (The Citizens League, which sponsored the agreement, hopes to increase tax sharing to 100 per cent and extend it to the rest of the state.) Nonetheless, what they did in the Twin Cities is a major first step—doubtless more important than the frequent exposés of industrial tax breaks which, valuable as they are in showing people what's happening, do nothing to remove the underlying causes of underassessment.

Another way to end competition for taxpaying businesses is to uproot its cause by equalizing the property tax. This might in part be accomplished through the series of school finance cases now being argued by the Lawyers' Committee for Civil Rights Under Law. They argue from the fact that some school districts have ten or more times as much taxable property per school child as other districts to draw on for financing education. The lawyers' case is that these unequal resources make for unequal education and that this violates state constitutions. (A case arguing the same for the U. S. Constitution lost in the Supreme Court on a 5–4 vote.) The California Supreme Court, in the landmark 1971 case of *Serrano* v. *Priest,* agreed with that argument, but the principle remains to be put into practice. A similar New Jersey case led in 1976 to a tax act that is supposed to equalize the tax dollars available per child; whether it will do so remains to be seen. A dozen similar cases are banging around inconclusively in the state courts: making the property tax fairer via the courts has yet to happen. Since the Serrano case, a few state legislatures have made a pass in the same direction by voting state aid for the most property-poor school districts, but the results to date are modest at best.

Attractive in principle, the school-tax cases are likely in practice to have evil side effects. What happened in New Jersey—and will doubtless happen in California and elsewhere—is that local property taxes for schools were equalized downward by substituting other kinds of taxes. That spells income and sales taxes, both of which hit the average man harder than the property tax they replace. (New Jersey, in the process of adopting a state income tax, managed to discard its tax on unearned income.) And so we find big landowners incongruously applauding the right of every child to the same dollar education—as long as the result is to lower the tax on their holdings. As he contemplates this situation the average man is in a dilemma: he can get more equal treatment on his property tax, but only at the price of being hit harder on the income he earns by work.

A bold and well-connected entrepreneur may simply skip underassessment and aim for the jackpot: tax exemption. You don't have to be a church or a school to get around the property tax. All you need to do, the hustlers who know government have long since learned, is get government to build what you want, making it tax exempt, and then lease it to you. The Houston Astrodome is one of the more notable monuments to this form of tax evasion. In the past such deals have slipped routinely through under a wave of civic propaganda that drowned out anyone who was trying to calculate the tab to be picked up by the rest of the taxpayers. Recently, because watchdogs are more diligent and the public more aware, at least two such pirate ventures have run onto the rocks. One was in Indianapolis and involved Mayor Richard Lugar, who only yesterday was hailed as the nation's model Republican mayor. Lugar said he wanted the city to buy a four-acre downtown block, clear it, and sell it to a developer who would put up $45 million of new buildings to be known as Lincoln Square; this, said the mayor, would cause taxes paid on that property to multiply tenfold. Bonds were sold for the city's costs on that basis. Along the way, however, the deal was quietly changed so that the developer would lease—not buy—the property, thus escaping the tax. Prudential blundered into the act here too; it offered to finance part of the deal around the same time that the city was shifting its health insurance to Prudential, at higher cost, from Blue Cross. A coalition ranging from citizen groups to unions to teachers and even developers left out of the action raised so loud a howl that, in mid-1974, Mayor Lugar gave in; the developer would pay his taxes.

The other hustle occurred in 1975 in New York City, where the Port Authority pioneered industrial tax evasion way back in the 1920s, and involved Madison Square Garden. The timing of this one was grotesquely bad. Even as the city was floundering on the edge of bankruptcy, its administration made a secret agreement with the Garden's owners to buy it and then lease it right back, accomplishing nothing more than freeing the owners of $2.5 million a year in property taxes, plus other benefits totaling $50 million over ten years. This time it was journalist Jack Newfield who exposed the deal; the unusually strong public response may have been due to the fact that the adjoining news story was likely to be about the city's inability to collect enough taxes to pay its bills. The Beame administration, which by then had lost its grip on anything bigger than its city limousines, quickly gave in and the deal went down the drain. Such victories, though negative, are rare enough to celebrate.

Governments have found ways of reducing the property tax on various categories of people, always for the worthiest of purposes, but the reductions seldom make sense in terms of their purported goals. The most familiar of these is the deduction on assessment given to elderly and veteran homeowners. It has little to do with need. The millionaire who is over sixty-five or a veteran gets a tax break (if he's both he gets two deductions), while those in the same categories who are too poor to own a home get no break at all. Thus the deduction helps those who, as a group, need it least, at everyone else's expense.

Partly in response to this observation, the states have been adopting the so-called circuit-breaker. Wisconsin was the first, in 1964. By 1975, twenty-three states had circuit-breakers and others were thinking about it. Circuit-breakers come in several varieties, but all are intended to provide a rebate to people who are considered to be paying more than they can afford for their housing. The usual plan limits eligibility by income, but few have any limit on wealth. People within the income limit get a rebate on their property taxes if their housing cost goes above a specified percentage of their annual income. Some states limit the circuit-breaker to the elderly; some do not. Some even include renters—the first time this put-upon category has been recognized as worthy of a tax break.

The circuit-breaker, though clearly superior to the flat elderly and veteran deduction, still doesn't do what it claims to do. It offers no help to those who don't spend *too much* of their income on housing; it is geared to those who are temporarily down on their luck, not those who have always been down. Since you only get a rebate by spending more than a given proportion of your income on housing—and the more you spend over the limit, the bigger the rebate—the circuit-breaker helps those who spend the most on housing and denies aid to those who spend the least. Those who spend the most on housing typically have the most wealth, if not income—to give them a tax break, economist Mason Gaffney commented, is to "distribute welfare in proportion to wealth, surely an odd notion." In *Who Pays the Property Tax?* Henry J. Aaron of the Brookings Institution observed that circuit-breakers tend to subsidize "those within each income bracket who consume unusually large amounts of housing"—and here we sense the fine hand of the housing operator who, with a little help from his legislative friends, gets the taxpayers to help people buy more of his product. It's the modern strategy of those industries that, having priced themselves out of the average man's reach, now attempt to third-party their missing customers onto the public's back so that they can enjoy the benefits of high prices without suffering the free-enterprise penalty of a shrinking market.† Food stamps provide that service for agribusiness, and Medicaid and Medicare do the same—although organized medicine was at first too dense to see it—for the health industry. Recently we have been treated to proposals for clothing stamps, and, incredibly, gasoline stamps, the latter presumably to be decorated with a picture of John D. Rockefeller shaking hands with the Shah of Iran.

Massachusetts was the first state to attempt to cope with the problems of the elderly homeowner without cost to the rest of the public. Homeowners over sixty-five whose income is under $20,000 can defer their property taxes, depending on their equity, up to a total of half the value of the property. When the owner dies or sells the home, the back taxes are repaid with 8 per cent interest. The Massachusetts law was enacted in 1974, and similar laws are now in effect in Oregon, Texas, Virginia, and Utah.

The subsidy the housing industry gets from circuit-breakers is puny compared to the giant support payments

---

† In chapter 2 we saw the proponents of prepaid law trying to get this kind of tax break.

it gets through the homeowner deductions in the federal income tax. These deductions subsidize buying a home, through the property tax deduction, and also subsidize borrowing to pay for it, through the interest deduction; the more you buy and borrow, the greater the subsidy to the builders and banks. The great bulk of the benefits goes to those in the upper-income brackets, at everyone else's expense. Renters get no deductions though their landlords, who do, may in some cases pass on part of their savings in the form of lower rents; whether they do so depends on the state of competition in the local rental market. If the extent to which renters are screwed by the federal homeowner's deduction is in dispute, there's no arguing about what happens to them in those districts that tax apartments at a higher rate than single-family homes. Sometimes, as in Boston, this is because the assessor by custom hits apartments harder. But some states actually set a different and higher tax rate for apartments. One of these is Minnesota. In 1975 Minnesota apartment house owners brought a suit against the discrimination against their properties and their tenants, but settled eventually for a cricuit-breaker deduction for tenants on their state income taxes, similar to, though smaller than, that already enjoyed by homeowners.

In California a group of people in 1976 hit on what they thought was a way of short-circuiting the federal screwing of tenants. The group was the Santa Cruz County Community Economic Ownership Foundation, an offshoot of LEAF, a San Diego foundation which is part of the Georgist movement described below. According to its spokesman, Robert Colonna, they found a quirk in California law that seemed to make it possible for tenants to become eligible for the property tax deduction on their federal taxes. California law allows a tenant to request that his share of the property tax be charged directly to him rather than to the landlord, while the IRS gives the deduction to whoever pays the tax, whether or not he is the owner. While the change benefits the tenant, it does not hurt the landlord: he loses the deduction, but his taxable income is reduced by exactly the same amount, so he comes out where he started. (The cost of the tenants' reduced taxes is third-partied to all other taxpayers.) Part of Colonna's sales pitch to landlords and local officials was that if tenants paid less taxes, they would have more money to spend, benefiting local merchants and sales tax collections. In mid-1976, Colonna's group was helping tenants and willing landlords negotiate new leases that would make these the first tenants in the nation to achieve tax equality with owners.

So far we have described efforts, of varying importance and success, to make the property tax as it now exists fairer to the average person. None cuts to the fundamentals of how we tax property. None would greatly change how much homeowners in general pay, nor alter the impact of the property tax on how we use land. There is, however, another way to look at it.

Scattered around the country are a number of people who take a radically different view of the property tax: their aim is not tinkering but major surgery. They are the present-day followers of Henry George, the nineteenth-century economist and author of *Progress and Poverty*.‡ Today Henry George is remembered, if at all, as the author of the single-tax idea: tax land value and nothing else. Few advocate the single tax nowadays, but that wasn't all George had to say. George—who in some respects was the Ralph Nader of his day—began with the basic understanding that the property tax is not one but

‡ The Georgist movement is primarily based at the Henry George schools that exist in many of the larger cities. The works of Henry George, and other Georgist writings, are kept in print by the Robert Schalkenbach Foundation, 50 East Sixty-ninth Street, New York, N. Y. 10021.

two fundamentally different taxes: one is a tax on the land itself, the other is a tax on what man builds on the land.

Land is a prime target of the monopolist. It was made, not by human effort, but by the god of your choice, and she's not making any more these days. Its value rises for two reasons that require no effort on the part of the owner. An increasing population demands more land, but the supply is fixed: the price goes up. When the society settles around a piece of land, building a city and commerce and transportation, its value goes up astronomically, even if it remains vacant or is used far below its capacity (a parking lot in midtown, for example). In neither case has the landowner contributed to the increased value of his property; as John Stuart Mill wrote, "landlords grow richer in their sleep without working, risking or economizing." It is the purest kind of unearned income.*

By contrast, improvements—what's built on the land—are the result of human effort, and are not limited in quantity by nature: if we need more homes or factories or offices, we can build them. There is no natural monopoly in improvements as there is in land. But the property tax makes no distinction between the two. State law usually requires that both be taxed at the same rate, and in practice the assessor is likely to appraise vacant land lower than the land under an income-producing property. Thus the land hoarder is rewarded, not punished, by the property tax.

A century ago, long before the great slurbs of Los Angeles and North Jersey, Henry George foresaw the awful price we would have to pay for the way the property tax is applied. Since land in a valuable location—near population or transport centers—will continuously rise in value,

---

* Mills's point was restated recently in a paperback title: *How to Get Rich While You Sleep: Let Real Estate and Land Do Your Work.*

and since building improvements will raise the taxes, the landowners' greatest profit derives from hoarding: holding the land vacant, or underused, while the price inevitably rises. But a growing society has to expand somewhere. So development is forced to bypass its natural sites and reach out past the hoarded land into the countryside, where property is still relatively cheap—suburban sprawl is our current name for the result. The price paid by society is enormous: the cost of bringing services like utilities and transport to artificially distant settlements; the physical and environmental cost of needlessly butchered countryside; the lost value of underused services back at the underdeveloped urban center. (It should be said that the property tax is not the only villain. The huge federal subsidies to highways and single-family housing are also powerful inducements to sprawl and waste. So are utility price structures which, by charging everyone the same rate, in fact overcharge those close to the power source in order to subsidize the sprawlers.) Only the land hoarder benefits; everyone else pays the bill. The bill is a huge one. The Southern California Research Council figured out that the cost to other taxpayers to make one new home in that area reachable and livable was $18,500. Looking at sprawl from another angle, a federal study calculated that new cluster housing within the urban area would require 50 per cent less land, 55 per cent less capital investment, create 55 per cent less air pollution, and consume 44 per cent less energy than sprawl development in the countryside. The high price of hoarded land—up 60 per cent in five years—is one of the main reasons that the average man can no longer afford to buy a house.

The solution, in the Georgist view, is to tax land value much more heavily and improvements much less or not at all. The tax on land now seldom exceeds 1 per cent of its value; since most land increases in value in an average year by much more than that, the owner is under no pressure to do anything but hoard. But the tax on buildings and other improvements falls very hard. In income tax terms, an annual 3 per cent of true value tax is likely to tax away three quarters of the net income the building can earn. That same 3 per cent tax will add 25 per cent either to the rent a tenant must pay or to the costs the owner must absorb for him. Taken together, the two taxes provide a powerful incentive to hoard rather than improve. The incentive can be reversed: a higher land-value tax to reduce or eliminate the profit in hoarding, a lower improvement tax to increase the motivation to make the land productive. The slumlord, for example, would find he could no longer hold onto his rundown property waiting for the price of the land to go up high enough; on the other hand he could improve it without being socked with a prohibitive tax increase. That's why partisans of land-value taxation believe that a simple shift in the structure of the property tax could accomplish, at no cost to other taxpayers, what urban renewal has failed to do, at great cost to the rest of us. The high land tax would also encourage the thrifty use of land by raising the cost of wasting acreage. As Henry Aaron points out, tax-exempt institutions are among the most wasteful of landowners, and with good reason: once they own the land, it costs them nothing to hang onto it, while the value goes up.

The benefits of shifting the property tax off improvements onto land remain mainly theoretical, since it is virtually untested in practice, at least in the United States; some places in Australia and New Zealand, joined recently by Jamaica, practice land value taxation. The United States is far from the worst offender, in the Georgist view: we at least tax land along with improvements, while some nations in Western Europe and the Third World let the landlord's holdings go virtually untaxed. Only in two states does the law even permit taxing land and improve-

ments differently, and only a few cities have tried to reverse the assessor's traditional bias in favor of vacant land-
holdings. (Several cities—Boston, as noted earlier, is one
example—have offered lower taxes as an inducement to
owners to improve downtown properties. But this does
not shift the tax to land; it simply third-parties the missing taxes onto all other property owners of any kind.)

The tiny Georgist enclave of Arden, Delaware, practices land-value taxation, but only in a very small setting.
Arden was founded in 1900 as a Georgist new town; it now
has 1,500 people living on 432 acres. The land is held in
trust and leased to residents. Only land value is taxed, not
homes or other improvements, and the tax currently
amounts to about $600 on a half acre worth $12–15,000.
This is less than half the rent that land can earn, and yet
the tax is sufficient to pay the costs of local government.

Pennsylvania, back in 1913, adopted a law permitting
"second-class" cities (a category which, W. C. Fields to
the contrary, does not include Philadelphia) to tax land
twice as heavily as improvements. The law later was extended to third-class cities. Two cities, Pittsburgh and
Scranton, have applied the differential for many years;
Harrisburg joined them in 1974. But because the law
applies only to city taxes, not to overlapping school and
county property taxes, the difference in practice is so
diluted that nothing conclusive can be said about its
effects.

Hawaii adopted a similar law in 1963, but it is so
riddled with qualifications as to be close to meaningless.
Some categories of property are exempted, land is so un-
derassessed that improvements remain overtaxed even if
their apparent rate is lower, and, finally, the total property tax is so low that there isn't enough to shift to make
much difference. Land hoarding is still good business in
Hawaii.

Attempts to implement land-value taxation occur occasionally around the country. In Pennsylvania, Steven Cord, an active Georgist and professor of history at the University of Pennsylvania at Indiana, Pennsylvania, has been lobbying third-class cities to take the opportunity the law offers to shift taxes from improvements to land. In San Diego, Floyd Morrow, a member of the city council, used his swing vote between growth and environmental factions to force the developer of a new town in the city to have the cost of the new public services the new town would require raised from a tax on land value only—thus putting the cost on the owners of the land instead of shifting it to the rest of the city taxpayers. In three western states—Montana, Idaho, and Colorado—Georgists have been campaigning for a change in state law permitting land-value taxation. Perry Prentice, the Time Inc. vice president who has spent much of the last fifteen years on the road arguing the Georgist case, felt in 1976 that "the temperature's gotten warmer." But if the audience is more receptive, the change itself has not happened, nor does it seem about to happen. One reason for this, in the view of another active Georgist, William W. Newcomb, a real estate man in West Melbourne, Florida, is that the Georgists have remained a sect apart rather than building bridges to such alternate political movements as Common Cause and Ralph Nader's Public Citizen.

Arlington County in Virginia and Southfield, Michigan have shifted some of the tax burden to the land, within the limits of the law, simply by forcing land to be assessed at something resembling its true value. The results of even this modest change have been substantial. Southfield, according to its assessor, Ted Gwartney, assessed land at its full market value, "whether it is being used, used poorly or not used at all." Shifting part of the tax to land reduced most homeowners' taxes, and the city stopped increasing the tax on a home when the owner improved it. Land speculators received "a whopping increase in assessed value," Gwartney wrote. The result was very rapid growth—growth that otherwise would have sprawled into the countryside at much higher cost—and a property tax rate only one third that of neighboring Detroit. When Arlington County brought its assessments into line with reality, the Rosslyn district, which lies right across the Potomac from downtown Washington, began to boom with construction that would better have been located in the city itself. Similarly, when, as noted earlier, Ramapo, New York, went to assessing property at full market value, the heaviest increase fell on vacant land, and one result was that several new businesses chose to locate in the town.

Washington is the largest city in which an active campaign for land value taxation is being conducted. The capital has the advantage that it needs no county or state authority to make the change; a recent act of Congress, passed with the help of testimony by local Georgists, allows the District of Columbia to tax land and buildings at different rates. Other circumstances made the issue timely. Washington being the home of one of our few remaining non-military growth industries, the area is suffering an acute housing shortage and a rapid, partly speculative, rise in property prices. At the same time, much of downtown Washington is decayed and underused. The organization attempting to put land-value taxation on the agenda as one solution to Washington's problem is the five-hundred-member League for Urban Land Conservation, of which Walter Rybeck is president. The league in 1976 was circulating the results of a computer simulation of what would happen if the entire property tax were collected from land, with no tax on buildings and other improvements. Taxes would drop considerably on all kinds of housing, especially apartments, and on intensively used commercial property like large office buildings. But taxes would go up on underused property, like filling stations and parking lots, and most of all on vacant land—motivating the owners to use it more efficiently. As of this writing, it is too early to tell what effect the Georgist message is having in Washington.

One state, Vermont, has attacked one aspect of the land problem in a modest way by picking it up by its hind legs. In 1973 Vermont adopted a law imposing a state capital gains tax on land bought and resold within six years. The tax is far from prohibitive: the top rate is 60 per cent, and that applies only if you buy and sell within a year and score a profit of over 200 per cent—that still leaves you with a net of at least 80 per cent in less than twelve months, which obviously beats working. If you hold the land five years and make the same 200 per cent, you only pay 10 per cent to the state. If you resell within the year for a measly 99 per cent profit, you pay 30 per cent; if your profit was between 100 and 200 per cent, your tax is 45 per cent. Even this rather mild measure was hotly contested in the legislature and the courts. The tax was politically possible, it seems, because the target of Vermonters' wrath was not land hoarding as such, or profiteering—it was profiteering by out-of-staters. The six-year limit of course exempts those who hoard for the long pull; in that sense, the tax, far from discouraging land hoarding, actually seems to encourage it. The bias in the Vermont law came into focus in 1974 when it was amended to exempt a property bought as a principal residence—i.e., by a once or future resident of the state. Governor Thomas P. Salmon later explained that this change took care of "a rather serious philosophical problem" and added that "our statistics indicate that this new exemption is being put to use rather frequently." For all its shortcomings, the Vermont tax was the first of its kind. Similar bills have been introduced in several other states.

The rate at which the countryside is being devoured has led to various schemes for slanting the property tax in the interests of preserving open space. One of the most widespread, and least effective, of these schemes is the differential tax on farm land. Starting with Maryland in 1956, more than thirty states now impose a lower tax rate on farm land, on the theory that this will permit the farmer to resist the temptation of the demon developer. The idea is appealing, for everyone loves the farmer and the American values he supposedly symbolizes. In practice, the lower tax doesn't accomplish its purpose. All it does is permit the owner to hold out for a higher price, raising the eventual cost of development to everyone. Nor is the owner the sturdy yeoman of the myth—he's likely to be Farmer ITT or some other speculator in overalls. In New Jersey, the Center for the Analysis of Public Issues collected estimates that half the "farm" land was in the hands of hoarders and developers who rent it to farmers until they're ready to sell or build; all the lower tax did was provide them with a windfall at everyone else's expense. In 1972, according to the center, other taxpayers had to pay an extra $48 million to make up for the lower farm tax—and, of course, will eventually have to pay higher prices for the land that the speculators are holding. The owners were also enjoying a rapid increase in their capital: in just one year, from March 1973 to March 1974, the market value of that undertaxed New Jersey farm land rose by no less than 31 per cent. The assessor was his usual co-operative self: during that year, assessments on that farm land rose by only 1.8 per cent.

The latest open-space panacea is something called transferable development rights (TDR), and Hillsborough, New Jersey, became in 1975 the first municipality to give it a try. It works like this: a community contains a limited number of development rights—so many units per acre, let us say. You can build more intensively on one property by buying the development rights to an-

other property, which, without those rights, must hence-
forth remain open space. If, for example, one hundred
acres are all zoned for one unit of housing per acre, a
developer can put all hundred units on ten acres by buying the rights to the other ninety acres; the result is housing concentrated on ten acres and ninety acres of open
space or farm land. TDR has the merit of reducing the ri-
gidity of zoning, but it appears to be based on the curious
assumption that development in a given community
should and can be limited for all time by fixing the number of development rights.

TDR is, ultimately, no more than a sophisticated form
of zoning. In the contrast between zoning and land-value
taxation as approaches to the problem of land use, we find
illustrated our own ambiguous attitudes toward free markets and regulation. Although the free market is praised
in our mythology, we usually find it buried under a
strange mixture of monopoly and regulation. Nowhere is
this more visible than in land use. Of all our forms of regulation, zoning is the most pervasive; even the ICC at its
worst cannot compare with the lunatic detail in which
zoning codes attempt to dictate the shape of our communities. Zoning succeeds with the weak, but fails with
the strong, for money and market pressure can always
punch a variance through the zoning code; as the Philadelphia *Inquirer* once observed, "Zoning is the most sophisticated form of white collar crime." Most conser-
vationists want to save the land by better regulation
while leaving the property tax, with all its perverse
effects, pretty much as it is now. Land value taxation, on
the other hand, is intended to make the property tax a
force that will guide free market pressures toward better
land use, rather than hoarding and waste and sprawl. So
far the regulatory philosophy has prevailed: the free
market remedy remains on the shelf.

8

The Nader Conglomerate

So FAR WE HAVE reported on ways in which the average person is beginning to demand and get a better deal from the institutions that govern his life. Sometimes he's able to do this as a lone individual, but more often change has been brought about by new forces challenging the monopoly on public decisions that had kept the subject of the screwing of the average man off the nation's agenda.

The most familiar aspect of that monopoly is the two-party system—some see it as a conspiracy—that controls politics and government. While the monopoly obviously is still unbroken in terms of what we are usually offered at election time, competition is growing outside the party system: as fewer people vote in elections, more find other ways to cast a ballot. In this chapter we report on the best-known of these alternatives, the people and organizations grouped around that household name, Ralph Nader. In chapter 9 we will describe the growing variety of political organizations that are challenging the two-party monopoly out in the states and the municipalities. These movements and the threat they present have not gone unnoticed within the monopoly. Just as the automobile companies shook themselves out of their profitable sleep when Volkswagen drove on the scene and began to produce smaller cars, so some of the actors in the two-party system have sensed that there's a market out there for which their industry now offers no product. In chapter 10 we report on the growing number of officeholders who are basing their political careers on issues that only yesterday were excluded from the political marketplace. Because of its long-standing complicity in the monopoly, the press has been all too accurately called the fourth branch of government: in chapter 11 we describe the growth of Action Line, through which the press is beginning to report on the concerns of the average person.

The Nader conglomerate provides a variety of alternatives to the failed political system. What began as a one-man attack on one automobile, the Corvair, and was later a series of one-shot assaults on assorted sinners, is now sinking institutional roots. Though still too heavily dependent for both its identity and its money on the leader himself, the Nader operation is becoming less transient in both its methods and its goals—"Public Citizen" rather than "Nader's Raiders." The pay is still lousy, but Nader people stay around longer than they used to, and though a shift in the winds of fashion can dry up the source, public support in 1976 seemed reasonably stable at something better than one million a year (almost all in fifteen-dollar donations); some Nader operations are approaching self-sufficiency. Similarly, Nader goals have shifted toward creating lasting ways for the average person to fight back: not exposing the unsafety at any speed of one brand, but breaking up the monopolies that shackle the marketplace; providing means for their customers to cope with such antagonists as airlines and utilities, and a flow of information that, increasingly, describes how to fix it rather than what's wrong. (Nader periodicals and reports are all available from P. O. Box 19404, Washington, D.C. 20036.)

Most Nader operations are based in Washington: the Tax Reform Research Group and the Health Research Group, some of whose work we noted in chapter 3; the Litigation Group, a public-interest law firm; the Corporate Accountability Group; in and around Congress, the Congress Watch, a lobbying group, and, now an independent spin-off, the Capitol Hill News Service. Outside Washington, Nader's Public Citizen has tried to plant grass-roots organizations; because of its funding mechanism, it has been more successful among students than with other kinds of people. We shall now see what all this activity—some 200 full-time workers and about $2.5 million a year—means to the average person.

The most far-reaching victory of the Naderites, and potentially the biggest break for the average man in recent years, was the landmark Goldfarb case won by the Litigation Group in 1975. The Supreme Court decision in Goldfarb, which we described in chapter 2, brought lawyers, and by implication all professionals, under the antitrust laws. It was the first step toward restoring free enterprise —and, therefore, better service at lower prices—to all guild-controlled occupations. A year later the Litigation Group won a second major victory in the same arena: the Supreme Court decision overturning guild-inspired state laws that forbade pharmacists from advertising the prices of prescription drugs. Both cases were argued for the Litigation Group by Alan Morrison. The Litigation Group has been involved in another case against a professional monopoly: it brought suit when the Maryland Medical Society threatened to discipline any members who answered questions put to them, by the Nader Health Research Group, for use in a doctors' directory. Also because of the Health Research Group, the Nader lawyers have successfully fought for better protection of workers against various industrial poisons; they have won cases on behalf of truck drivers fired for refusing to drive trucks that were overloaded or in poor repair. The Nader movement's support of the Aviation Consumer Action Project, a passenger advocacy group, has brought the Nader lawyers into a series of airline cases; twice they have helped hold travel costs down by defeating the CAB's efforts to give the airlines whatever fare increase they wanted. Others among the hundred-plus cases handled by the Litigation Group's ten lawyers include two suits that forced executives of 3M and American Airlines to repay to their companies money they had used for illegal campaign contributions.

Industrial monopoly is professional monopoly's big brother, and the Corporate Accountability Group's proposal for federal chartering of the biggest corporations is their attempt to do to the industrial monsters what the Goldfarb case is doing to the guilds.* The proposal, made public in early 1976, was the outcome of some five years' work; it was far more carefully researched and thought out than some of Nader's earlier and hasty works. Mark Green, its principal author along with Joel Seligman and Nader himself, is the author of *The Closed Enterprise System*, a previous Nader work on monopoly, and *The Other Government*, a 1975 book on Washington lawyers. His current idea is aimed of course at the source of the biggest screwings the average person is forced to endure: the corporate monopolies and shared monopolies that are responsible for the sluggish, wasteful performance of the American economy, with its evil combination of inflation and unemployment. Were free enterprise to be installed in our industrial economy, some two thirds of which is now ruled by the Invisible Handshake of shared monop-

---

* It was published by W. W. Norton under the title *Taming the Great Corporations*.

oly, the public would reap huge benefits. The Green group decided that requiring the biggest seven hundred or so corporations to get charters from the federal government is the likeliest way to get from monopoly to free enterprise.

At present corporations are chartered by the states, any state, no matter where they do business, but Delaware by preference. Little Delaware has managed to make even fewer demands on corporations seeking a charter than its forty-nine rivals, and so by 1974, 251 of the 500 largest firms were chartered there. As Green observed, "Our largest corporations are far larger than Delaware and could buy it—if it hadn't already sold out." Delaware wasn't always on top. Selling itself for corporate charter fees was an idea pioneered in the nineteenth century by New Jersey; Delaware topped the offer around the turn of the century; other states entered the fray; Delaware regained the title with a decisive outburst of corporate permissiveness. (This sort of competition among state governments has as much relation to free enterprise in the marketplace as does a war among Mafia families. In its noxious effects, it is similar to the competitive undertaxing of industry described in chapter 7.)

Under state chartering, then, anything goes. If there should happen to be any rules still lying around, the states solve the problem by not enforcing them: eighteen of twenty-two states answering a Nader query said they did not employ anyone to enforce their corporate regulations. Among the first principles to go under is that of democracy within the corporation. In theory, the stockholders elect the board of directors, who choose and supervise the management and make general policy decisions. In practice, directors are chosen by the management, not the other way around. According to Green, 99.7 per cent of elections for director in the biggest firms are uncontested—a figure that compares favorably with election returns under Stalin's 1936 constitution, which was hailed, you will recall, as "the most democratic constitution in the world." The antitrust laws have had little more impact on corporate misbehavior than has the state of Delaware. After almost a century, antitrust law is enforced, if at all, against the smallest rascals in the market, while the monster monopolists remain unscathed.

Federal rather than state chartering of corporations is not a new idea, as Green points out. James Madison proposed it at the Constitutional Convention, long before the rise of ITT, and the idea had the support of three successive presidents—Roosevelt, Taft, and Wilson—in the early years of the century. In its Naderite incarnation, the proposal has three main parts. Democracy in the corporation would be promoted by requiring a full-time board of directors made up of outsiders, by making it much easier for employees and dissident stockholders to elect directors, and by banning any retaliation against employees who blow the whistle on management misdeeds. Corporations would be required to give out much more information, for example on how much they are polluting their neighbors, and the communities in which their plants are located would have a say in what to do about any health hazards created by the corporation. Monopoly would, for the first time, be defined by an objective standard: four firms controlling 50 per cent or more of the market. The remedy, in most cases, would be to force the firms involved to give up part of their holdings.

Federal chartering of course will not automatically free the markets that the monster monopolies have gone to such pains to close. As conceived by the Naderites, it does, however, try to meet the most obvious objections. Since it would apply only to the seven hundred-odd biggest among the country's two million corporations, its enforcement would not be administratively impossible. In response to the objection that regulators always end up in the hip pockets of the regulated, Green and Nader argue that their provisions for internal democracy would make the rules to a large degree self-enforcing. In any event, it will not happen tomorrow. Any proposal that puts all seven hundred monster firms on the same side has little chance of early success, certainly in the saber-toothed version put forth by Nader and Green.

The more modest goal of tax reform has better prospects. The Nader Tax Reform Research Group is one wing of a movement that did not exist before the 1970s. Its monthly publication, *People and Taxes,* is the best single source of news about state and local as well as national tax issues. Louise Brown, its specialist on the Internal Revenue Service, is a leading critic of the way IRS administration of tax law affects the interests of the average man; it was she, for example, who brought to public attention the incredibly high rate of error in the tax advice given by local IRS offices. The group's director, Robert Brandon, is also its lobbyist in Congress. Although Brandon cannot swing the big stick of an oil company, he provides the information, and the threat of publicity, that can swing a close vote in favor of the public. Nader's is not the only Washington-based tax-reform group. Tax Analysts And Advocates are two organizations. The Advocates part is a public-interest law firm that brings class-action law suits on tax issues. The Analysts is the research part: its weekly publication, *Tax Notes,* reports only on federal taxes, but does so in much greater detail than *People and Taxes.*

The Nader conglomerate has been responsible for two new ways in which the public can fight back. In recent years the courts have greatly extended the citizen's rights to intervene in a governmental decision affecting him, but that right remains an empty one as long as he lacks the means to intervene with some hope of accomplishment. When, for example, a regulatory agency in Washington makes a decision that will affect all of us, after months of obscure hearings conducted in technological Sanskrit, no one is ever there to fight for the average man. The citizen has neither the time nor the money to be there, he wouldn't understand what they're saying anyway, and no one is going to do it for him, least of all his elected representatives from the two-party monopoly. Or take your utility bill. When you compare it to the bill for the same month last year, you may strongly suspect that another monopoly is taking you to the cleaners. Other than smashing the meter, what are you going to do about it? You can complain to the state utility commission, or, if you are particularly enterprising, you can attend the hearing after which the commission will give the utility the rate increase it wanted. But the last time the commission did anything to defend the customers was before you were born, and at the hearings you'll quickly be lost in the endless intricacies of rate-making. So you stay home and snarl at the bill.

Nader's Congress Watch, a nine-person Capitol Hill lobby, was the main promoter of a 1975 law that for the first time provides the means for the public to take part in the little-known but costly decisions of federal regulatory agencies. The Magnuson-Moss Act, drafted by Joan Claybrook, director of Congress Watch, provided half a million dollars to pay the cost of lawyers and expert witnesses for the public appearing before one agency, the Federal Trade Commission. Among the first public groups to get this kind of funding, and the subjects on which they testified, were the Center for Auto Safety, on mobile homes; Consumers Union, on food advertising; the National Council of Senior Citizens, on prescription drugs, and Consumer Action of San Francisco, on vocational schools.

The other new channel for fighting back is called RUCAG, a resoundingly ugly acronym that stands for Residential Utility Consumer Action Group. Putting together the resources you need to fight the utilities on a continuing basis—as opposed to a one-shot Lifeline campaign—is virtually impossible by the usual tactics, but the Naderites hit on the idea of utilizing the utilities themselves: the idea is related to what is being done to represent utility customers in New Jersey (see chapter 10). Under the RUCAG scheme, each utility bill would include a box which the householder could check and then add to his payment a voluntary donation to his chosen utility-watching group. The utility would have to collect the donations and pass them along, in effect biting its own tail. (If this sounds crazy, consider the difficulty the utility would have in diverting the money without word leaking out.) Those voluntary contributions would then finance the crew of people—lawyers, accountants, engineers—that would show up as informed opponents the next time the only phone company in town wants to raise the price of talk, or when the electric company says what it really needs in this town in a nuclear plant. The RUCAG might also challenge the common utility practice of giving industrial users lower rates, leaving the residential customer to make up the difference. (The principle here is the same as the Lifeline described later in this and in the following chapter.)

Nader has also been at war with the utilities over nuclear power plants. Since 1974, the Naderites have been helping to bring organization to the widespread public unease about the safety of nuclear reactors. The opposition, known as "Critical Mass," gathers annually in Washington and keeps in touch via a newsletter. Early in 1976

citizen groups were collecting signatures in at least six-
teen states to put on the ballot "safe energy" laws that
would require the utilities to get a two-thirds vote in each
house of the state legislature in order to build a nuclear
plant or keep an existing one in operation. The utilities
won the first round, the California referendum on June 8,
by a vote of two to one. Utilities all over the nation
helped out their endangered brethren with a war chest of
$3.5 million, much of which they will be able to charge to
the public in higher rates. But their victory was considerably less than total, for the California Legislature on
the eve of the referendum adopted legislation tightening
the rules on putting up new nuclear plants. In Washington, Nader's Congress Watch lopped off one of the nuclear industry's tentacles when it persuaded Congress to
eliminate the $1 million budget of the Office of Nuclear
Affairs, an agency that the Federal Energy Administration had created to promote the use of nuclear power
plants.

The Capitol Hill News Service was started with Nader
seed money but is now leading an independent, self-
financed life of its own. Its founder and director, Peter
Gruenstein, wanted it to plug an important hole in the
news we get about government. While the pages are filled
with presidential pronouncements, people back home
don't learn of government decisions affecting their local
concerns, and hardly anyone knows what his congressman
is doing down there. All most of his constituents ever
hear, even if they're listening hard, are the incumbent's
self-serving boasts, and, every two years, the equally
empty claims of his opponent, who typically knows little
more than the public about the congressman's record.
The purpose of Capitol Hill News Service is to help fill
that gap. It has seven reporters covering Congress for seventy local newspapers and radio and television stations.

Capitol Hill differs from the other news services in two ways: it is dirt cheap, and it provides superior coverage of news of local and regional interest. The clients are small stations and papers—circulation around 30–40,000—in the smaller towns of mid-American states like Kentucky, Indiana, Montana, upstate Pennsylvania. In a typical week, Montana might get a story on a new federal regulation about strip mining, Kansas a piece on beef promotion, and Indiana a report on how one of its congressmen voted on tax reform. Since most of its clients hold conservative editorial views, Capitol Hill tends to play down its Naderite origins.

On the face of it, Nader's campus-based PIRG (for Public Interest Research Group) would seem to be the conglomerate's most successful effort to build a popular constituency outside Washington. By 1976, the PIRGs could claim affiliates at 150 campuses in twenty-two states; in each of those states, they maintained one or more offices with paid professional staffs, each autonomous and in theory responsible to a student board of directors. PIRG could, it proclaimed, "successfully overcome the weaknesses and transitory nature of past student movements." It claimed that "more than 500,000 students are participating in PIRGs, raising revenues of more than $1 million annually"—an income roughly equal to the combined revenue of all other branches of the Nader network. By contrast, the non-student Citizen Action Groups only existed in six locations, and made no comparable claims about either membership or income.

But there was considerably less there than met the eye. Those student-participation figures were inflated by what on Wall Street they call creative accounting. The key to both PIRG's apparent success and its inherent weakness is how it gets its money. It's called the "negative check off" and it works like this. PIRG organizers solicit student signatures on a petition to the university. If they collect signatures from a majority of the student body, and if the university authorities agree, then dues for PIRG— typically $5–10 a year—are added to the activities fee charged all students. Those who don't want to support PIRG can get a refund, but they have to ask for it. Thus the student who does nothing at all—including signing the petition, which may have happened before he was around—finds himself among that half-million "participating" in PIRG. In fact, he makes up the majority of that superficially impressive figure.

The difference between this passive participation and the real thing became evident during the 1975–76 battle of Penn State. The PIRG organizers had collected 24,000 signatures, a majority of the students at the multicampus university, in favor of a negative check-off of $6 per student per year. But the university trustees voted, by 19 to 7, to eliminate the negative in favor of a positive check-off: PIRG dues would be collected only from students who requested it. PIRG refused the offer on the grounds that the positive check-off was "tantamount to killing the program." The stakes were high. A negative check-off would have collected $270,000 a year, PIRG said, while the positive version would only bring in $10–30,000—a telling commentary by PIRG itself on the depth of student commitment. Penn State was not the only campus where PIRG's method of collecting dues had become an issue. At Ivy League colleges the students themselves rejected the negative check-off, and in Minnesota, where it had existed for three years, the authorities in 1976 were preparing to switch to the positive system.

The issue was cloaked with irony. While PIRG's method of meeting the payroll was hardly consistent with Nader's own goal of citizen participation, the universities were poorly positioned to make the point—indeed, "you're another" was PIRG's most effective response. As PIRG partisans were quick to say, other student-activity fees, at Penn State and elsewhere, were mandatory: no one had a right to get a refund on the grounds that he didn't want to take part in one or any given activity. And, stretching the analogy further, all universities enjoy the mandatory third-party benefits of tax exemption: other property owners in town have no way to refuse to pay extra taxes so the university can pay none. In practice, Nader's response was to open a second front. He announced that PIRGs all over the country were going to start investigations of the inner workings of universities—with, of course, Penn State as the first subject—though PIRG had previously avoided targeting universities, presumably on the grounds that it was risky to bite the hand that was collecting the dues.

Whatever the merits of its financing, PIRG had found a way to maintain a substantial number of people working on a wide variety of public issues. They were doing it, moreover, not in Washington but in parts of the country that had received little such attention. Oregon PIRG, for example, with a budget of $170,000 from seven campuses, supported a staff of ten that included four lawyers in a state where public interest law was virtually non-existent. Most of those who ran PIRGs were young lawyers, some were clergymen, many were veterans of what now seems like the old New Left. The future, they felt, was being determined out there in the states. Fritz Wieking, the Director of Indiana PIRG, who has a divinity degree from Yale, was a native who returned: "When I left here I swore I would never come back, and when I finished college I said it again. But I found out that like it or not, places like Indiana would have to change if there was going to be social change." Students, when they do take part, do so as researchers and lobbyists, but it is unlikely that more than a tiny fraction of the student body at its member campuses has made PIRG part of their educational experience.

Only a minority of the issues taken up by PIRG are of special concern to students. The most interesting of these was the investigation it undertook in 1975–76 of the Educational Testing Service. ETS is of course the "non-profit" (as usual, this only means non-tax-paying) organization that holds a near-total monopoly over the tests that determine whether you will be accepted in, or included out, not only of colleges and universities, but also organizations as varied as the CIA and the Peace Corps. It is, as one ETS executive said, "the nation's gatekeeper," and it is accountable to no one, certainly not to those it either does or does not admit through the golden gate. The idea of investigating ETS originated at PIRG's office in Albany, New York—appropriately, since that was where ETS managed to lose the transcripts for two hundred law school applicants. New York PIRG set up a complaint center to gather everyone's gripes about the testers. By spring of 1976 PIRG had collected about 150 student complaints mostly concerning errors and delays and other administrative sloppiness characteristic of a monopoly; some students refused to make formal complaint because they feared it would jeopardize their applications. PIRG convinced the Higher Education Committee of the New York State Senate—ETS is chartered in New York, though its home is an estate is Hopewell, New Jersey—to hold hearings, at which PIRG representatives urged some form of public regulation of the testing monopoly.

On another front, Maryland PIRG successfully contested the state's refusal to allow a bank offering free checking to open a branch on the University of Maryland College Park campus—a victory that, PIRG claimed, was worth $300,000 a year in lower banking costs for the uni-

versity community. Several PIRGs have put out tenants'
rights handbooks useful to student renters, and, in recognition of the boom both in the riding and the stealing of
bicycles, three PIRGs conducted separate studies of the
respective merits of various brands of chain and cable
locks—but disagreed in their recommendations. Strangely
enough, as of 1976, no PIRG had reported any action on
an obvious target, the student life insurance hustle that
we described in chapter 5.

Most PIRGs have devoted most of their time to issues
of concern to the public at large. Typically these are undertaken with other citizen groups. Michigan PIRG, for
example, joined with others in 1974 in a successful campaign for passage of a bill permitting pharmacists to substitute generic for brand-name drugs and requiring them
to post prescription prices—issues that we dealt with in
chapter 4. Like other parts of the Nader complex, PIRGs
have sought to change the balance between the utilities,
whose prices have ballooned in recent years, and their
customers. Earlier we saw that the Nader movement is
pushing the RUCAG idea to give residential bill payers a
vehicle for fighting both the amount of the bill and how
it is determined. In San Diego PIRG took part in the successful state-wide campaign for Lifeline (described in the
following chapter), which means laying the burden of
utility rate increases on the big users who now pay the
lowest rates. The outcome in San Diego was that the public utilities commission cut the local gas and electric company's $105 million request to $27 million and required it
all to be laid on the largest users; bills for major industrial
and commercial users went up by half, residential and
small commercial users paid no increase at all, and those
using the smallest amounts of electricity got a slight
decrease in their bills. The Connecticut PIRG, one of the
few that is not student-supported, lobbied through its leg-

islature a bill forbidding the utilities from figuring advertising costs in their rates—since utilities are, with only rare exceptions, in a monopoly position, advertising their products is of no value to the public.

It is worth noting that PIRG headquarters in Washington gives pride of place in its proclamations not to these events but to a "major victory" that was neither major nor an unmixed blessing for the public. This was Indiana PIRG's success in defeating three local telephone companies' requests for ten-cent charges on calls for directory assistance (in one case, only for numbers available in the book). Now, few among us go broke calling information, and, if the principle that the dime that stays in one person's pocket comes out of another's applies here, the effect of PIRG's "victory" will be that people who look numbers up in the book rather than calling information will continue to pay a bit more to make up for those who don't.

Several PIRGs have gone in for producing information that the public can use in coping with the experts. PIRGs in Massachusetts and New York City have compiled local directories of doctors along the lines pioneered by Nader's Health Research Group, and Maine and Massachusetts PIRGs have put out guides on how to use the small-claims courts. Other PIRG research is less directly connected to everyday concerns. New York PIRG compiled a voters' guide to its state legislature—considering the dismal quality of that body, the voter can only read it and weep. Michigan PIRG got considerable attention when, building on the work of Yale's Professor Bruce Russett, it published the first figures on which states lose how many jobs in what fields because of the money Washington draws out of the private economy to finance the weapons industry. On balance, the nation as a whole loses jobs, and the biggest losers are New York and the industrial states of the Midwest, including Michigan. While the

general conclusion might be sensed in his bones by anyone who looked simultaneously at the weapons budget
and the unemployment figures, the hard figures published
by PIRG could stiffen a congressman's spine into voting
against a defense appropriation touted as "producing
jobs."

The Nader movement has traveled a long road since he
burst on the scene in 1965 with *Unsafe at Any Speed*.
Their record of accomplishment on behalf of the average
person is unmatched. Were it possible to run the Nader
complex on the equivalent to a lawyer's contingency fee,
collecting a percentage of everything gained for the client, the Naderites would be swimming in cash. Just the
fees on the Goldfarb and drug advertising cases won by
the Litigation Group would finance Nader operations for
decades to come. But of course the movement would
starve if it depended on donations from those who will
get a lawyer cheaper because of Goldfarb, or those who
will find the right doctor through the Health Research
Group's guides, or who will get screwed less by Internal
Revenue because of the Tax Reform Research Group.
Forced to recognize this sorry fact of life, the Nader
movement has explored enduring methods, like RUCAG
and helping the public appear before regulatory agencies,
of making it possible for the public to fight back. For
that reason alone, the Nader movement is the most
important of the alternative political systems available to
us. But far from the only one, as we shall see in the next
chapter.

9

Acorn and Other Seeds

A WIDE VARIETY of citizen groups has sprung up around the nation in recent years in reaction to the failure of the political system to provide a vehicle for the interests of the average person. They share a desire to bring together the great majority against the privileges and parochial concerns of the few. They address a spectrum of issues, with utility rates and property taxes currently getting the most attention. Though their styles and aims are varied, they all seek their goals outside the two-party political monopoly, and they concentrate their efforts in the states and municipalities, where tangible results can be achieved with far less power than it takes to move anything in Washington. Here we shall describe a geographic sampling of these groups, beginning with ACORN.*

ACORN is an alternate political system for the average person in Arkansas: the only organization that represents the interests of the 70 per cent of the state's residents who earn less than $7,000. Since its birth in 1970, it has grown from winning small local skirmishes to taking on, and sometimes defeating, the state's most powerful institu-

---

* The acronym stands for Arkansas (later American) Community Organizations for Reform Now.

tions. A coalition of about fifty local groups with names like Cavanaugh Neighborhood Association, ACORN can make its growing clout felt in a small town hall or in the state capitol at Little Rock. This is the South, where traditionally those in power have kept white and black at each other's throats, but ACORN has bridged the color line: its membership is 60 per cent white, 40 per cent black, and the issues it fights join rather than separate the races. By 1976, ACORN employed ten organizers, was trying to become self-supporting, and had planted its seed in other states.

ACORN originated with Wade Rathke, now in his late twenties, who is its chief organizer. Rathke is from Louisiana, went to Williams College in the late sixties, dropped out and became an organizer for the National Welfare Rights Organization. He found that organizing people on welfare led nowhere because his constituency was a minority. Later Rathke said: "I wanted to build on a majority constituency rather than on a minority, where the next-door neighbors are in it together, not fighting each other." This led him to Arkansas and ACORN, whose purpose he defined as organizing that 70 per cent of the people into 70 per cent of the political power. Today there are probably more people on public assistance in ACORN than ever belonged to the earlier welfare rights groups, but neither they nor ACORN suffers the stigma of being an organization for welfare recipients, because it has chosen to represent a wide spectrum of people against the institutions that oppress them.

ACORN organizes. When it moves into a new area, ACORN typically begins with highly visible local issues for which its organizers think a quick solution can be found. Take its 1975 arrival in Mountain Pine, as described by Andrew Kopkind in an article on ACORN in the 1975 summer issue of *Working Papers*. Mountain Pine is an obscure back-country papermill town with 310 households, a number of whose residents had called ACORN after a favorable piece had appeared in the nearest newspaper, the Hot Springs *Sentinel-Record*. ACORN organizer Steve Holt showed up, knocked on doors, sent around a flier, and called a meeting. Thirty people showed up and aired their problems. From a list of ten or so issues, Holt steered the group toward two he thought could be quickly won: the telephone company's poor service and high prices, and the need for a traffic signal at a railroad crossing where someone had recently been killed. Holt knew the phone company was seeking a state-wide increase, and was anxious to avoid trouble with ACORN: it would probably be willing to do better by little Mountain Pine, where subscribers were paying more than twice as much as in nearby Hot Springs, and waiting years for a new phone. The traffic signal, often promised and as often postponed, arrived after Holt got pictures of the site in the papers and called the state highway commissioner to say a delegation of Mountain Pine people would soon be coming to see him. Three weeks after the first meeting, eighty families, almost one third of the households in town, were dues-paying members of ACORN and, Holt recalled, three local officials, the judge and two members of the legislature, "called up the papers and said they'd support us." The Mountain Pine story has been repeated, with endless local variations, all over Arkansas.

Often ACORN can win an issue simply by kicking a somnolent local government that has never been kicked before. In Jonesboro and Little Rock, it was getting the authorities to make landlords either tear down or repair dilapidated housing. A Jonesboro sign next to one such house read: "I'm tired of looking at this mess—aren't you? Call ACORN." Once ACORN gave the Little Rock budget a hand by needling the city into collecting long-overdue charges for weeding vacant lots; ACORN dramatized the issue by tacking up its own "bills" on the delinquent owners' doors. Gradually the issues grew bigger: in Little Rock, ACORN organized the residents, both white and black, of the integrated Oak Forests neighborhood to combat an effort by real estate interests to panic the whites into selling their homes, and, later, they were fighting a proposal to bisect the neighborhood with a road—the Wilbur D. Mills Freeway.

Those were typical of ACORN's earlier days. By 1973 ACORN had assembled enough backing by its local successes to take on real power: the utilities. It organized well-publicized opposition to the Arkansas and Louisiana Gas Company's request for a twelve-million-dollar rate increase; the campaign included convincing people to withhold a dollar from their bills, after a "temporary" increase, and send it to the state Public Utilities Commission. Under pressure orchestrated by ACORN, the commission finally cut the increase to half what the company had asked, despite a recommendation by a commission "consultant" that the company should get almost all it wanted. The company had to send some 300,000 customers refunds totaling $4.5 million, which is more than forty-five times ACORN's annual budget.

That wasn't all. ACORN also got the commission to begin changing how the utilities charge different kinds of customers. In the Arkansas and Lousiana company case, the commission required the company to put most of its increase on the big users, thus reducing the discount they get at the expense of residential customers. This is the essence of the "Lifeline" idea that, as we shall see later in this chapter, was first instituted in California and has been promoted in other parts of the country. By mid-1975 ACORN had made Lifeline a major issue all over the state. Because towns can set utility rates under Arkansas law, though they prefer to let the state do it, ACORN local groups in a dozen towns simultaneously asked their governing bodies to set rates that would guarantee residents a minimum amount of electricity and gas at minimum rates, while allowing the utility companies to get their added revenues from the big users. Not just residents: ACORN was careful to include small-business men, who would also benefit, among the promoters of Lifeline. ACORN members presented data showing what the Lifeline rates would mean in each community: in Pine Bluffs, for example, a small user would pay $12 a month for electricity instead of $17.21.

In another utility case ACORN organized the kind of people not usually found under the same tent with welfare recipients. The case was Arkansas Power & Light's plan to build a giant coal-burning generating plant near Pine Bluffs, and ACORN's allies were well-to-do farmers whose land was downwind from the plant site. Not so long ago they were wearing white sheets to political meetings and even now, as Arkansas Journalist Martin Kirby put it, "they were the type who would go to their graves believing in the righteousness of racial segregation and who could afford to send their children to the nearby segregationist private school." But the issue here was not race, nor even income; it was the power of the power company to put in a plant whose sulfur emissions would, the farmers feared, damage their cotton and soybean crops. In this context, the farmers saw themselves as underdogs. They accepted ACORN's help because, as one of the farmers said, "They helped us get organized. We were concerned about this, but we didn't know where to get started in filing a protest." ACORN had a couple of ideas about how to get started. The new Protect Our Lands Association filed a demand with the power company for a deposit against damages to their fields, pointing out that, since they had to pay a deposit to get electricity, it was only fair for the company to do the same. ACORN researchers discovered that the biggest stockholder in the

holding company that owned Arkansas Power & Light
was Harvard University; that resulted in a letter to Harvard's president asking for his help. Harvard's answer was
unresponsive, but there was a bit of publicity on the East
Coast for the embattled farmers of Pine Bluffs. The eventual outcome was that the power company was forced to
cut the size of the power plant in half. If it was less than a
complete victory, what ACORN and the farmers won was
half of a very large loaf.

Like the American Association of Retired People,
ACORN has found that the elderly are particularly easy
to organize in their own interest. Meg Campbell, ACORN
organizer in Hot Springs, the spa that has an unusually
large percentage of retired people, said to Andrew Kopkind: "You have no idea how many issues old people have.
They have a lot of free time and on the other hand, not
much time left, so they're raring to go. Health care is a
tremendous issue, and bus fares, housing, rent control,
even the matter of how long the WALK signs are on at in-
tersections. They want old people on the city council and
participation in running all these programs which are
supposed to help them. No one else thinks of that. An organizer has to hold them back sometimes, they're so ener-
getic." ACORN first organized around the familiar issue
of reducing legal restrictions on the use of generic drugs
and prescription price advertising. When ACORN
brought enough members to Little Rock to appear before
the pharmacy board and the inevitable press conference,
the new governor, David Pryor, who had made a name as
a nursing-home reformer when he was in Congress,
scrambled to hop aboard, and the legislation passed. The
governor's legislative assistant said of ACORN's role:
"They get the credit for the legislation—some might say
the blame." In 1976 ACORN was pushing price advertising for eyeglasses, another issue of particular interest to
the elderly, and a natural for Arkansas, which borders

Texas and Missouri, states where eyeglass prices are both advertised and lower. ACORN drew attention to the subject by launching its campaign around the time that the other side, the American Optometric Association, was holding its annual meeting in, of all places, Hot Springs. The optometrists' guild predictably denounced price advertising as being promoted by an "unholy alliance of consumer groups and retail optical companies," and one of its leaders described low-price Texas as a "sewer" for eye care. The Arkansas press reported that prices were indeed twice as high in Arkansas for the same glasses, thereby attracting to ACORN's support many citizens who doubtless had not thought about the question before.

ACORN is one of those groups around the country that, as we saw in chapter 7, have been trying to make the property tax be applied less unfairly to the average homeowner. The saga of one such ACORN effort illustrates what happens when reformers intrude into the cozy world of small-town tax politics. The scene was Pulaski County, which includes Little Rock, and ACORN's antagonists were the members of the county Equalization Board, which hears taxpayers' appeals and is supposed to assure that everyone is assessed by equal standards. ACORN members had studied the assessment rolls and found the usual patterns: wealthy homes assessed at a lower fraction of their value than less valuable dwellings; industrial and commercial property assessed lower than residential. ACORN asked the board to do its equalizing, and was told it could only handle individual cases. The chairman threatened to resign. ACORN argued that the state's freedom of information law required that meetings where appeals are heard be open to the public. This violation of political protocol infuriated the board. As one board member pointed out, "a man's taxes ought to be between himself, the board and God"—though the latter was not known to have expressed any interest in attending the meetings. Another board member offered the unique view that meetings must be closed because letting the public in would create a "fire hazard." ACORN won that round, and soon thereafter its members and a reporter from the *Arkansas Democrat* were watching when a friend of the chairman applied for a lower assessment. She lost the case, over the chairman's protest, and when he saw the reporter taking notes, the chairman announced that the subject wasn't newsworthy. This time he asked the whole board to resign. They didn't, so the chairman took another tack. Maybe, he said, the board should investigate the newspaper's tax assessment. And ACORN's, another member chimed in. The chairman promised to resign next year. It didn't all add up to very much, even for Pulaski County, except that such persistent prying is the only way to prevent the tax favors which assure that the average homeowner's taxes will keep going up to make up for those whose appeals find a receptive ear when no one else is listening.

ACORN has so far avoided becoming a conventional political party, but it doesn't stay out of electoral politics. It endorses candidates, and a number of its members have been elected to town and school board offices. That doesn't necessarily increase their power, Wade Rathke observed: ACORN's clout lies not in officeholders but in its ability to mobilize people. ACORN's best-known political exploit was a quiet campaign that netted its members almost half the 407 seats on a moribund county legislature known as the Quorum Court: ACORN won a niche in county government and added respect for its political skills. By 1975 ACORN felt confident enough to expand beyond its home state. It responded to invitations to help organize local groups in two towns in South Dakota—Sioux Falls and Huron, and two in Texas—Dallas and Fort

Worth; soon the Fort Worth group claimed credit for the first defeat in twenty-eight years of a utility rate increase.

More than most such organizations, ACORN has been aware that it is unlikely to endure without a solid financial base. The problem as always is that people who are happy to join ACORN in winning themselves something today are too often gone by tomorrow. ACORN has gone the standard route of providing services available only to its paid members: for example, members get a 10 per cent discount at forty-five stores around Arkansas. ACORN also promises help in individual problems. A brochure proclaims:

> Every group stands behind its members in problems they have getting their rights. ACORN members and staff have advocated for countless members in such things as workmen's compensation and consumer problems. In ACORN, no member ever goes alone, for an injury to one is an injury to all!

By 1976 ACORN had 5,300 member families paying one dollar a month dues (on paper: collections in fact ran far below that rate). Dues and income from such projects as rummage sales cover little more than half ACORN's budget, the rest coming from donations. A second potential weakness of ACORN is that its shock troops, the organizers, are elite outsiders whom you would not expect to spend a career working for four thousand dollars a year (ACORN's top salary) in the back country of Arkansas. Its founder and chief, Wade Rathke, is one such person. Steve Holt, whom we met in remote Mountain Pine, is a Harvard graduate, and Meg Campbell, who was organizing old people in Hot Springs, is out of Radcliffe. It's doubtful that ACORN's membership can provide replacements for them when they go, as most of them surely will.

It's a long way from Arkansas to the Twin Cities of Minnesota, and the Citizens League of Minneapolis and

St. Paul doesn't look a bit like ACORN. It does not recruit its members from the 70 per cent of the powerless; the Citizens League is an elite organization, comfortably financed, that draws its membership of three thousand from the business and academic establishments of its communities. You can of course find such civic organizations in any metropolitan area—the difference is that the Citizens League has scored a rare success in bridging the gap between city and suburb. That accomplishment can be of lasting benefit to the people of the Twin Cities area.

The Citizens League was largely responsible for putting through a unique device for sharing the property tax base among the two cities and their surrounding suburbs. Under the League's plan, which we touched on in chapter 7, 40 per cent of all net growth of industrial and commercial property goes into a tax pool which is then redistributed among the three hundred tax districts in the area in proportion to their population. It is intended to discourage the destructive competition among tax districts for new business properties, and to encourage new housing, because the tax-sharing will most benefit those districts with the most residents. Put into effect in 1974, but retroactive to 1971 (it had been held up in court), the so-called "fiscal disparities" plan was already producing results by 1976. The difference in business tax rates among the various districts was gradually being reduced, with revenue going from those with the greatest industrial growth to those with the largest population. It was what every metropolitan area in the nation needed, but, as of this writing, it had only happened in the Twin Cities.

It wouldn't have happened there without the Citizens League. It was their idea, and they rounded up the necessary backing, included that of the business establishment, to edge it through the legislature, where it got by with little to spare: it only passed the state senate by three votes.

By 1976 the Citizens League had pushed its thinking further in the same direction. It was advocating an ambitious land use plan that, by banning road and sewer construction in large parts of the area, would save the Twin Cities region the gigantic costs of unnecessary sprawl: $2 billion by 1990 was their estimate of the potential saving to the taxpayers of the region.

Out in the thinly populated states of the northern Rockies the big issue is land use of a different kind. Here against the spectacular mountain background cattle graze over huge deposits of coal that the energy companies would like to strip-mine. Strip mining is cheap today and costly tomorrow: the land is wrecked beyond repair, and so too are the lives of people, by the boom-and-bust cycle of coal towns that mushroom and vanish within a decade or two. For some, the goal is preserving an agrarian lifestyle from bulldozers and immigrants. For Indians, whose reservations lie over much of the coal, the issues are more complex than they seem to doctrinaire environmentalists: the Indians would like to preserve what's left of the land that was once all theirs, but the coal money might enable them to escape the poverty to which white rule has subjected them. As one native American observed, "We're told, 'You Indians won't like middle-class life.' How in hell do we know when we never had the chance to try it?"

Bridging the Indian-environmentalist gap is one of the purposes of the Northern Rockies Action Group. Headquartered in Helena, Montana, and fueled mainly by foundation grants, NRAG began operating in 1973. Its founder, Bill Bryan, intended NRAG to be a support organization for the citizen groups scattered across Montana, Idaho, and Wyoming who are attempting to cope with such distant Goliaths as the energy companies and the federal government, notably, in the case of native Americans, the ineffable Bureau of Indian Affairs, which administers the Gulag Archipelago of the reservations. By 1976 the people of the three states had substantially increased their capacity to fight back. The paid staff of citizen groups had risen from two to forty-five and they were meeting budgets totaling about $400,000. What has been happening is illustrated by the experience of the Wyoming Citizens Lobby, one of the groups NRAG helps and the first of its kind in that state. The Wyoming legislature only meets for general purposes for forty days every other year, and traditionally hardly anyone but the special interests show up in Cheyenne for its session. The legislators were free to sell themselves to those interests, and their constituents didn't even know it, since votes weren't recorded and press coverage was perfunctory. In 1975 the citizens lobby mounted its first successful onslaught on the legislature. Two participants later described how it went. They rented a house in Cheyenne for the duration and kept it filled with about a dozen citizen lobbyists who spent their days watching the legislators, who weren't used to having the public peering over their shoulders. Members contributed food to nourish the lobbyists; one rancher sent in a suitcase full of frozen meat each week. A toll-free WATS line made it possible for anyone in the state to call for information about what was happening in the legislature; calls averaged thirty to forty a day.

The participants felt they had made the legislature aware for the first time of some pressure other than that of the special interests. One way their influence manifested itself was in the appointment of members of the citizens lobby to state boards and commissions where many of the decisions affecting their lives are made. A land-use planning bill was passed in that session, and the first state controls on the locating of industrial plants were adopted. Another bill, said to be the first of its kind in the nation, required the landowner's consent for strip mining (homesteaders only acquire surface rights, mineral rights remaining federal property)—though this seemed more likely to enrich lucky landowners than to serve the interests of the average person even in Wyoming. Of course the Rocky Mountain states are still threatened by the short-term greed of strip mining, and fundamental decisions concerning the future of this land remain to be made, but the people of the area have more power to influence those decisions than they ever had before.

On the West Coast, California was the scene of a major victory for the interests of the average person. Starting in 1976, the residents of the nation's most populous state have enjoyed the benefits of Lifeline rates for household electricity and gas. As we've seen, Lifeline has been adopted elsewhere in part and on a small scale, but this was the first time it had been embraced by an entire state.

This is what Lifeline means to Californians. Rates on a basic minimum of energy for household use—three hundred to five hundred kilowatts per month of electricity depending on the area, and seventy-five therms of gas—are frozen at the 1976 level until the rates on big users reach a point 25 per cent above the Lifeline rate. Only then can the utilities raise the minimum household rate. Since the big industrial and commercial users in California as elsewhere have been paying much less than the household rate, it seemed clear that they, not the householder, would have to bear the entire burden of rate increases for years to come. As estimated by Lifeline's proponents, the immediate saving to householders amounts to ten to twelve dollars a month (compared to what they would have had to pay if the utilities' pending increases had been applied according to the old pattern). The savings will increase, of course, each time the utilities raise their rates.

Lifeline in California was won by a broad coalition of

people and organizations: nothing less would have sufficed to overcome the entrenched power of the utilities, their big users who get rate breaks (in California this category includes agribusiness), and the oil companies that provide their fuel. That alliance has traditionally had its way with the utilities commissions that theoretically regulate them. It's another example of Catch-85: the householders who are 85 per cent of the utilities' clients are forced to pay more so the other 15 per cent can pay less. The Lifeline victory, like others, has a hundred fathers: here we shall examine the Lifeline struggle through the experience of one citizen organization, the Bay Area Citizens Action League of San Francisco.

Bay CAL was born out of Lifeline. Its organizers were veterans of the movements of the sixties who, like Wade Rathke of ACORN, had absorbed the basic lesson that an effort to get a better deal for an oppressed minority will arouse the fatal opposition of working and middle-class people who rightly consider themselves also among the losers, if they are left out of, or asked to pay for, what is being proposed. The organizers had seen utility rates, then increasing rapidly, as a unifying issue, and they wanted an approach to it that would bring them the support of the elderly. Tim Sampson, the stocky, bearded professor who was the head of Bay CAL, later recalled:

> We needed an issue that was going to be important in reaching [the elderly]. As we experimented with it, it was apparent that everyone was really responsive to the notion, particularly to the notion that Lifeline would be for everybody. Seniors and poor people were responsive to the idea that it was not another special program for them, not another "welfare program." Middle class consumers were very clear that it was something that would affect everyone. I think the one thing that is significant about Lifeline is that it constitutes what I would call an understandable positive alternative.

The Bay Area organizers put together a coalition that included labor unions, churches, environmentalists, consumer groups, and, for the elderly, the American Association of Retired Persons, whose efficacy we have earlier observed. It also attracted many other people who were upset about their escalating utility bills. This was in 1974. In the state elections of that year, the coalition was able to make utility prices an issue, and the new governor, Edmund G. Brown, Jr., appointed two Lifeline sympathizers to the state Public Utilities Commission, which under his predecessor, Ronald Reagan, had been a rubber stamp for rate increases. Lobbying was focused on the state legislature in Sacramento. On one occasion about a thousand people showed up to support a Lifeline bill. Sampson described how it went:

First, we had a major public rally at which we got the Assembly Speaker, [Leo] McCarthy, and a number of other legislators to come and pledge their support to our bill. We also showed off the depth of our coalition by having speakers from labor and the churches and environmental, consumer and senior groups that were supporting us as well as members of our own campaign organization. Then we broke up into small delegations and actually went and made a lobbying visit to each of the 120 members of the legislature. We did that with the advantage of a very careful and appropriate knowledge of how it's done. We had consulted with a number of lobbyists as to some of the pitfalls. Of the 120 we probably only directly saw maybe 30, but in each other office we saw someone whether it was a secretary or an aide and we said "we're going to get back to you, we want an agreement," and we had an accountability agreement and a fact sheet on the bill and some literature which showed that it was a national idea whose time had come. We got high marks on the orderly process in which we kicked off this bill. That was a really good combination of a traditional mass demonstration with the other kind of quiet meet and confer technical lobbying procedure which many of the public interest groups follow.

Bay CAL debated Pacific Gas & Electric, the utility company that serves northern California, at a series of hearings before the Public Utilities Commission. Interestingly, the company evidently had also learned the lesson of the sixties, for it tried to use the divisive strategy that Bay CAL had avoided. PG&E proposed that those too poor to pay its rates should get subsidized "utility stamps." This is the standard third-party maneuver that we saw earlier in property taxes and "employer-paid" contributions to health and pension plans. In this case the effect would have been to make all taxpayers pay more to subsidize the stamps, while leaving untouched the low rates for big users and increased rates for non-poor households. The supporters of Lifeline rejected the idea. At a PUC hearing, Bay CAL was able to bring out in public the corporate connections between PG&E and both its big clients and its suppliers of fuel. Under questioning, Shermer L. Sibley, PG&E's chairman of the board, testified that he belonged to the boards of General Motors and Del Monte, two of the biggest users who get low rates; other members of the PG&E board sit on the boards of some twenty other big users; Shell Oil, which sells natural gas to PG&E, has a director on the utility's board.

The campaign came to a successful head in 1975: the legislature voted the bill requiring the PUC to put Lifeline rates into effect in 1976; the governor signed it; the Public Utilities Commission put it into effect for PG&E customers in January 1976. The coalition that won Lifeline might not survive its victory. Although Bay CAL was casting around for other issues, both its mass support and its financing—from churches, foundations, and individual donations—were based on Lifeline. But whether or not it survived it had made its point: with organization and the right issue, the average person can fight back against the opposition of those who are screwing him despite the apathy of the two-party political monopoly.

Meanwhile, back on the East Coast, a Massachusetts group called Fair Share was seeking Lifeline rates for another utility, the telephone. Their goal was a minimum amount of service at a low price: thirty calls a month for $2.50, or sixty for $3.75. The issue was of a particular importance to invalids and the elderly who have to do most of their communicating by telephone. At this writing, the telephone Lifeline had not been won, but its proponents had managed in 1975 to hold a rate increase to less than half the amount the company requested, for a consumer saving of $50 million a year, and kept the monthly minimum at $4.50. They had also convinced the Department of Public Utilities to reject the company's lobbying expenses as a cost that it could pass on to the customer. In the case of electricity rates, which in Massachusetts had doubled in only two years, Fair Share was seeking a flat rate for everybody. Under the existing rate structure, big users paid 1.8 cents per kilowatt hour, households paid 4 cents and small businesses paid almost 6 cents. Fair Share collected enough signatures on a petition to force a 1976 referendum on the question of equalizing everyone's electricity rates at 3 cents per kilowatt hour. In the city of Boston, Fair Share won a limited Lifeline: the utilities commission exempted the first 384 kilowatt hours, which meant about 65 per cent of its customers, from its 1975 increase.

Massachusetts Fair Share, a kind of Yankee ACORN, is four years old, has staff members in a dozen cities and towns, and tries to organize people of middle income around a variety of issues. In 1975, for example, it lobbied in Washington to prevent the premature foreclosure of FHA-insured mortgages on eight hundred homes; the usual outcome of such foreclosures is that the owner loses his equity, the bank gets its money back to reloan at higher interest, and the FHA inherits the house which it will allow to deteriorate to the detriment of the neighborhood. In 1976 Fair Share was organizing support for an amendment to the state constitution that would permit a graduated state income tax with higher incomes paying at a higher rate. The existing tax imposes the same rate on all earned income, but in one respect was already fairer than the federal income tax: it taxed unearned income twice as heavily as income from work.

Not all the groups we have described will enjoy long lives. Some, like ACORN, have made a deliberate effort to ensure their survival; those that have not may soon vanish. It doesn't really matter, for their importance lies not in themselves but in the sense of possibility they can arouse. They have demonstrated to their participants that it is indeed possible to fight back and win measurable gains. In the political marketplace, these groups provide an alternative to the two-party monopoly, and they attract support because they deal in issues—utility pricing is an excellent example—that the monopoly had managed to keep off the market. As we shall see in the following chapter, the potential in issues that concern the average person has been glimpsed by a growing number of participants in state and local government.

10

Progressives in the States

His first week on the job, Herbert Denenberg refused to give Greater Philadelphia Blue Cross a $74 million rate increase. The rest is history. In a few months, Denenberg revolutionized the previously obscure post of state insurance commissioner and turned insurance into an attention-getting consumer issue.

Denenberg was one of the first state officials to grab a headline by some means other than proclaiming a crime crackdown. His legacy to state government is thriving. Far more important than the specifics of his battles with the insurance industry is the sense of possibility that he brought to state government. Since the days of the New Deal, liberals have either mistrusted or ridiculed state government; "states' rights" was no more than a code word for racism. The criticisms generally involved one of two themes—either those in state government were corrupt or they were reactionaries. And in some states they were both. Even when a governor briefly caught the attention of the national press, those serving under him were still considered to be mediocrities. (The press's taste in governors was always erratic; it's hard to believe that in the late 1950s "Soapy" Williams of Michigan, Robert Meyner of New Jersey, and Nelson Rockefeller were thought to be our leading governors.)

These days state government is becoming fashionable in a different way. The efforts of the Nixon administration to decentralize the Great Society have given governors control—sometimes reluctantly—over large portions of federal spending in their states. The press, taking its lead from David Broder of the Washington *Post*, discovered such governors as Reuben Askew of Florida, Daniel Evans of Washington, and Dale Bumpers (now a U. S. senator), of Arkansas. But it wasn't until Denenberg burst on the public scene in 1972 that anyone realized it was possible to be creative and become a household name in little-known state offices as well.

Denenberg's unsuccessful attempt to return to public office does not reflect a lasting eclipse in his career. After he lost a primary race for the U. S. Senate in 1974, Denenberg's appointment to the Pennsylvania Public Utilities Commission was blocked by state senators still bitter over his outspoken criticism of them while he was insurance commissioner. As a television and newspaper commentator in Philadelphia, Denenberg found another route to remain in a position of influence. The established route for ex-insurance commissioners is that fat job in the insurance industry as a reward for their non-critical posture while in office. Eventually, Denenberg realized that his rewards were not likely to come within the two-party monopoly. Consequently, he and other reformers who have followed him into hitherto obscure state and local offices haven't adopted the pat formulas of political success imprinted on our minds by two generations of mass media. An officeholder's potential depends less and less on his or her looks, youth, or ability to turn a catchy phrase. While many candidates still make waves in the selection process for precisely these reasons, there is also encouraging evidence of constituencies caring about issues and performance rather than image or party affiliation. The strategy and reward for the bulk of officeholders described in this chapter concerns effectiveness—one can be powerful in a key position, no matter how unglamorous it may seem.

The sneakiness of this procedure is not unacknowledged. The *Texas Observer,* in covering a convention of state and local reformers, refers to them as "the Sixties activists who have now wormed their way into elected or appointed offices." Sam Brown's race in 1974 for state treasurer of Colorado symbolizes this changed attitude. Brown, one of the leaders of the antiwar movement, shares a common background with many of the new congressional freshmen. But instead of asking the voters to send him to Washington, where only yesterday he challenged the power of the presidency before a world audience, Brown campaigned for a traditionally minor state post. In an interview with *The Village Voice* before his election, Brown made clear that he understood the difference between legislative and administrative power:

> I spent the last year studying the state budget and state laws, trying to see where power really lies in Colorado . . . and I finally hit on state treasurer. Here was an office that has been virtually ignored for years, yet the treasurer has incredible powers which, if wielded conscientiously, could benefit communities and people all over the state.

Brown's first months in office were rocky ones. His widely announced plan to create a public banking system in the state was jarred by the loss of his first proposal—to limit the size of banks—in the Colorado state senate. Brown lost his cool a bit over that, announcing in an interview that he would not "give the legislature a candid budget next year. I'm going to bury everything I can and fund as many programs as I can with soft dollars." Just exactly what he meant by that is not clear, but it didn't sound like the stuff which will bring us governmental reforms.

Fortunately, that approach changed, and by the end of his first year in office, Brown was beginning to live up to the publicity that surrounded his campaign. With some $125 million in state funds under his control and looking for a bank to call home, Brown set up unprecedented criteria for banks to meet in order to be eligible for these state funds. These criteria, dubbed "Brownie points" by the press, include willingness to make loans to small farm and small business ventures; loans to students, women, and minorities; and most importantly, loans for low cost housing in order to combat redlining (the practice of denying mortgages to entire neighborhoods).

With this reform, Colorado is on the way to having a banking system responsive to public needs. With victory, Brown's rhetoric reflected caution. "I am inclined to believe that state banks will be necessary," he told *Harper's Weekly*, "but I can't prove it, and I'm certainly not prepared to go out and argue with a bunch of people until the facts and figures are in better order."

Although still far from typical, Brown, like Denenberg, is not unique as a state officeholder. A conference in Madison, Wisconsin, in mid-1975, on radical innovations in state and local government, sponsored by the Institute for Policy Studies, drew an encouraging crowd of officeholding reformers. The trading of innovative ideas at that conference was to be followed up at regional meetings across the country. The "star" status awarded such reformers as Madison's Mayor Paul Soglin and Brown belied the grass roots nature of these meetings. In the southwest conference held in December 1975, participants paid their own way and were housed in vacant monks' cells (an appealing image of government reform— one that seems, as well, rather fitting for ex-novitiate Jerry Brown of California).

The accomplishments of some delegates were noteworthy. Judge Justin Ravitz of Detroit—the "Marxist judge" who was profiled in *Time* magazine when he was elected in 1974—had gone far to equalize justice in his court for the poor and rich. He instituted a twenty-four-hour court to speed up the arraignment process, thus enabling suspects of minor crimes to be released within twelve hours of their arrest. In the previous system, suspects would have to stay in jail overnight if arrested in the evening, or over the weekend if arrested on Friday night. Shortly after he got onto the bench, the prosecutor brought in a case of short-weight found in one of Detroit's leading supermarket chains. The defendant pleaded *nolo contendere* and the prosecutor, as a matter of course, had planned to drop the charges (it has always been easier to get prosecution for street crime than for corporate crime). Ravitz refused to go along with the prosecutor and insisted that the meat manager be indicted. The manager spent the next few days in prison, a happenstance billed in the conferee's notebook as a historical first in the area's white-collar-crime annals.

Three other examples stood out in this crowd: Richard Applebaum, a sociologist from the University of California at Santa Barbara, described how a local citizen group drove a development-minded consulting firm out of the Santa Barbara City Council. Alarmed at the firm's proposals, the group offered an alternative growth plan that included the pursuit of land-use measures that do not have a regressive impact on the poor and low-income people and the elimination of elite neighborhood parochialism. The growth plan offered by the citizen group also carried a lower price tag than the plan offered by the professional group. As their concerns became policy, Santa Barbara responded by initiating population impact and growth studies before allowing any new housing projects.

Houston Controller Leon Castillo, who calls himself the

city's "official gadfly," gained attention at first in the manner of Denenberg by naming a "Dirty Citizen of the Tax Week" as part of his self-described "guerrilla warfare" against tax abusers. After three years in office, however, his tactics have become more substantial. By casting a cold eye on exemptions for individuals—the department never had an assessor for individual taxes before—Castillo found that 30 per cent of Houston's dentists, for example, were not paying property taxes. Castillo's zeal totaled up to some $921 million extra added to the city's valuation, and that's $921 million less to be carried by the rest of the population.

In a more rural part of Texas, Judge José Angel Gutierrez is the highest elected official for the largely chicano Zavala County. One of the few locales where La Raza Unida is a dominating political force, Zavala has been locked in a fight with the local utilities that are using Zavala resources. Gutierrez, when dealing with the utilities, likens his county to an underdeveloped nation in danger of exploitation by outside forces. He has proposed, consequently, county control, by eminent domain, of the gas wells and pipelines in their jurisdiction. Adoption of such a policy by the local governments across the country would no doubt hasten the retirement and nervous breakdowns of utility officials—unless, of course, they invited the CIA in to protect American interests. Crystal City, in Zavala, unilaterally rolled back the gas rates this year to 1972 levels in the first skirmish of this war. A Texas court has ordered the city to pay the utility company back some $200,000 its move has cost, but, at this writing, the city and Zavala County are vowing not to pay without more control over the resources in their area.

These IPS conferences do not exhaust the track record of sixties reformers in state and local government. The proliferation of consumer affairs positions at both levels has attracted its share of attention. One of the first and best known, Bess Meyerson of New York City, doesn't exactly fit into the category of the people described above, but two newcomers to these positions are worthy of mention. New York and California are among those states who have made the consumer affairs department a cabinet-level position. These positions have been filled, interestingly enough, by two veterans of Nader's Raiders—John Esposito and Richard Spohn. Spohn moved over from the California Citizen Action Group to accept the post and was instrumental in the Lifeline victory in the state legislature described in the preceding chapter. Esposito has been supporting that peculiarly Naderesque notion of the RUCAG (see chapter 8), and seemed to have secured Governor Carey's support should the bill ever reach his desk.

Not all the good news involved recycled activists. Good administrators are appearing in the wolf's clothing of party politician, or in that thought-to-be-extinct shape of the citizen–public servant. One of the latter is Stanley Van Ness of New Jersey. Van Ness was appointed as the State Public Defender in 1969—an office created in the sixties to provide indigent defendants with legal counsel. While his work in that office has been impressive, it represents only a fraction of his duties. His other job is unique: Van Ness has worn two hats in the state government since assuming the newly created office of Public Advocate in 1974. New Jersey is the only state in the nation to have such an office, and its appearance is symptomatic. The notion of Public Defenders, a product of the sixties, reflects the concern of that era with individual rights of, for example, war resistors, civil rights workers, or drug users. That the seventies has brought the first Public Advocate into being is an indication of how priorities have changed between decades, for it is the nature of Van Ness's new office to go beyond individual rights to community rights.

Thus we find him involved in many of the issues described in earlier chapters.

The Public Advocate is free to pick his issues, like a private consumer group, within the limits of his resources. Van Ness's office has challenged the advertising bans on prescription drugs and the composition of state licensing boards in an effort to cut the middleman's profit in service industries. His Division of Public Interest Advocacy has filed suits in various land use issues. A suit to sustain rent control in inner-city areas, a class action on behalf of consumers allegedly bilked out of millions in an illegal mortgage scheme, a challenge to the composition of the state real estate commission, and a suit seeking public access to New Jersey's private beaches are a few of the targets selected in their first year. Van Ness's Division of Rate Counsel attempts to serve the purpose for which RUCAG was designed. By providing public representation in rate cases, this division influenced six major utility rate decisions in its first year of operation and saved utility consumers an estimated $63.7 million. The Atlantic City Electric Company—the very germ of Parker Brothers' Monopoly—got a stiff lesson in public interest finance when its $30.7 million rate package was siphoned down to $10.7 million as a result of the PA's involvement in the case. That cut of $20 million shows that when it's the consumers' game the price of landing on the utility need not be the classic four times the total of the dice. The Public Advocate also represents victims of child abuse, mental health patients, as described in chapter 4, and inmates up for parole.

While Van Ness's ombudsman role has drawn more attention than the rest of the New Jersey cabinet put together, he has had to watch his budget shrink to half its size and suffer massive reductions in staff and therefore capacity to act. Those who remain, however, point out with conspiratorial glee that they are being sued in various counties across the state for lack of services. Should they "lose," the state will be forced to provide additional manpower.

Los Angeles created in 1975 an institution as unique as New Jersey's Public Advocate: a public fraud unit, in the county district attorney's office, that prosecutes local anti-trust cases. The idea may seem exotic to those who, when they hear the words "antitrust," think only of mul-tinational monsters like Exxon and ITT, but in chapter 4, we saw that the attorney general of Ohio has been bring-ing antitrust actions against state-wide guild practices, and local government is if anything a more fertile field for anyone who chooses to plow into it. Contracting for municipal services, most notoriously garbage collec-tion and construction, has traditionally been rigged to preserve high prices to be passed on to the taxpayers. In their direct dealings with the public, local businesses create a variety of devices to prevent competition, devices that will never come to the attention of the federal anti-trust lawyers in Washington, occupied as they are in failing to control nation-wide monopolies. Examples are the first three cases taken on by the Los Angeles anti-trusters: a suburban garbage monopoly; a board of real-tors that kept out competitors unless they agreed to charge a standard fee, and two medical laboratories owned by physicians who steered all their patients to their labs and their higher prices. The first case to be suc-cessfully resolved was that of the doctors' labs: they agreed to give up ownership of the laboratories and to pay $435,000 in penalties and refunds. James Knapp, the director of the fraud unit, estimated that the public had been overcharged by $1 million in three or four years by the two labs alone—a figure that suggests there are many billions out there that could be recovered for the public if the Los Angeles antitrust operations were extended to all the nation's municipalities.

Another state official has resorted like Van Ness to outside forces in order to increase his effectiveness. James Stone, the young insurance commissioner of Massachusetts, pushed a bill through the state legislature ordering him to hire more actuaries in his department. Massachusetts now has more actuaries than any other state; without them it is nearly impossible to analyze insurance company practices. Stone is worthy of the Denenberg legacy if only because the insurance companies have no fewer than four higher court appeals and one temporary restraining order clipped to some of his rulings.

Plucked out of the Harvard junior faculty by Governor Dukakis, Stone quickly produced results. He realigned a Blue Cross/Blue Shield good- and bad-risk pooling system and effected a 15 per cent decrease in non-group good risk rates, while limiting the offsetting increase in the bad-risk pool to only 1 per cent. When auto insurers threatened en masse to leave the state in protest against a consumer-oriented rate adjustment proposed by Stone, he was able to stop them by pointing out they would be violating an antitrust statute. The auto insurers currently have him in court over this adjustment, but Stone managed one barb in the meantime. He put out a buyer's guide to basic auto insurance and required the auto insurers to mail it out at their expense. The pamphlet drew blood among the insurers with such lines as "Most of our drivers buy far more insurance than they really need . . . Remember, do not buy what you do not need." Stone calls the pamphlet his "Why you don't need to buy auto insurance" guide. He added a personal touch as well: "My own car is a 1972 Chevrolet Vega, garaged in Boston. On the charts below, I have compared my intended insurance purchases . . . with those that a more eager buyer might make. The price difference is dramatic." The response to the mailing has often taken the form of complaints from insurance agents writing to Stone about the stream of buyers demanding "the same insurance as the commissioner has."

But, for all this publicity, Stone is not a remodeled Denenberg. The pamphlet, in his eyes, is the least of his accomplishments. Most of his activity involves the direct pocketbook effect of his rulings rather than publicity. In this way, he is, perhaps, the "second generation" of state government reformers chronicled in this chapter. Denenberg put the issues in insurance in the headlines; however, the actual recouping of the vast sums of consumer money that disappears up the insurance chimney is still in its earliest stages, and this is the direction that Stone has taken. His latest three regulations—two of which are being challenged in court—illustrate this approach. He has ruled that insurance companies must pay for an annual audit by a CPA firm (in court), extend the pooling of inner-city fire insurance packages to include crime and liability insurance as well, and hire more minorities (in court). Attorney for the insurance industry is, by the way, James St. Clair, counsel to Richard M. Nixon in his last days as President.

It is not easy to be recognized for good deeds when you work in a Springfield, Albany, or Harrisburg. Still, an arbitrary glance at the states post by post reveals officials at the cabinet level who demonstrate that state government need not be a political backwater.

LIEUTENANT GOVERNOR: Martin Schreiber, Wisconsin

It is not known as the most demanding job in state government—somehow being one heartbeat from governor does not quicken the pulse—and from New York to California it has had its share of trouble in recent years. The nation's best-known lieutenant governor is Mary Anne Krupsak, but that is almost entirely because of her symbolic importance to the women's movement. Martin Schreiber of Wisconsin, whom we met in chapter 6, stands out for transforming his largely ceremonial office into something far more substantive. Two major programs in health care—an ombudsman for residents of nursing homes and a system of home-based care for shut-ins—have given him both a name and plenty to do. The one million dollars he has collected for these projects has mushroomed his staff from two to twenty-seven since his first election in 1970. Schreiber himself serves as the nursing home ombudsman, collecting complaints from inmates, relatives and staff. His work in this area has done as much as any of the gory exposés of recent years to alleviate the problems of nursing homes in his state, and he has been on the road testifying before state legislatures in an effort to get a federal ombudsman program off the ground.

SECRETARY OF STATE: Gloria Schaffer, Connecticut

In a state that has been kinder to women politicians than most, Gloria Schaffer has enjoyed the largest state-wide vote totals her last two times on the ballot. (She is, at this writing, trying to extend that appeal to her race for U. S. Senate.) It might be that Schaffer does so well at the ballot box as a result of her work in election reform. When the Connecticut state legislature passed an Irish stew of election reforms in 1974—a total of fifteen bills covering everything from justices of the peace to disclosure of campaign finances—Schaffer huddled with the state-wide candidates to make sense of this Watergate-inspired overkill. Eventually, her staff was instrumental in a recodification of these reforms in 1975, and Connecticut has one of the better systems of disclosure of contributions and financing of campaigns in the country. In Connecticut, voters can register practically on demand. Under Schaffer's reforms, any group of twenty-five or more can require a registrar to come to them—a boon to shut-ins, students, and workers. One can also take advantage of cross-town lines registration and register to vote at work to cast a ballot at home even if there are different jurisdictions involved.

ATTORNEY GENERAL: John Hill, Texas

Given the conservative political cast of the state, it would be easy to envision the Texas attorney general leading well-publicized campaigns against subversives, pornography or marijuana. Although formerly a highly successful Houston malpractice lawyer, Hill has departed from the narrow traditions of Texas government. His major accomplishment has been the passage and interpretation of the Texas Open Records Act, one of the broadest and most rigorously enforced freedom-of-information statutes in the country. The mandate that has opened up Texas state government began with the Sharpstown Bank scandals which swept Hill and Governor Dolph Briscoe into office in 1974.

Hill retains many ties to the John Connally wing of Texas politics, but he has not shied away from battles with Southwestern Bell and other utilities. He successfully blocked a telephone-rate increase, getting a ruling from the state supreme court in the process that the attorney general has the power to challenge all future changes in utility rates. Much of Hill's success is a result of the young, aggressive attorneys who were brought in to replace the patronage-heavy staff of his office. Their effectiveness might be measured by the experience of one—Bill Flanary. Flanary was investigating an oil-well-speculation scam when his car was firebombed—presumably by someone who doesn't appreciate governmental reform. (Flanary was uninjured.)

SUPERINTENDENT OF PUBLIC INSTRUCTION: Wilson Riles, California

Riles defeated archconservative Max Rafferty for administrator of California's vast school system. (It wasn't much of a campaign—a major Rafferty issue was that Riles, who is black, wasn't putting his picture on billboards or campaign literature.) As superintendent, Riles has been willing to tangle with the powerful teachers' unions. For example, he has made no secret of his belief that the practice of tenure should be curtailed. Riles once actually proposed abolition, but quickly backed down in face of union objections. Even so, they are not hard and fast against him—Riles was the first to include all the unions in policy-making councils. Riles has been a firm supporter of the California Supreme Court's *Serrano* decision, which ordered that disparities in funding between rich and poor school districts be eliminated. Serrano, however, has been sitting in the hopper for the five years since that decision.

Riles's office has been actively involved in the arguing of this continuing court case, in addition to sponsoring bills in both houses of the state legislature to implement the original decision. Riles's major accomplishment has been the development of an Early Childhood Education Program, serving about one third of the state's elementary school pupils below fourth grade. The goal of the program has been to reduce adult-child ratios in the classroom from 25:1 to 10:1 through the imaginative use of paraprofessionals and teacher aides. Although it is notoriously difficult to measure the success of educational programs, ECE seems to have been a significant factor in raising the test scores of those who participated.

TAX COMMISSIONER: Byron Dorgan, North Dakota

Byron Dorgan is the only elected tax commissioner in the nation, and as such he enjoys unique independence in the state government. Appointed to fill a vacancy in 1969, Dorgan unleashed a team of four auditors on the books of multistate corporations operating in North Dakota. They raised corporate tax revenues by 33 per cent—largely by discovering that corporations claimed in other states that they made their money in North Dakota and argued just the opposite in North Dakota itself. Dorgan's tax work has accounted for a 50 per cent increase in the number of returns filed in a state that is actually losing population. Dorgan has served two terms as chairman of the Multi-State Tax Commission, an organization of twenty-three member states and fifteen affiliates that co-operates on corporate auditing across state lines.

"You can always audit the businessman on Main Street," says Dorgan, "but up until now nobody has been auditing the giants." Dorgan's efforts have resulted in a number of lawsuits—an effective measure, it seems, of innovation—initiated by such giants as U. S. Steel, General Brands, Colgate-Palmolive, Procter & Gamble, as well as the Rock Sioux Indian Tribe.

CORRECTIONS COMMISSIONER: Kenneth Schoen, Minnesota

A major function of state government is to run prison systems. During an era when crime is a major social issue, a corrections commissioner could win easy headlines with a policy of "getting tough" with prisoners. Kenneth Schoen is not this kind of prison administrator. He has begun an intelligent program of de-emphasizing incarceration. Under Schoen, Minnesota's prison population has decreased significantly, and the state's maximum security prison will close in 1977. (Dangerous prisoners will be housed in maximum-security facilities in other prisons.)

Among the reforms which Schoen guided through the state legislature were a system of cost incentives to encourage local governments to place offenders in rehabilitation programs rather than in prisons, parole arrangements which take much of the arbitrariness out of the system, and pretrial rehabilitation programs for first offenders.

The Minnesota Restitution Center also characterizes the state's attitude toward crime. Dealing with property-crime offenders only, the center provides jobs for the criminals in order for them to pay back the victims of their actions. The participants in this program regularly meet with the victims of their crime. Like the night prosecutor described in chapter 2, the Restitution Center is one of those rare efforts designed to have the law serve the victims of crime rather than just the state. This return to the original principle of compensating the victim has had a remarkable effect on the criminals involved. The recidivism rate cited by Center Director Robert Mowatt is 30 per cent, whereas the national average is 70 per cent. "The guy has to deal specifically with a human being involved in his crime. At least once a month he has to confront the reality that he has ripped somebody off," says Mowatt. "On the other side, the victim gets a more realistic picture of who commits crime. Victims get to see that these are guys who haven't been able to solve personal problems." The program is being copied in Iowa and Georgia, and several other states are experimenting with it.

AGRICULTURE SECRETARY: Jim McHale, Pennsylvania

McHale is no longer in office, a victim, like Denenberg, of the Pennsylvania state senate in a confirmation battle. His career in office was characterized by acrimony, with such notables as Earl Butz and the National Farm Bureau lined up against him and the Food Action Campaign of Fred Harris and Jim Hightower solidly behind him. McHale was one of the few agriculture secretaries whose sympathies were with the small farmer instead of the agribusiness conglomerates.

McHale tried to establish a system of small farmer co-ops that would work directly with inner-city buyers, a project that never really got off the ground in his own

tenure, but which may expand the one small farmer co-op near Harrisburg currently operating. With a flair characteristic of his cohort Denenberg, McHale initiated an "anti-inflation" garden program by distributing vegetable seeds and renting out state-owned lands for cultivation. His most tangible success came in providing rural Pennsylvanians with transportation to medical facilities through the use of already existing but underused transportation programs. McHale was also the main administrator involved in providing relief for victims of the state's debilitating floods in 1974.

Most of all, McHale is remembered for his feistiness in taking on the big agricultural combines, creating havoc, for instance, when he tried to challenge the use of state land by colleges actively spreading the agribusiness gospel. McHale, along with other state officials like Vermont Health Commissioner Tony Robbins and Massachusetts' Transportation Commissioner Fred Salvucci, provided delightful copy for newspapers if not increments of success at the issues they attack. Robbins, for example, dueled Yankee Electric to a standstill over emissions from their nuclear power plant. (He is the only health commissioner in the country with the power to monitor nuclear power plants.) Salvucci outlined an antihighway, inner-city-oriented transit policy that was hailed in public interest circles. By standing up to an industrial enemy, Robbins, Salvucci, McHale, and others like them have earned the title of defender of the average man. They are indicative of the shift in strategy from the sixties to the seventies—the latter focusing their efforts on power rather than protest, new laws rather than exposés. Since many of these offices are non-partisan, their accomplishments chip away at the two-party political monopoly as well.

There is one office unmentioned so far that is by no means non-partisan—the governor. When it has attracted

attention of late, the issue has been government involvement, or spending. Handled with such conspicuous thrift by Jerry Brown in California or Michael Dukakis in Massachusetts, government spending blossomed into a major issue in 1976. The jury is still out on their administrations, with confused early returns alternately hailing them as the wave of the future or condemning them as pale photocopies of Ronald Reagan. The evidence is mounting, however, that government thrift might have value far beyond the immediate effect of reducing waste and frills. Reducing government's role means different things to different people. For industry, it means fewer safety regulations and less effort to prevent monopoly. For others, however, the meaning could be almost insidiously progressive. Consider that eliminating government also means, for a Jerry Brown, eliminating state income taxes for individuals under $5,000 and for couples under $10,000. Beneath the labels of austerity and attacks on pointy-headed bureaucrats—if that's what is bothering you about the Jerry Browns—there is that effect of progressive tax reform.

Eliminating government also takes on different meanings in different economic contexts. In times of prosperity, it has overtones of benign indifference, and it has been often criticized within this context. On the contrary, this movement presents itself in a time of recession, and the thrift of state governments is, after all, a response to the economic climate. Cutbacks in hard times reflect, on one hand, a desire to do away with dead weight that affects everybody. Not unrelated to that is the opportunity to equalize the economic status of those citizens over which the state has the most direct control. In this light, Brown's proposal to put state workers on a flat dollar-salary-increase schedule rather than the top-heavy percentage schedule currently in use represents a desire to capitalize on popular sentiment in order to bring about progressive wage reform. Under the percentage system, a worker earning $20,000 gets twice as much at raise time as one earning $10,000, and the increases compound themselves over time in favor of the higher-paid workers. On a facetious level, one can describe this reform as part of the effort to streamline government—it means, after all, less paperwork—but taken as part of Brown's platform, it is further evidence of the ease with which significant reforms can be instituted within a philosophy of austerity.

What Brown offers is in line with the observation that some businesses are better off without restrictive entry rules, and that some people are better off without expert advice. The marketplace effect of these ideas is one of more competition and more savings. Similarly, less government, while producing the immediate effect of saving tax dollars, will also challenge the marketplace monopoly of the two-party system. Already in California, one sees that Lifeline utility rates were implemented not at the urging of the Democratic caucus in Sacramento, but as a result of the efforts of the Bay Area Citizen's Action League and others outside the two-party system. The void in two-party control of the political process being set up by Brown is there to be filled by forces outside that system. Essentially, there will be more opportunities for the citizen to take government in his own hands, and there will be more competition in the political marketplace—a situation from which the average man can only stand to gain.

11

Action Line

THE PRESS, LIKE SO many among us, has grown more skeptical of our institutions in recent years. In its most noted form, that skepticism has been expressed in the new willingness of the larger newspapers to disobey the wishes of government—the publication of the Pentagon papers supplied by Daniel Ellsberg is an example. But the press (as used here, the term includes radio and television, in order to avoid the word "media") has shown little interest in providing better news coverage of the mundane daily screwings of the average citizen by, say, the health industry or a local bureaucracy. There is, however, one exception: the Action Lines that now appear in more than 350 newspapers and a few radio and television stations. For all its flaws, and they are multiple, Action Line is in many respects the most important new contribution journalism is making to the defense of the average person.

Action Line presents itself as the champion of the little guy. The Washington *Star-News* announces, for example, that "Action Line serves readers by getting answers, solving problems and cutting red tape." Here is a day in the life of that Action Line: C.W.S. complained about a real estate promotion of land in Florida, not, as you might expect, because his lot was half a mile out to sea, but because his promised dinner passes hadn't shown up—Action Line reported that "you should have your free dinner passes by now"; M.A.E. wanted some counseling—Action Line said to "start with the Mental Health Association of . . ."; M.O. wanted all his money back on a deposit he had put down on an apartment—Action Line told him he was lucky to get back as much as he did; G.B. couldn't pry his check out of the Veterans Administration—Action Line reported that "your August and September payments have been authorized and you should receive them within a week. No explanation was given for the delay."

Not a bad day, and, in fact, better than most days at most Action Lines. Although Action Line comes on as dedicated and all-powerful when it pries a check out of a bureaucracy or makes the store refund your payment on that chair that collapsed the first time you sat in it, much of these columns are occupied with fluff and trivia chosen to satisfy curiosity rather than need. Action Line now seems to be getting those late-night barroom calls that usually begin with: "We've got a bet going down here about whether . . ." The too frequent result is items like (in the Los Angeles *Herald-Examiner*): "Can you please tell me when Irving Berlin wrote 'God Bless America' for Kate Smith and when did she first record it? We should adopt this song as our national anthem, it really sends chills up my spine."

This love of the cute item is explained in trade publications like *Editor and Publisher* in which articles on Action Lines list the cases the papers most fondly remember. Here are some of the highlights of the Detroit *Free Press*'s crusades (and it's one of the better columns):

> Action Line's accomplishments have been both plentiful and unique. It has campaigned successfully on behalf of a woman reader who complained that D-cup bras unfairly cost more than smaller sizes; defeated a braggart bass fiddler who claimed he was the fastest-plucker in town by

arranging a contest with someone still faster; provided the proverbial two front teeth for Christmas for a boy who really needed them.

Moreover, the requests for hard-to-find items—"Where can I find a pink llama-skin coat?"—often amount to little more than plugs for local businesses. And in fact, many of these questions are actually planted by friends of a merchant seeking free advertising.

Arthur Levine, in his article on Action Lines in the April 1975 issue of *The Washington Monthly*, on which much of this chapter is based, described the limitations in both capacity and will that he found in the three columns in the Baltimore-Washington area—the Washington *Star-News*, the Baltimore *News-American*, and the Baltimore *Evening Sun*. At these afternoon papers, the Action Line consists of an editor plus clerical help who work from recorded telephone calls and letters. In addition, the *Star* has three staff reporters at work on the column. The papers all seemed passive about their work: they refused to print offenders' names and they were all too eager to accept official promises or excuses.

The two Baltimore papers simply forward their readers' complaints to the agency or business in question and ask the accused to respond. They usually get some kind of answer—the *Evening Sun* claims a 70 per cent "effective response rate." But that figure apparently includes cases where the target of the complaint simply says he can't do anything. The *Star* won't even make that much effort, although it occasionally sends batches of complaints to agencies and department stores, casually followed up by a phone call. "We get a good response rate," editor Dan Poole told Levine. "We get a complaint put at the top of the pile, although it probably would have been taken care of anyway."

This kind of Action Line tends to enter into a tacit alliance with the agencies it is supposed to be fighting. One official observed about the Action Line that simply forwards complaints without follow-up: "The public thinks the Action Line goes to bat for them, shakes people up, exposes them. It doesn't work that way. The Action Line doesn't make us look too bad and we supply them with material to fill their columns."

The clearest indication that many papers never intend to act on the vast majority of complaints is their use of tape-recording systems to handle complaints over the telephone. This device, which nearly one third of the Action Line papers now use, generates such a volume of complaints that all attempts to select the most serious cases are overwhelmed. The cynicism of the arrangement is shown by the Chicago *Daily News,* which several years back decided to erase the recordings of phone calls it didn't consider interesting. For all the good taped complaints do, other papers might as well follow the example of the *Daily News.*

At the *Evening Sun* in Baltimore, Levine found a sense of dreary routine in the office of Direct Line editor David Woods. A former PR man, he spent most of his time at his desk, reading through letters and marking them for referral. At times he would pick up a slip of gray paper with an inarticulate phone message typed on it and say, "Here's another! People are really stupid." A secretary wearing earphones typed up the litany of troubles coming off the tape recorder. The paper received an average of 150 queries a day. A few were put aside to be handled by phone, but most were routinely mailed out to the offending businesses. Woods was particularly proud because he had managed to fulfill a dying Briton's request to find the man's old World War II chum from Baltimore. "It's very gratifying," Woods said.

Like other Action Line editors around the country, Woods had to be selective about what he published. Near his desk there was a pile of corporate and government responses to the *Evening Sun*'s routine inquiries. They would not be followed up, except for a few of the publishable items, because of time and staff limitations. One letter, from a puzzled welfare lady seeking to sublease a friend's apartment in a housing project, was answered by a housing official who outlined all the reasons why he could not satisfy her request. Woods told Levine, "I think I'll use that in the column. . . . At least the guy explained why he couldn't do it." Other letters in the pile asked questions about sales tax, faulty tires, Social Security insurance, and excise taxes. Many of the official replies did not resolve the original complaint, but were likely to be chalked up as part of the "effective action response."

The *Sun*'s Direct Line refused to print company names. Time after time, a reader had to guess about an item like this: "Last July, I purchased a bean-bag chair from a Washington department store for delivery to my son in Baltimore. I paid $35 and have my canceled check, but my son never received the chair. I've tried to resolve the matter both by telephone and by letter but without success. Can you help me get my money refunded?" The *Evening Sun* replied, "A note signed by J. Young stated that 'a check for $36.19 was issued in full refund on payment of the bean-bag chair which was never delivered.'" As Levine observed, the readers might have had a few more questions about this correspondence: What department store takes from July to February (when the column appeared) to acknowledge the complaint? Why didn't phone calls and letters work? Why didn't the company deliver the chair in the first place?

The *Evening Sun* was far from alone in its timidity. According to a 1973 survey of Action Lines by David Beal, now with the Milwaukee *Journal*, fewer than half the columns regularly named names. The reason is obvious. As the Baltimore *News-American*'s Jon Stewart explained to Levine, "We have to survive as a business. We are more sensitive about advertisers, because they put food in our mouths and money in our pockets." There are several variations to the no-name policy. Even the most craven Action Line will run the name if the company is declared bankrupt or is indicted for fraud. Charles Walsh, a former Action Line editor in Connecticut, said: "It was okay to attack small merchants, but we didn't name department stores, because they were big advertisers." Beal found ten papers that named only out-of-town or out-of-state firms. At the Sacramento *Bee*, Action Line reporters tried to outmaneuver their editors' no-name policy in the manner of foreign correspondents trying to fool censors. One column discussed calling a credit card company and drawing "a blanche," while another handled a subscription complaint by calling "the famed men's magazine and talking to a bunny there."

What kind of clout the no-names papers are forsaking can be seen in the case of an Action Line on a Rochester newspaper, the *Democrat and Chronicle*. Until 1972 the column was run by Jim Blakely, who made it a powerful consumer advocate. The willingness to print names was the key to its success. The staff consisted of Blakely and one secretary; later he got an assistant. Blakely viewed the column as a "court of last resort," so he used a screening process which allowed him to handle the most serious complaints. From an average of fifty letters a day (he didn't accept telephone complaints), he selected those that had made "reasonable attempts to solve the problem." Trivial questions were dropped, and he ignored those that could be answered by a trip to the public library.

Blakely would repeatedly publish the names of companies and agencies that received complaints—until they became more responsive. "After beating the hell out of

Social Security for a while," he said, "we didn't have to bother. They became co-operative." He would also print the names of stores that "told us to mind our own business." He noted, "It was our way of telling the community that a certain store wasn't interested in you, the consumer." Nor did the column back away from occasionally naming doctors or lawyers who were screwing the public —a move that was, and is, almost unknown among Action Line columns. Most refer those kinds of complaints to the local toothless bar association or medical society, and they are quickly forgotten. Blakely also referred cases to the medical society—but followed up to see what kind of action was taken. As a result of the column, one doctor was expelled from the local medical society. With lawyers, Blakely simply went over the head of the bar association to an appellate court judge with disciplinary powers —one lawyer ended up reimbursing a couple for tax penalties caused by his own laziness. The column also served to strengthen the local consumer movement, including the usually weak Better Business Bureau. In this case, the bureau co-operated with the column, and Blakely took to printing the names of businesses that didn't satisfactorily reply to bureau inquiries within thirty days.

Its willingness to name names also enabled the column to put heat on slow-moving government bureaucrats. Blakely remembered one Albany official who simply refused to send out state college scholarship money due Rochester residents. If he didn't respond, Blakely promised to run his name every day in the paper until he changed his mind, coupled with daily telegrams to the governor. "He became co-operative," Blakely said.

A persistent Action Line column can have a dramatic effect on services in its area. Blakely cited the case of a national insurance company that was the subject of frequent complaints to his column because of poor service to policyholders. "We just kept running the complaints until none of their insurance salesmen in a nine-county area was able to make a sale. People refused to deal with them. Finally the executives from the national office came down to straighten things out."

Blakely said that he received no managerial or advertising pressure, and that the publishers and editors were pleased with the column. "In three-and-a-half years, we didn't get one lawsuit. . . . The smart businessmen in town saw it as a good check on their customer relations department."

The excuse given for almost any flaw in an Action Line is the staggering volume of complaints, which is, in fact, a serious problem. The *Star* received a thousand complaints a week. The bulk of complaints tends to be similar: delayed government agency benefits, unreturned refunds, faulty repairs, mail-order fraud, and municipal services, like road repairs or garbage collection. The editors feel they must be selective; the complaint against them is that they make the wrong choices. Overly concerned about "reader interest," the columns print a surfeit of light, fluffy items to the exclusion of the "duller" items which may be of more genuine concern to readers—in fact, the Beal survey demonstrated that columns that stress problem solving are more popular with readers and, not surprisingly, solve more problems. The result of printing fluff is that the serious but unpublished complaints are simply ignored. A recent study by Berkeley anthropologist Laura Nader indicated that over half the columns don't try to solve problems unlikely to be published, and those that do rarely go beyond routine referrals to the complained-against company or agency. Many papers contain a disclaimer similar to this one printed in the Philadelphia *Inquirer:* "Action Line editors consider every request you send us. We publish the most interesting and helpful answers. We regret that we cannot answer, or even acknowledge, individual requests."

The first broadcast help service, Call for Action, started in 1963 by New York's radio station WMCA, is an exception to most of the rules. By 1976, Call for Action was a national organization with help services at forty-two stations, all based on the WMCA model. It operates entirely on volunteer help, and, according to Ellen Straus, its founder, accepts only as many calls as it can follow up. The service costs a fair amount—in WMCA's case, $21,000 a year—and it provides nothing to fill the station's air time; none of the cases is reported. All that is broadcast is a daily announcement that the service is available.

With a few exceptions like WMCA, stations and newspapers make little or no use of volunteer investigators and researchers. Most of the legwork for the Action Line column can be done by hard-working people capable of learning two basic reportorial skills, asking questions and checking facts. And most communities of any size have dozens of law and journalism students eager to put their talents to work. The addition of volunteers would enable Action Lines to go beyond referrals to become day-to-day ombudsmen, while giving the students invaluable experience. Most editors, however, prefer the old ways, content to rely solely on their own reporters, while complaining about understaffing.

The potential, both in accomplishment and the need for more resources, can be seen in an Action Line that is not restricted to the habits and means of the press. The Consumer Help Center of New York City is jointly operated by New York University Law School and Channel 13, the local public television station. It depends for its funding on foundations and donations, and for its manpower on volunteers, including NYU law students, all of whom are trained and supervised by members of the law school faculty. (A similar joint operation in Washington is run by WRC-TV and George Washington University Law School.)

The Consumer Help Center handles all the complaints it accepts. Unlike most Action Lines, it doesn't refer without follow-up, and, of course, it doesn't tape phone calls only to erase them if they bore the listener. Its volume of business, five thousand a year as of early 1976, is small compared to the mail that comes to the larger Action Lines, but probably compares favorably to the numbers that those Action Lines actually try to resolve. Most of the Consumer Help caseload is the usual consumer fare—credit problems, no refund, faulty products, late delivery —but it accepts complaints against government and health institutions, and often finds itself arranging needed social services rather than answering a specific gripe. Sometimes just an explanation of the person's rights will enable the complainant to carry the case on by himself. Often the center has to intervene, and when it does, according to its annual report,

> Intervention is successful in resolving seven disputes out of ten. Sometimes just the introduction of a third party into the dispute does the trick. Sometimes there has been a real misunderstanding, and a neutral mediator can cut through this to hasten a settlement. More often, when intervention succeeds, it is a combination of persuasion and an explication of the consumer's legal rights to the vendor, coupled with the undoubted weight of the interviewer's identification with both a law school and a TV station.

If intervention fails, the center may explain to the complaining person how to bring a case in small claims, and the center itself has brought some suits where it felt a worthwhile precedent could be established. Overall, the center claims that 64 per cent of its cases are resolved to the consumer's satisfaction. Interestingly, the consumers' satisfaction with the center's *performance* runs much higher—90 per cent—than their own winnings. As Beatrice Frank, the center's associate director, sees it, a lot of people out there are satisfied just to have someone explain the situation to them, even if they have a no-win case.

The center's clientele is the average man or, about two thirds of the time, the average woman. Fully three quarters of those who call earn between six thousand and fifteen thousand dollars a year; about half are workers wearing blue or white collars, and almost 40 per cent are housewives. A surprising 47 per cent are between twenty-one and thirty years old. Those in the greatest need, the poor below six thousand dollars, provide fewer than one in ten complaints. This may reflect the isolation of the poor, or just the nature of the audience for Channel 13, which is how most New Yorkers hear about the center.

The center can claim to have had some impact on the system as well as solving individual cases. When it received hundreds of complaints from victims of pyramid sales swindles that were then rampant in the city, the center forwarded the names to the State Consumer Protection Board, which then supplied them to their representatives in the state legislature—the result was passage of a bill outlawing pyramid sales schemes. (The scam works like this: you are offered an "opportunity" to buy a sales franchise in which you will recoup and profit by selling many more franchises to other people. It's a sophisticated variant on the old pyramid chain letter, and collapses for the same reason: there aren't enough people in the world to keep it going.) Beatrice Frank also felt that the Abraham & Straus department store had become "more co-operative" after the center identified it as its leading source of complaints. Some of the cases brought by the center may change aspects of consumer law, and the center was among those pushing for the improvements in small claims which we reported on in chapter 2.

The Channel 13 programs produced by the center in 1976 went beyond answering complaints to explain how institutions—small claims, the health services system—work and how to use them.

The Consumer Help Center limits its intake of cases by rationing the number of hours its telephones are open. With unlimited capacity, Beatrice Frank says, the center could easily get 100,000 cases a year—twenty times its present caseload. Frank feels the need for its services, already far greater than its capacity, will only increase as the city reduces its services to its people. Already in 1974, its second year, the center was getting "far more serious" complaints than the year before—many more cases dealt with welfare, Social Security, housing, and health-related problems. Much the same point was made to Arthur Levine by Reporter Lea Thompson of Washington's WRC-TV "Contact 4" program: "My God, we're filling such a void. Consumers are pretty desperate."

Action Lines do not begin to meet the need out there, and much of what most of them do is timid or token or trivial. They seldom force institutions to behave differently except in the tiny handful of cases Action Line is reporting, and that is because the press doesn't see the potential in those messages cascading in to Action Line: a fertile source of leads for news stories about how institutions fail the people. Still, between the news columns (and air time) devoted to governmental pronouncements and the advertising columns devoted to commercial pronouncements, there is, in Action Line, a small section that reports on the daily problems of the average man, and sometimes even helps him fight back. And that's a lot better than nothing.

12

Good News in Hard Times

IN EARLIER CHAPTERS we have described what amounts to a set of promising beginnings. Today those beginnings have had little impact, but tomorrow, if what is now under way is not aborted, the outcome will be a great improvement in the circumstances of the average person.

The professional monopolies are on the verge of breaking up. The first effects are now being felt in legal services, the subject of the historic Goldfarb decision and the other trends described in chapter 2. Similarly, the efforts by the Federal Trade Commission and others to bring price competition to such guild-controlled markets as eyeglasses and prescription drugs are in their earliest stages. What today has affected only a minority of our encounters with professional guilds can tomorrow spell an end to what Jethro Lieberman called the "tyranny of the experts." On one level this means getting a fair price when we go to buy drugs or a divorce. In a less measurable way it means getting on a more equal footing with the experts, for their tyranny has been as much over our minds as over our pocketbooks. We can see the beginnings of this new equality, even in the case of the two most awesome professions, in the growth of do-it-yourself law and the increased willingness of the public to talk back to the doctor and demand a second opinion before submitting to the surgeon's knife. In both these examples, people are not just saving money: they are getting a firmer grip on their own destinies.

Even government has begun, occasionally, reluctantly, and under great pressure, to screw the public somewhat less—while still trying, whenever we're not watching, to do the contrary. One example from 1976 is the abolition of "fair trade" laws, which had allowed manufacturers to set retail prices on their products, this preventing price competition. When Congress voted to repeal the fair trade laws remaining in twenty-one states, the decision was worth an estimated $2 billion a year to consumers.

It may seem hard to believe, especially as April 15 rolls around, but the public has even won some tax battles. The 1975 federal tax act, continued in its essentials in 1976, was the fairest in a generation, though admittedly that wasn't saying much. Ever since 1954 successive federal tax acts had cut taxes on the income of the wealthy, either openly by reducing their rates or covertly by drilling them new loopholes, and thus had left the person whose income was earned by work carrying an ever-larger share of the burden. The 1975 act took a couple of small steps toward fairer taxation. One was the thirty-five-dollar credit (instead of a deduction) for each personal exemption: this benefited the typical family of four earning up to about $20,000, whereas the deduction favored those of upper income. The earned-income credit provided a cash rebate of up to $400 for low-income working families: a limited form of the negative income tax discussed in the early 1970s. These benefits, if small, were direct. Indirectly, the working taxpayer benefited from Congress' closing of one of the oil industry's loopholes, the depletion allowance; if oil pays more, the rest of us will pay less. Add to that the new loopholes that were *not* drilled, a benefit no less real for being negative, and though it still does not total very much, it is the first time the trend has gone our way. As in the case of the professional monopolies, what has happened in the income tax is more important for its potential than for what has so far been delivered.

It wasn't government's idea. The Administration actively opposed making the income tax fairer, and Congress, left to its own devices, would doubtless have continued to produce its annual crop of special-interest loopholes through which the incomes of the wealthy could escape taxation. What happened is that a small number of people have succeeded in putting tax reform on the political agenda. Earlier we mentioned the two Washington-based organizations: the Tax Reform Research Group and Tax Analysts and Advocates. Through their publications, *People and Taxes* and *Tax Notes*, they have created a constituency that understands the basics of the tax system. Though their combined circulation is small, their readers include reporters who pass on what they have learned to a much wider audience; the coverage of tax news is much improved in recent years. Outside Washington, the local tax reform groups have created informed grass-roots pressure; some have concentrated their efforts in the home districts of members of the House Ways and Means Committee, where tax legislation originates. John Gardner's Common Cause lobbied through measures opening up to public view the procedures that lead to a tax bill. Because loopholes can no longer be drilled in the dark, Common Cause and other tax reformers were able to defeat efforts to gain tax privileges—in 1975 it was for the cigar and beer industries —of the kind that used to slide silently through the Congress.

By contrast, the other monstrous federal screwing of people who work, the payroll tax by which Social Security is financed, has yet to come under serious attack. Those who might be expected to be its leading critics, the unions, seem fearful that an attack on the payroll tax would undermine the security of their members' retirement income. The public is largely unaware that much or all of the so-called "employer's share" of the tax is ultimately paid by themselves in the form of lower wages, making the tax up to twice as heavy as it appears to be. Nor is the issue easy to dramatize: although the payroll tax is even more unfair to working people than the income tax, it does not have any spectacular individual beneficiaries: no Rockefellers or Reagans escaping taxation on large incomes. The payroll tax is just rising over the horizon as people like Samantha Senger, formerly of the Tax Reform Research Group and now at the Senate Finance Committee, are explaining its evils to what is still a small audience. As an issue, it is roughly where income tax reform was in, say, 1970, two years after Stanley Surrey first published the total cost of tax loopholes. But, since the pressures described in chapter 6 will inevitably push it upward, the payroll tax seems certain to become a primary target of tax reform.

The pressures of the market have even caused substantial change in that most torpid of industries—education. Only yesterday college was one of the fastest-growing industries in the nation. New campuses sprouted everywhere, almost supplanting highways as a source of political and contractor boondoggle. If you wanted a well-paid job, you had to go to college: it was touted as the best of investments. What happened to you during those four years didn't particularly matter. With an ever-increasing clientele, the colleges had no reason to be concerned about the quality of the product. So in the main the experience consisted of passively accepting the thin gruel dished out by bored professors thinking about their next research projects.

All this was said in the growth years, but it had no impact until the market spoke with its particular authority. Suddenly the value of a college degree shrank: in only five years, from 1969 to 1974, the return on investment in going to college dropped from 11–12 per cent to 7–8 per cent. During those same years, the advantage in earnings of college over high school graduates fell from 53 to 40 per cent. Now college degrees were in surplus, and an increasing number of graduates were either unemployed or making do with something less than a "college-level" job. In one exotic example of the trend, a Sarah Lawrence graduate who was going back to work advertised for a daytime babysitter. The first applicant she got was another Sarah Lawrence graduate. So, a few hours later, was the second applicant, and this one also had a master's degree. With the value of the degree in eclipse, the percentage of people of college age actually in college also began to drop. One gloomy 1975 forecast held that one in ten colleges would have to close or merge within five years.

The go-go years were over, and now the colleges had to try to lure customers instead of simply conscripting them out of high school. The happy result is much greater freedom, and sometimes lower costs, for the person who wants to learn something. The conventional four full-time years in the classroom from age eighteen to twenty-two is no longer the only way. Colleges now sought out those they had previously avoided: older and part-time and offbeat students. By 1976, 10 per cent of college students were over thirty-five. In one Sunday New York *Times*, the first three education ads were for "weekend colleges" for part-timers; "Our Great Idea," one college called it. In a 1976 report to the Ford Foundation, Ronald Gross listed symptoms of the growth of what he called "open learning." Among them were the University Without Walls, with centers at twenty-seven colleges, through which off-campus students can earn degrees by independent study, and the University of Mid-America, a four-state effort to use television to take education off campus; students can talk to instructors on a toll-free line and visit drop-in centers where tutors and learning materials are available. Also notable was the growth of work-study programs, the most familiar of which is Antioch College, from 50 in 1962 to almost 1,000 in 1976: these programs are one way to break the rigid separation between the worlds of work and learning. In these and other ways, the pressures of the market were forcing the education industry to give the average man a better and more varied diet.

When we look back over the good news reported in earlier chapters, we see a remarkable variation in what has been accomplished in one state, sometimes one town, and another. To define the potential for good in the present situation let us ask ourselves how much the public would benefit if what is available somewhere were available everywhere:

Van Nuys, a suburb of Los Angeles, is the birthplace of the legal clinic, which delivers legal services at far below the standard cost, and is also the headquarters of the Wave Project, which helps you divorce yourself for seventy-five dollars. Suppose that legal clinics and Waves existed everywhere outside Van Nuys. Further suppose that someone made Waves for other legal services: probate and real estate are logical candidates.

Wisconsin and *Minnesota* permit and encourage do-it-yourself probate.

New York City provides a growing number of people

the opportunity, paid by health insurance, to get a second opinion before submitting to surgery.

Three states—*New York, Connecticut,* and *Massachusetts*—allow savings banks to sell life insurance, and in *Wisconsin* the state itself sells life insurance. Both are substantially less expensive than the comparable insurance available in the other forty-six states. Some states have no-fault auto insurance, some don't; some permit low-cost group insurance, others do not.

Connecticut assesses property three times as accurately as North Dakota. In *Manchester,* New Hampshire, and *Louisville,* Kentucky, the average error in the assessment of single-family homes is less than 10 per cent, while in Philadelphia it is more than 40 per cent, and in Trenton, more than 50 per cent. *Southfield,* Michigan, has shifted some of the property tax off improvements onto the land. The twin cities of Minnesota, *Minneapolis and St. Paul,* and their neighbors share the benefits tax of industrial and commercial growth.

California has Lifeline utility rates for the entire state.

These examples plucked from preceding chapters should be enough to make the point. Conditions vary widely across the country, and if the average person had access to the best available somewhere, the savings to the public would be measured in tens of billions of dollars; the savings in self-respect cannot be counted in currency but would amount to at least as much.

But is it possible? Farmers know that what grows in one field may not grow in the next, and the same might be true of the plantings we have described. But in those places ranging from Van Nuys to New York there are no peculiar local conditions that would lead us to conclude that what happened there could not happen elsewhere. In each case a group of people, often small in number, sometimes even a lone individual, decided to give change a try, and succeeded. Doubtless a historian could find the bleaching bones of a dozen failures for each success, and yet the number that have won out in recent years suggests the great opportunities waiting to be realized.

The leadership that can realize those opportunities is already on the scene. Though varied in their origins and the issues they espouse, the present generation of political activists has shown itself increasingly sophisticated in devising ways to change the economic system for the benefit of the average man. They have absorbed the lessons implicit in the omissions and failures of the recent past, and, whatever their ideological backgrounds, we find them now devoting themselves to issues that can bring together rather than divide the great majority that are losers in the present economic system.

The consumer protection movement has evolved from a narrow concern with individual products to challenging the institutions that put out those products. Both Consumers Union and Ralph Nader, for example, have shifted their focus from cars to monopolies. Consumers Union has for many years been testing products, and more recently services, and publishing the results in *Consumer Reports*. But anyone who does that must eventually see that some kinds of services and information are denied to the consumer by monopoly rules. So Consumers Union, which first evaluated the life insurance on the market, moved in 1975 to challenge the rules that keep some kinds of insurance off the market: it brought a court action seeking to make savings bank life insurance available to those who do not live in the three states where it is now legal. Consumers Union also filed one of the suits that, in the wake of the Goldfarb decision, are intended to eliminate the barriers to lawyer advertising: the suit took the form of an appeal from a local bar association's action in forbidding its members to supply information for a legal serv-

ices directory. In both cases, Consumers Union went beyond evaluating what is now on the market to attacking the monopolies that control entry to the market.

Nader has gone through a similar and much more publicized sea change. He started out tilting with one company, General Motors, over one product, its Corvair: the narrowest kind of consumer issue. In the next phase, that of Nader's Raiders, he and his followers went around exposing the sins of government and industry, doing in essence what the press failed to do. The benefits were transient at best. Only in recent years has the Nader movement attempted lasting change in the economic system, with the Goldfarb case as its greatest achievement and the plan for federal chartering of the largest corporations, including GM, Nader's original antagonist, as its boldest proposal.

Coming down another track, the American Association for Retired Persons has arrived on the same territory. As we have seen, AARP started out selling insurance and later drugs to its members with no visible thought of changing the rules of the marketplace. But by the mid-seventies it was doing battle with the professional guilds and denouncing "concentration of market power"—the same issues pursued by Consumers Union and the Naderites.

The largest number of those active in causing the changes we have described are the survivors of the various movements of the 1960s. They burst on the national stage in those delirious years demanding an instant transformation of society, and their style and rhetoric were as offensive to the majority as their aims were just; many of them seemed to be working out personal needs at the expense of both the audience and the cause. Sometimes the point is obvious. Wading naked through the Reflecting Pool in Washington clearly did nothing for the cause of

peace, nor, in most cases, for the cause of nudity. Similarly, the surest ally of the polluting industrialist, surer even than the purchased regulator, is the ecofreak who will blindly oppose any kind of economic development regardless of human needs. The phony reformer is harder to diagnose. John Lindsay, during his glamorous passage as mayor of New York City, substituted style for performance, charged the bill to tomorrow, and escaped to television—always his best medium—just before the roof fell in. While in office Lindsay was the darling of reformers who might have been expected to notice all that he was failing to do; Mary Perot Nichols, his most perceptive critic, was the first to observe the basic truth: "John Lindsay is giving reform a bad name." Today the flamboyant style is gone, though hardly the phony one, and so is the espousal of the causes of minorities against (or so it was perceived) the interest of the average man. Thus we find Wade Rathke in Arkansas and Tim Sampson in California working on issues that serve the interest of the majority, and Sam Brown in Colorado seeking to make banks more responsive to the needs of the public.

Others we've met in earlier pages, like Joseph M. Belth in insurance and Mary Adelaide Mendelson in nursing homes, do not fit easily into any definable category. Yet all share a profound distrust of government as it presently functions, and most seek their goals outside the two-party system. The old ideological lines have gotten blurred. The people we've described would seem to belong on what we used to think of as the left, which is supposed to believe in government control, but in fact most of their efforts are directed toward freer enterprise and a more competitive private market. Their opponents, the supposed economic conservatives, are in fact supporters of government coddling of monopoly; their ideology is best described as socialism for the rich.

The present generation of reform leadership is beginning to find ways to escape the familiar dilemma of the
inability of government to regulate in the public interest.
The essence of that much-debated dilemma is this: an un-
restrained private economy leads to monopoly control
and the screwing of the public, while government regulators fall under the control of those they are supposed to
regulate, leading once more to monopoly and the screwing of the public. The way out of that trap is to put the
power to regulate in the hands not of government but of
the public, and in each case in the hands of that part of
the public most directly affected by the industry in question. One example is the organization of the relatives of
nursing-home patients that Mary Adelaide Mendelson
was putting together in 1976: it would give the most interested members of the public a means to put pressure
on the nursing-home industry and its official regulators.
Another example is the Nader-sponsored 1975 act that
provides funding for the public to take part in the decisions of the Federal Trade Commission.

Far more important in its potential, however, is the current effort to give the public a say in the regulation of the
utilities. The first phase of this new kind of utility politics
is, as we've seen, what is called Lifeline: removing from
the rate structure the present discrimination against the
householder in favor of the big users. The second phase is
what currently goes by the name of RUCAG: creating institutions by which utility customers can hire the skilled
help they need to intervene in the regulatory process. It is
a major confrontation. On one side, the customers of
course include everyone who doesn't live in an unmetered
cave. Against them are arrayed the heavyweights of the
American political economy: the utility companies themselves; the companies that supply them with oil and coal
and gas and now uranium, and the manufacturers who

benefit from the utilities' preferential rates. Given the power packed into that lineup, it is no surprise that utility and energy policy is the area in which the two-party monopoly has most dismally failed the public. None of the state utility commissions, nor the elected officeholders who appoint them, thought of Lifeline rates—the idea and the political pressure to implement it had to come from outside the monopoly. Similarly, what started out a couple of years ago as a national debate on energy ended in a whimper as both parties and the Administration and the Congress decided after the usual invisible handshake to hang the messenger bearing bad tidings and let the future shift for itself.

Public control of utility regulation could have far-reaching effects on our lives. Lifeline rates are only the first small step. Next the public could undo the egregious swindles, routinely approved by the present utility commissions, that bloat our bills and offend our senses. The common practice of letting utilities charge advertising and lobbying costs to the customers could be laughed right out of the rate base. Advertising a product that is both a necessity and provided by a monopoly is the sheerest waste; we hardly need Con Ed's ad about the low cost of electricity per kilowatt-hour to remind us to turn on the lights when the room grows dark. Lobbying costs us double: the utility buys up enough commissioners and legislators to get itself a rate increase, and we then have to pay not only the increase but also the costs the company incurred in getting it through. The customer pays for his own screwing. Two other inviting targets are the swollen executive payrolls and other internal inefficiencies of the utility companies, and the common practice of letting them pass along increased fuel costs to the customers dollar for dollar, thus removing any reason for the utility to try to hold down the prices it pays to its suppliers. These changes, though worthy and aesthetically pleasing, are minor compared to the potential that lies beyond.

Control of utility pricing provides a handle on energy policy. An effective RUCAG could prevent the cancerous growth of utilities which is a leading cause of both rising prices and waste of our resources. Utilities dependent on fossil fuels like oil and coal are distinctive in that growth means higher costs to everyone. A manufacturer who expands his production can reasonably expect to lower his unit costs or at least hold them stable, but the opposite is true of the utility. Because the fuels they consume are increasingly difficult and expensive to obtain, the next barrel of oil or ton of coal will cost more than the last one; expansion can only mean higher unit costs and, naturally, more pollution. Meanwhile, the present pricing system encourages waste of energy, and the end result is the artificial "need" for nuclear power plants. A pricing system that penalizes waste could encourage industry to save energy and to explore, in its own self-interest, alternate power sources that are non-polluting and, in the long run, cheaper than fossil fuels. At one remove, the present system produces lunatic boondoggles like the "energy independence" scheme for spending $100 billion of taxpayers' money to uncover still more expensive fuels; appropriately enough, that idea was being touted in 1976 by the man who in his person uniquely symbolizes the conjunction of big fuel and big government: Nelson Rockefeller. It is difficult to overestimate how much a continuation of the present utility and energy policies will cost us in waste and devastation. The beginnings of a public effort to gain control of the utilities is, at this writing, the single best hope of avoiding that ruinous future.

Admittedly we have stretched the implications of Lifeline and RUCAG pretty far in the preceding paragraph.

The point, however, is that such techniques offer the attractive possibility of putting the public in control of public policy without crossing the treacherous swamp of the two-party monopoly. It will only succeed, of course, if the public responds to the invitation.

The conventional view for some time has been that the average man is either indifferent or torpidly supports the present order. This is the conservative-majority thesis, "conservative" in this context meaning acceptance of the doctrine of socialism for the rich. It is symbolized by the Dayton Housewife, that statistically average American, forever forty-seven, forever married to the same machinist, and forever willing to forego political change as long as those in power continue to distract her with such menaces as communism or blacks or marijuana. The tax loopholes of the rich are not something she resents; she aspires to them for her 2.2 children. Besides that, we are solemnly warned, she is authoritarian at heart, and, if the rich ever lost control of the two-party system, she would vote us into fascism. The Dayton Housewife is the dream goddess of the ruling class.

It doesn't make much sense, when you stop to think about it, but then it never has. Richard F. Hamilton, in his authoritative 1972 work, *Class and Politics in the United States*, methodically demolished the factual base of the conservative-majority thesis. Hamilton found by working his way through an accumulation of opinion surveys from the fifties and sixties that working-class people were not in fact prone to support the self-serving economic policies of the rich, and that—despite the image of hardhats beating up peace demonstrators—they were less warlike than those above them on the ladder. In *The Working Class Majority*, published two years after Hamilton's work, Andrew Levison reached similar conclusions.

The opinions Hamilton found in what now seem to be

the good old days, by the mid-seventies had become too obvious to ignore. The Dayton Housewife's loss of faith (if indeed she ever had it) in our economic and political institutions was repeatedly documented in the polls. In 1975, for example, the Gallup poll found that people had even less confidence in "big business" than they did in Congress, a finding that moved Gallup to declare that "The business community in this country needs to undertake a large-scale public relations effort with the American people." Around the same time, a New York *Times* survey found a diminishing hope for the future among families earning less than $15,000. The People's Bicentennial Commission, in a Hart Research Associates poll, found that a substantial majority believed both parties favor big business, and that corporations dominate Washington. A majority favored employee ownership of corporations, but, reflecting the current mood, only a small minority advocated government ownership. Two questions in the Hart poll bore indirectly on utility politics: about half thought public ownership of oil and other natural resources was desirable, and three quarters thought consumers should be represented on the boards of corporations operating in their areas. Granted that Hart found evidence supporting the radical beliefs of the PBC, but his results differ little from other polls.

These statistical findings are paralleled by the author's own unscientific sampling of public opinion. In 1974 and 1975, after the publication of *The Screwing of the Average Man*, I appeared on about fifty of those radio and television programs on which listeners telephone in to talk to the guest. The calls on all those programs totaled about one thousand. Reflecting on the wide variety of opinions that came back over the telephone, the most striking result is a negative one: the almost total failure of the callers to defend the existing order. Only two callers said anything along the lines of "You're trying to tear down our economic system" (as one of the two put it). And no one, not one among those thousand callers, had a good word to say for our political system; indeed, no caller even bothered to mention either political party nor any officeholder or candidate. This was not for lack of concern. Many callers said, in effect, we know we're being screwed, and what can we do about it? But no one seemed to think the answer to that question lay in the two-party monopoly.

The collective picture that emerges is one of a disenchanted public. The average man—or the Dayton Housewife—is alienated and ready for a change. But a willing public is not enough, for, as Richard Hamilton observes, change doesn't happen without competent political leadership. People by themselves are too isolated, too preoccupied with their daily lives, to be a significant political force. In the 1950s the voice of the average person was muffled by the two-party monopoly, which found it profitable to keep his concerns off the political market. Then came the intoxicated amateurs and egomaniacs of the sixties, who succeeded briefly in giving change a bad name.

But today—and this is the message of this book—skilled and experienced leaders have emerged who by the results they have achieved are in the first stages of creating a new kind of political constituency. Despite the bad news that is our daily bread, it is a time of hope for the average person.

Selected Bibliography

Chapter 2

DACEY, NORMAN F. *How to Avoid Probate.* Crown, 1965. The original do-it-yourselfer.

Juris Doctor: This magazine, which non-lawyers can read without difficulty, is a good source of news about the field.

MATTHEWS, DOUGLAS. *Sue the Bastards.* Dell, 1975. A guide to using small-claims courts in any state.

NADER, RALPH, and MARK GREEN, eds. *Verdicts on Lawyers.* Crowell, 1976. Good collection of critical views.

Divorce-yourself kits are available in New York State from James Winder (local offices are listed under "Divorce Yourself") and in California from Nolo Press (Box 544, Occidental, CA 95465). Winder also sells kits applicable in other states on personal separation, bankruptcy, and wills. Nolo's other titles include *Tenants' Rights, Protect Your Home* (how to make a declaration of homestead), *Beat the Bill Collector, Change Your Name,* and *Sex, Living Together and the Law.*

Chapter 3

FUCHS, VICTOR R. *Who Shall Live?* Basic Books, 1974. Excellent statement of the issues involved in the economics of health.

ILLICH, IVAN. *Medical Nemesis.* Pantheon, 1976. Mind-stretching views from a great iconoclast.

KLAW, SPENCER. *The Great American Medicine Show.* Viking, 1975. Good survey of the current state of the industry.

LEVIN, ARTHUR. *Talk Back to Your Doctor*. Doubleday, 1975. Provides a solid factual base for doing what the author says.

SAMUELS, MIKE, and HAL BENNETT. *The Well Body Book*. Random House/Bookworks, 1973. For those who want to take self-help considerably further than Levin goes.

Local directories to physicians, dentists, and psychotherapists are available through the Health Research Group, P. O. Box 19404, Washington, D.C. 20036

Chapter 4

LIEBERMAN, JETHRO K. *The Tyranny of the Experts*. Walker, 1970. The classic statement of the problem.

SHIMBERG, BENJAMIN, BARBARA F. ESSER, and DANIEL H. KRUGER. *Occupational Licensing: Practices and Policies*. Public Affairs Press, 1973. A nuts-and-bolts companion to Lieberman.

Chapter 5

BELTH, JOSEPH M. *Life Insurance: A Consumer's Handbook*. Indiana University Press, 1973. The most thorough of the guides.

DENENBERG, HERBERT S. *The Shopper's Guidebook*. Consumer News Inc., 1974. Covers several other fields besides insurance.

A Guide to Life Insurance. Consumers Union, 1974.

The Insurance Forum: Belth's monthly newsletter is an excellent source of news about the industry. Available from P. O. Box 245, Ellettsville, Ind. 47429.

MINTZ, JOE A. *A Shopper's Guide to Individual Retirement Accounts*. Consumers News Inc., 1976.

Chapter 6

ALDER, JOAN. *The Retirement Book*. Morrow, 1975. Good compendium of facts for those preparing for retirement.

BUTLER, ROBERT N. *Why Survive?* Harper & Row, 1975. An expert's passionate indictment of what we do, and don't do, about the problems of the aging.

EISELE, FREDERICK R., ed. *Political Consequences of Aging*. The Annals, September 1974. Informative collection of articles.

MENDELSON, MARY ADELAIDE. *Tender Loving Greed*. Vintage 1975. The exposé of the nursing-home industry.

Chapter 7

AARON, HENRY J. *Who Pays the Property Tax?* A good general statement.

People and Taxes: This monthly is the best general source of news about tax reform. Available from Tax Reform Research Group, 133 C St., S.E., Washington, D.C. 20003

Sample Property Tax Investigations and *Urban Residential Speculation Taxes*. Tax Reform Research Group. Mimeo. 1975. Very useful to the activist.

BRANDON, ROBERT M., JONATHAN ROWE and THOMAS M. STANTON. *Tax Politics*. Pantheon, 1976. Excellent combination of description of the tax system and do-it-yourself for tax reformers. Covers income as well as property taxes. By members of the Tax Reform Research Group.

Chapter 12

HAMILTON, RICHARD F. *Class and Politics in the United States*. Wiley, 1972. If you think the working class is conservative and hawkish, read this.

LEVISON, ANDREW. *The Working Class Majority*. Penguin, 1975. Reaches conclusions similar to Hamilton's, without the data, and in less academic prose.

Index